READERS GUIDES TO ESSENTIAL CRITICI·

CONSULTANT EDITOR: NICOLAS TREDELL

Published

Lucie Armitt	George Eliot: *Adam Bede – The Mill on the Floss – Middlemarch*
Simon Avery	Thomas Hardy: *The Mayor of Casterbridge – Jude the Obscure*
Paul Baines	Daniel Defoe: *Robinson Crusoe – Moll Flanders*
Richard Beynon	D. H. Lawrence: *The Rainbow – Women in Love*
Peter Boxall	Samuel Beckett: *Waiting for Godot – Endgame*
Claire Brennan	The Poetry of Sylvia Plath
Susan Bruce	Shakespeare: *King Lear*
Sandie Byrne	Jane Austen: *Mansfield Park*
Alison Chapman	Elizabeth Gaskell: *Mary Barton – North and South*
Peter Childs	The Fiction of Ian McEwan
Christine Clegg	Vladimir Nabokov: *Lolita*
John Coyle	James Joyce: *Ulysses – A Portrait of the Artist as a Young Man*
Martin Coyle	Shakespeare: *Richard II*
Justin D. Edwards	Postcolonial Literature
Michael Faherty	The Poetry of W. B. Yeats
Sarah Gamble	The Fiction of Angela Carter
Jodi–Anne George	Chaucer: The General Prologue to *The Canterbury Tales*
Jane Goldman	Virginia Woolf: *To the Lighthouse – The Waves*
Huw Griffiths	Shakespeare: *Hamlet*
Vanessa Guignery	The Fiction of Julian Barnes
Louisa Hadley	The Fiction of A. S. Byatt
Geoffrey Harvey	Thomas Hardy: *Tess of the d'Urbervilles*
Paul Hendon	The Poetry of W. H. Auden
Terry Hodgson	The Plays of Tom Stoppard for Stage, Radio, TV and Film
William Hughes	Bram Stoker: *Dracula*
Stuart Hutchinson	Mark Twain: *Tom Sawyer – Huckleberry Finn*
Stuart Hutchinson	Edith Wharton: *The House of Mirth – The Custom of the Country*
Betty Jay	E. M. Forster: *A Passage to India*
Aaron Kelly	Twentieth-Century Irish Literature
Elmer Kennedy–Andrews	The Poetry of Seamus Heaney
Elmer Kennedy–Andrews	Nathaniel Hawthorne: *The Scarlet Letter*
Daniel Lea	George Orwell: *Animal Farm – Nineteen Eighty-Four*
Sara Lodge	Charlotte Brontë: *Jane Eyre*
Philippa Lyon	Twentieth-Century War Poetry
Merja Makinen	The Novels of Jeanette Winterson
Matt McGuire	Contemporary Scottish Literature
Jago Morrison	The Fiction of Chinua Achebe
Carl Plasa	Tony Morrison: *Beloved*
Carl Plasa	Jean Rhys: *Wide Sargasso Sea*

Readers' Guides to Essential Criticism

Series Standing Order ISBN 1–4039–0108–2
(outside North America only)

You can receive future titles in this series as they are published by placing a standing order. Please contact your bookseller or, in the case of difficulty, write to us at the address below with your name and address, the title of the series and the ISBN quoted above.

Customer Services Department, Macmillan Distribution Ltd Houndmills, Basingstoke, Hampshire RG21 6XS, England

Bram Stoker
Dracula

WILLIAM HUGHES

Consultant Editor: Nicolas Tredell

First published 2008 by
PALGRAVE MACMILLAN

Palgrave Macmillan in the UK is an imprint of Macmillan Publishers Limited, registered in England, company number 785998, of Houndmills, Basingstoke, Hampshire RG21 6XS.

Palgrave Macmillan in the US is a division of St Martin's Press LLC, 175 Fifth Avenue, New York, NY 10010.

Palgrave Macmillan is the global academic imprint of the above companies and has companies and representatives throughout the world.

Palgrave® and Macmillan® are registered trademarks in the United States, the United Kingdom, Europe and other countries.

ISBN-13: 978–1–403–98778–5 hardback
ISBN-10: 1–403–98778–5 hardback
ISBN-13: 978–1–403–98779–2 paperback
ISBN-10: 1–403–98779–3 paperback

This book is printed on paper suitable for recycling and made from fully managed and sustained forest sources. Logging, pulping and manufacturing processes are expected to conform to the environmental regulations of the country of origin.

A catalogue record for this book is available from the British Library.

A catalog record for this book is available from the Library of Congress.

10   9   8   7   6   5   4   3   2   1
18 17 16 15 14 13 12 11 10 09

Printed and bound in China

For G
A long overdue acknowledgement

Contents

Dracula criticism from the nineteenth to the twentieth century; the life and writings of Bram Stoker; twenty-first-century criticism of Stoker's novel. Critics and biographers discussed include Harry Ludlam, Daniel Farson, Peter Haining and Peter Tremayne, and Paul Murray. The chapter also makes extensive reference to Stoker's own semi-autobiographical work, *Personal Reminiscences of Henry Irving*.

Psychoanalysis and Psychobiography: The Troubled Unconsciousness of *Dracula*

Sexual guilt, taboo and the Oedipal; psychobiography; child sexual abuse; divided psyches and abjected bodies. Critics discussed include Ernest Jones, Maurice Richardson, Phyllis Roth, C. F. Bentley, Marie Mulvey-Roberts, Joseph S. Bierman, Seymour Shuster, Daniel Lapin, Elisabeth Bronfen and Jerrold Hogle.

Medicine, Mind and Body: The Physiological Study of *Dracula*

The physiology of the mind; the multiple meanings of blood; sexuality, infection and the obsessive consumer; scientific criminology; vampires and the definition of deviance. Critics discussed include William Hughes, David Glover, John Greenway, Victor Sage, David Hume Flood, Marie Mulvey-Roberts, Diane Mason, Leila S. May, Ernest Fontana, and Robert Mighall.

Invasion and Empire: The Racial and Colonial Politics of *Dracula*

The conquest of the West; anti-Semitism in Stoker's fiction; Transylvanian superstitions and Balkan politics; Anglo-Saxon alliances. Critics discussed include Branka Arsić, Stephen Arata, Jules Zanger, Carol Margaret Davison, Vesna Goldsworthy, Eleni Coundouriotis, Matthew Gibson, Franco Moretti, and Andrew Smith.

Acknowledgements

Many friends and colleagues have supported my work during this book's unusually long gestation. My special thanks are due to Diane Mason, to Andrew Smith (University of Glamorgan), John Whatley (Simon Fraser University) and Matthew Gibson (University of Surrey), as well as to Victor Sage (University of East Anglia).

Among the many colleagues who have supported my work in this and other projects, I would also like to express my gratitude to Sue Zlosnik (Manchester Metropolitan University), Avril Horner (Kingston University); Terry Hale (University of Hull); Nick Freeman (Loughborough University); David Punter (University of Bristol); Glennis Byron (Stirling University); Marie Mulvey-Roberts (University of the West of England); Richard Walker (University of Central Lancashire); Nigel Kingcome (University College, Falmouth); Helen McGrath (Antix Productions); Richard Dalby; Clive Leatherdale (Desert Island Books); Albert Power (The Bram Stoker Society, Dublin); Dennis McIntyre (The Bram Stoker Centre, Clontarf); John Bak (Université Nancy 2); Gilles Menegaldo (Université de Poitiers); Max Duperray (Université de Provence); Gaïd Girard (Université de Brest); Jacques Sirgent (Musée des Vampires, Les Lilas); Lana Maht Wiggins (University of New Orleans); Benjamin Fisher (University of Mississippi); Jerrold Hogle (University of Arizona); Carol M. Davison (University of Windsor); Carol A. Senf (Georgia Institute of Technology); Ardel Thomas (City College of San Francisco) and Katarzyna Ancuta (Assumption University, Bangkok). Within in my own institution I acknowledge, with thanks, the support and practical assistance afforded by Tracey Hill, Colin Edwards, Stephen Gregg, Neil Sammells and Tim Middleton. I am grateful, also, for the diligent work of Nick Drew, and the Librarians and inter-library loan staff at Bath Spa University. I hope you will all forgive me for the necessary brevity of this acknowledgement:

Finally, I would like to express my lasting gratitude to those medical professionals, who are in many cases now my friends also, who supported me during the illness which delayed the completion of this book: particular thanks are due to Graham Howell and the staff of Cheseldon Ward, Royal United Hospital, Bath; to Richard Collins, who remains the only practitioner ever to extract my blood without protest; to Camelia Chifor, and to Ina de Souza. I am grateful also to Nicolas Tredell, to Sonya Barker, to Felicity Noble and to Penny Simmons not

merely for their professional production of this *Readers Guide* but also for
their flexibility and sympathy during my illness.

WILLIAM HUGHES
Trowbridge, Wiltshire

NOTE

All references to *Dracula* are taken from the Norton Critical Edition, edited by Nina
Auerbach and David Skal (New York: W. W. Norton, 1997). References to this edition
appear in parentheses throughout the Guide.

Introduction

DRACULA CRITICISM IN THE NINETEENTH CENTURY

The critical response to *Dracula* has been shaped by the preoccupations of the late twentieth-century academy, arguably as much as it has been determined by the content of Bram Stoker's 1897 novel itself. Though the earliest published critical appreciations of the novel, inevitably, came at the hands of Victorian reviewers, these were characteristically dismissive of what was at the time hardly a significant literary event. Stoker, known primarily as a successful theatre manager in London's West End was, at best, a minor novelist of the day, the author of but three moderately successful romance-cum-adventure novels prior to 1897. *Dracula*, indeed, was not an immediate commercial success on the scale of *The Woman in White* (1869), by Wilkie Collins (1824–1889), an epistolary novel to which Stoker's work was favourably compared.[1] Less favourable reviewers disdainfully remarked upon a somewhat hyperbolic intensity of gruesome spectacle in the novel – what the *Athenaeum* termed 'a determined effort to go, as it were, "one better" than others in the same field' – and, indeed, openly castigated the author for a lapse in taste on account of his selecting a 'theme [...] quite unworthy of his literary capabilities'.[2]

Given that Stoker was regarded, even by his closest associates, as a writer who merely 'wrote his books to sell', it is hardly surprising that *Dracula* should be initially dismissed as nothing more than, at best, 'a first-rate book of adventure', and, at worst, an assembly of 'horrid details' crafted in such a way as to simply 'please those for whom they are designed'.[3] In this and other contemporary reviews of Stoker's writings, the 'lurid and creepy kind of fiction represented by *Dracula* and other novels' is marginalised due to a perceived connection with the rising mass-market.[4] If the reviewers of Stoker's own time are to be believed, *Dracula* answered, first and foremost, the needs of a culturally undiscerning readership hungry for narrative and spectacle. There is no acknowledgement from contemporary sources that the novel engaged with any of the issues of the day, whether these be the scandalous marital or financial abuses that characterised the tradition of the Sensation Novel, or the more rarefied literary, cultural or political questions that preoccupied the metropolitan elite at the *fin de siècle*.[5] For Stoker's literary contemporaries there was seemingly nothing portentous or prophetic to be found in *Dracula*. Reviewers, whether favourable or hostile, did not acknowledge matters and interpretations central to modern criticism of the novel: the somewhat sexual postures adopted in the vampiric encounter, the racial and sexual politics of the *fin de siècle*, the question of assertive womanhood, the symbolism of blood, or even the speculations surrounding the author's own sexuality, are never considered.

Such things, of course, might be simply too obvious to require comment – or, indeed, their indelicacy could in itself motivate an eloquent silence on the part of a reticent reviewer. Their accentuation in a later century, though, might as easily suggest the power of a retrospective, as opposed to a contemporary, critical gaze. These issues, as persistent in modern criticism of *Dracula* as they are absent from contemporary reviews, arguably reflect as much the preoccupations of a later, commentating, age, as they imply a privy insight into the concerns of the past. They are an expression, in essence, of what twentieth-century criticism *understands* the motivating issues, conscious and unconscious, appropriate to a novel, an author and a culture poised uneasily on the edge of a new century, to be. The mobilisation of these issues in criticism through the relatively demotic Gothic medium of *Dracula* is equally significant. Whatever dismissive judgements have historically been passed upon its author or its generic worthiness, *Dracula* occupies a far from marginal position in the broad field of twentieth-century criticism. It is a frequently quoted work in critical debate beyond the Gothic, and has engendered its own dedicated academic journal.[6] It may be studied on the university curricula not merely of the English-speaking world, but also, as a compulsory element, through the *CAPES* and *Agrégation* of the French postgraduate system.[7] It is a novel worthy of translation and of meticulous scholarly annotation.[8] The persistence of *Dracula* in criticism is in part a consequence of the ease with which its incidents, and the issues conventionally associated with them, may be progressively appropriated by emerging theories and critical methodologies. Yet, perversely, the lingering ephemerality of the novel remains an important factor in its rise to critical attention. *Dracula*, indeed, may serve not merely as an index to the application of specific critical methodologies from the 1960s to the present, but may equally indicate how criticism, as a broad movement, has moved from a preoccupation with a limited canon of elite, 'literary' authors to a more inclusive liberal discipline whose boundaries touch upon those of cultural studies.[9]

The twenty-first century's interest in the nineteenth-century *fin de siècle*, and the pre-Millennium critical tradition of exposing the alleged neuroses of the Victorian period, both have their origins in how the twentieth century has conventionally viewed its immediate predecessor in time. For much of the twentieth century, 'Victorian' was a byword for little more than excessive formality, inflexible hierarchies and an intrusive morality which, nevertheless, could be easily dismissed as a comic prudishness typified by corsetry and concealed table legs. Cultural changes in the 1960s, however, as the French thinker Michel Foucault (1926–1984) intimates in Volume 1 of *The History of Sexuality* (1976), politicised the very concept of the Victorian, permitting it to be deployed as a rhetorical counterpart to all that is 'liberated' or 'modern'.[10] The 'progressive' credentials of modernity, in other words, whether expressed in academic writing or in a more general cultural consciousness, are established, in part at least, upon a discursive ability both to recognise and openly express issues that could be communicated in the past only by way of an elaborate process of encoding.

This institutionalised reassurance that modernity is 'liberated' may be, as Foucault suggests, illusory, but its overwhelming consequence is the concretisation of those associations which link the Victorian past in particular with repression and with indirect communication of distasteful or controversial issues. The current location of *Dracula* within criticism, and the accentuation of particular issues – and not exclusively sexual issues – apparently embedded within the narrative of Stoker's novel, are equally a consequence of this cultural moment. In the twentieth century, the ephemeral *Dracula* has come to be read as a text as much in tune with the pessimistic spirit of the *fin de siècle* as its close contemporaries, *Degeneration* (1892) by Max Nordau (1849–1923) and the poem 'Recessional' (1897) by Rudyard Kipling (1865–1936). *Dracula* is no longer what it arguably was in 1897, simply 'one of the most weird and gruesome tales of modern times'.[11] It is now a text that can seemingly be approached only through subsequent times, a novel whose critically accepted meanings both preface it and condition its reception, a quintessentially Victorian work whose preoccupations are apparently not wholly nineteenth century.

DRACULA CRITICISM IN THE TWENTIETH AND TWENTY-FIRST CENTURIES

There is no clear chronological succession to the criticism of *Dracula*, no distinct demarcation indicating the rise and fall of consecutive critical approaches following the entry of the novel into academic consciousness at the close of the 1950s. The criticism of *Dracula*, though subject to fashions in academic methodology, appears to defy the irretrievable changes associated with the passage of time as much as Stoker's fictional Count. Earlier assessments of the novel are often reprinted, anthologised or excerpted in their own right. Quoted briefly or at length, they form the starting point for many a rejoinder to, or expansion of, material already in circulation. Crucially, though, the novel continues to inspire critics publishing across the methodological spectrum, from Psychoanalysis to

Cultural Materialism, and from the most abstract theory to the densest of textual or structural analyses. Thus *Dracula* remains a novel suspended in critical coexistence, the Count a different vampire to every commentator, the novel's events variously literal or symbolic, repressed or liberated, as the critic's theoretical orientation directs. Read critically, *Dracula* is always a palimpsest of theoretical opinions, a point at which methodologies converge, compete and combine.

The earliest theoretical readings of *Dracula* were heavily influenced by Freudian thought, the novel first being read within a larger psychoanalytical exploration of the ghost story by Maurice Richardson in 1959. Seldom reprinted, though frequently cited, Richardson's 'The Psychoanalysis of Ghost Stories' effectively establishes many of the psychological tools – and, indeed, the key scenarios – which have characterised subsequent psychoanalytical and post-Freudian readings of the novel.[12] The Oedipal relationships noted by Richardson, for example, are developed at greater length and with more felicity by Phyllis Roth in both her 1977 article 'Suddenly Sexual Women in Bram Stoker's *Dracula*' and in her 1982 volume *Bram Stoker*. Similarly, Richardson's interest in totemism prefigures David Punter's subtle evocation of the boundary lines maintained through taboo in his short reading of *Dracula* in *The Literature of Terror* (1980), one of the most influential works in the development of Gothic from a literary curiosity into a discrete – and accepted – discipline within English studies. Richardson, finally, is also a pioneer in the application of psychobiography – the neurotic and unconscious history, as it were, of the author – in the criticism of *Dracula*. The article's passing suggestion of a father fixation within Stoker's psyche, associated with the author's employer, the actor-manager Sir Henry Irving (1838–1905), appears somewhat modest, however, when compared to later readings, such as those by Joseph Bierman and Daniel Lapin, which premise the novel's horrors upon childhood illness and infantile sexual abuse.[13]

Sexuality, of course, lies at the centre of Freudian criticism, and its implications, attractions and repulsions have been appropriated to the criticism of *Dracula* from the psychoanalytically orthodox 1970s to more recent analyses influenced by the French revisionist psychoanalysis of Jacques Lacan (1901–1981) and Julia Kristeva (born 1941).[14] One might recall, though, that sexuality, perverse or otherwise, has a cultural as much as a psychoanalytical identity, and that this has been explored in its own right – at times in reaction to the claims of psychoanalysis. This coexistence has been apparent from the earliest years of the critical response to *Dracula*. C. F. Bentley's influential 1972 article 'The Monster in the Bedroom: Sexual Symbolism in Bram Stoker's *Dracula*' might, like Richardson's 'The Psychoanalysis of Ghost Stories', depend upon the 1931 psychoanalytical study *On the Nightmare* by Freud's biographer, Ernest Jones (1879–1958), though Carol L. Fry's 'Fictional Conventions and Sexuality in *Dracula*', published in the same year, is premised upon an approach far more grounded in the acknowledged cultures of literature rather than the repressed drives of the psyche.[15] Other preoccupations recurrent in the criticism of *Dracula* were also established at this comparatively early stage of the novel's presence in critical discourse. Christopher Craft's frequently reprinted 1984 reading of ambiguous gender boundaries in the novel, ' "Kiss me with those red lips": Gender and Inversion in Stoker's *Dracula*' might be compared with later works in the field of queer studies, such as H. L. Malchow's consideration of homosociality in *Gothic Images of Race in Nineteenth-Century Britain* (1996), or Talia Schaffer's 'A Wilde Desire Took Me: The Homoerotic History of *Dracula*' in 1994.[16]

The relationships and identities portrayed within *Dracula*, and the changes that are undergone when a mortal encounters a vampire, appear to lend themselves readily to sexual symbolism. A note of caution might be extracted, though, from the somewhat revisionist work of Robert Mighall, the rhetoric of which at times makes clear its historicist antagonism to the perceived primacy of psychoanalytical and sexual readings of both the novel and the figure of the vampire.[17] 'A vampire', Mighall notes provocatively, 'is sometimes only a vampire'.[18] A vampire need not always be a sexual deviant, nor indeed need the novel itself be the exclusive preserve of a critical establishment which, Foucault might well have suggested, has become fixated upon expressing sexuality.

Sexuality, sexual identity and cultural gendering intersect in the discipline of Gender Studies, where *Dracula*, unsurprisingly, is a text frequently encountered in criticism. As a consequence of the earlier association of Gender Studies primarily with explorations of the depiction and consumption of women in culture, the earliest readings of *Dracula* in this field focus upon the novel's two central mortal female protagonists, Lucy Westenra and Mina Harker, with some attention being directed also to the Count's three apparent brides in Transylvania. Emphasis has long been placed in particular upon how the onset of vampirism provokes a state of mind in the victim that might be read as a sexual and social liberation, a departure, in other words, from the modest standards of a clichéd Victorian bourgeois culture underpinned by proprietary patriarchy. In this context, one might note the particular relevance of the New Woman, a much-maligned protofeminist figure of the *fin de siècle*, named with scorn more than once in Stoker's novel. The New Woman has been a recurrent feature of the criticism of *Dracula* from 1982, with Carol Senf's groundbreaking article '*Dracula*: Stoker's Response to the New Woman' and, as more recent considerations from divergent critical standpoints by Sally Ledger and Marie Mulvey-Roberts would indicate, this disquieting figure seems likely to retain her critical currency.[19]

The study of the representation of Victorian masculinities within *Dracula* is not confined to readings premised upon queer theory. The homosocial embraces professional cultures as much as socio-sexual ones, and recent studies have therefore taken time to explore the implications of the characters' involvements with the institutions of law and medicine, professions with which Stoker was himself associated.[20] Medicine, as a discourse, is acknowledged also in the study of the physical and social, as opposed to simply sexual, deviance depicted in *Dracula*, attention being drawn from the mid-1980s to the novel's embodiment of the racial, cultural and criminological theories of Cesare Lombroso (1835–1909) and Max Nordau.[21] Subsequent exploration of these theories would seem to indicate that atavism and scarce-contained savagery are the alternative faces of the domesticated Gentleman.[22] They are the faces, too, of the alien as both potential invader and successful colonist: *Dracula* has, from as early as the 1990s, been interpreted as a fearful warning of the vulnerability of the Anglo-Saxon West to the seductive and infectious East.[23]

Biography – sometimes, admittedly, in the guise of psychobiography – has been an important resource in gendered readings of *Dracula*, whether through the application of documented evidence with regard to the author's early education or personal politics, or in the more speculative form of assertions about the state of his marriage or sexual health.[24] Indeed, biographical details have at times supported most, if not all, of the debates associated with the novel. There is perhaps no single area, though, where biography has been most relevantly deployed as in the comparatively recent appropriation of *Dracula*, and indeed of Stoker as a writer, by Irish Studies. Irish Studies has been quick to expand upon Franco Moretti's 1983 contention that the Count emblematises an exploitative capitalism, an influential development of this being the interpretation of the vampire as an absentee landlord or colonial – and thus, in the Irish context, English – predator.[25] The East, in this case, is perversely rescheduled as imperial Britain, the conventional West of other colonial interpretations. Though ignored by Irish Studies for many years, Stoker is now arguably as institutionalised within the discipline as two other important Protestant Anglo-Irish Gothicists, the novelist and playwright Charles Robert Maturin (1782–1824) and the novelist and short-story writer J. S. Le Fanu (1814–1873). A persistent critical perception of Stoker as, in Joseph Valente's words, 'an ethnic social climber' seeking celebrity and success in the English capital has, however, undoubtedly compromised his status as a writer portraying a distinctively Irish cultural consciousness.[26]

It may be observed that much of the debate concerning *Dracula* has been conducted at relatively short length, rather than in the more expansive pages of the academic monograph. Though there are rare exceptions, criticism of Stoker's novel is emphatically the stuff of the academic journal, the discrete paper within a multi-authored collection of essays, or the chapter forming a component of a larger monograph under a single hand. While it is true to say that very few scholarly books have been published primarily upon *Dracula*, it must be acknowledged that many of these have exerted a lasting influence over both students approaching the novel as undergraduates, and critics responding to the debate as it appears in print. Rarely acknowledged in academic discourse today, Raymond McNally and Radu Florescu's somewhat populist *In Search of Dracula* (1972) was possibly the first book to provide the novel with a historical context, albeit one that privileged its alleged roots in sixteenth-century rather than Victorian culture. Stoker's novel itself is relevant to perhaps but a quarter of this work, which considers also the cinematic and folkloric vampire. Central to *In Search of Dracula* is a biography of Vlad the Impaler (1431–1476), historically styled 'Dracula' – variously 'Son of the Dragon', or 'Son of the Devil' – a Wallachian ruler whom the authors argue is the model for the Count.[27] Speculation on this identity, alternatively calmly scholarly and frenetically vitriolic, continues to this day. The relevance of this issue to the purely academic study of the novel, though, is debatable.[28]

Ten years after *In Search of Dracula*, Phyllis Roth published an important short volume, *Bram Stoker* (1982), the first detailed study of the breadth of the author's fiction. Written for the Twayne's English Authors Series, this psychoanalytically orientated survey divided Stoker's then largely unreprinted novels and short fiction into children's stories, romances, horror stories and, in a category of its own, *Dracula*. Roth's study upheld, and possibly concretised, the limited selection of key scenes from the novel that had already been made by earlier critics, emphasising in particular the menacing of Jonathan, the ritual despatch of Lucy, and the victimisation of Mina. However, it enhanced their application somewhat by linking them to other – for Roth psychologically significant – recurrent images across Stoker's *oeuvre*.

Roth's work was succeeded within three years by a far more methodologically disparate work, Clive Leatherdale's *Dracula: The Novel and the Legend* (1985). Leatherdale's work is divided into 11 chapters which provided a condensation of how the criticism of *Dracula* had evolved in 25 years: whilst acknowledging the psychoanalytical and sexual readings which had been fashionable for some time, Leatherdale's work took care to acknowledge the literary and folkloric background to the vampire, to chart an emerging awareness of Christian and occult symbolism in Stoker's novel, to consider the representation of both genders, and to read *Dracula* as a social and political commentary. Revised more than once, *Dracula: The Novel and the Legend* remains a good introduction to the breadth of approaches, though its ambition is somewhat undermined by Leatherdale's insistence that Stoker is 'a hack writer who in one solitary work wrote as if inspired'.[29]

Leatherdale enforces his dismissal of Stoker's allegedly 'hack' status through his concentration on *Dracula* to the relative exclusion of the author's ten less well known novels. This is not the approach taken, however, by his major monograph-length successors in criticism, all of whom have followed Phyllis Roth's early lead in both considering *Dracula* in comparison to Stoker's other novels, and exploring these as valid works in their own right. David Glover's *Vampires, Mummies, and Liberals: Bram Stoker and the Politics of Popular Fiction* (1996) might itself be taken as an index of the critical consciousness associated with *Dracula* in the ten years following Leatherdale's *Dracula: The Novel and the Legend*. Glover's work, though acutely aware of the gender polit-ics and sexuality of Stoker's fiction, is tempered by a thoughtful and subtly biographical reading of the Victorian author's avowedly Liberal politics and involvement in a more broadly liberal culture.[30] Beyond this, Glover applies the discourses of ethnology, sexology and criminal anthropology – the latter, admittedly, having been developed earlier in criticism by Ernest Fontana, Victor Sage, Daniel Pick and others – not merely to *Dracula* but also, as the thematic organisation of *Vampires, Mummies, and Liberals* betrays, to the Irish politics of Stoker's fiction, to the New Woman and to the racial (and racist) tenor of the novels.[31] Glover concludes his study by returning to the vexed question of the lineage between McNally's sixteenth-century warlord and Stoker's fic-tional Count. His study is unique, though, in its consideration of the portrayal of Count Dracula in twentieth-century vampire fiction, in Hollywood cinema, and in the political mythologies associated with the Romanian communist regime of Nicolae Ceauşescu (1919–1989; President of Romania, 1974–89).

Published four years after *Vampires, Mummies, and Liberals*, William Hughes's *Beyond Dracula: Bram Stoker's Fiction and its Cultural Context* (2000) also considers the breadth of Stoker's fiction. Foucauldian in temper and biographically informed, it examines the Protestant spir-ituality of Stoker's works, the discourses, social and scientific, which structure the portrayal of male and female in the fiction and, with par-ticular reference to *Dracula*, the author's deployment of contemporary medical and quasi-medical thought. As in Roth's psychobiographical *Bram Stoker* (1982), characteristic patterns in both incident and char-acterisation are noted across the author's fiction. These are projected, however, beyond the scenarios most often encountered in criticism, and are supported by contemporary reviews and unpublished archive material, in the form of letters and manuscripts, held in Britain and the United States.

The most recent monograph-length contribution to the debate, Carol Senf's *Science and Social Science in Bram Stoker's Fiction* (2002) must be taken in the context of her earlier *Dracula: Between Tradition and Modernism* (1998). Despite its subtitle, the latter is a work concerned less with genre than with close readings of the novel's major incidents and preoccupations. Following a contextual opening, which acknowledges both biography and literary antecedent, Senf reads *Dracula* through narrative strategy, empire, gender, religion, science and technology and social class. The separate chapters are succinct and the novel rather than criticism, arguably, is the primary focus of Senf's study, which is surprisingly little known outside the United States. *Science and Social Science in Bram Stoker's Fiction*, as its title suggests, considers a broader range of Stoker's writings, including the author's non-fiction. Senf develops further the distinction, expressed in her earlier volume, between science and technology, and her ethical vision of science as 'a neutral field that can be used for both fair means and foul' in many respects recalls Stoker's own consideration of literature as 'imagination – itself pure', a 'neutral' quantum which might yet be 'sullied' through the expression of 'impure or dangerous material'.[32]

Stoker's novel, likewise, has also found itself coloured over the years by the myriad critical interpretations imposed upon it. In the twenty-first century, *Dracula* no longer exists independently of competing interpretations striving to impose their own distinctive control and explanation over this apparent intersection of cultural and individual signification. Yet, what should be apparent from this introductory survey is that criticism of *Dracula* does not divide itself neatly into separate theoretical camps, each operating in relative ignorance of the other, or into discrete or successive methodological epochs. *Dracula*, as has already been suggested, remains the fulcrum-text of a vibrant confluence of older work and more recent studies. The enhanced availability of much of this material – through new or reprinted collections, by way of on-line archives or via simultaneous on-line and hard-copy publication of new work – underpins a sizeable resource for the student working on Stoker's novel from undergraduate to graduate-researcher level.[33] Just as there is no abiding justification for the mobilisation of a limited range of scenarios or characters from the novel in criticism, so too is there no reason for a critical response that draws only upon the best-known and most frequently encountered scholarly readings.

THE LIFE AND WRITINGS OF BRAM STOKER

As has already been suggested, biography is perhaps the only single extra-textual resource upon which almost all critiques of *Dracula* – psychological and materialist alike – have drawn at one time or another. A great deal of half-truth and often unchallenged misinformation parallels the documental facts of Stoker's life, and though a full biography is beyond the remit of this *Reader's Guide*, some acknowledgement of verifiable incidents in Stoker's youth and adulthood will serve to both preface and contextualise the following survey of twentieth-century biographers, as well as the criticism which they in many cases inform.

Abraham Stoker junior, the third of seven children, was born on 8 November 1847 at 15, The Crescent, Clontarf, County Dublin. He was a sickly child who, by his own admission, was not expected to live.[34] Educated first at home, presumably as a consequence of this undefined weakness, he was subsequently enrolled in a private Dublin day school run by the Reverend William Woods, a Protestant clergyman. The family was Anglican in religion, moderately Unionist in political allegiance, and Anglo-Irish in cultural temper, the author's father being a member of the British civil administration in Ireland and his mother the daughter of an army officer.[35] The family had historical connections to the Irish medical establishment, and these were perpetuated through three of the author's brothers who embraced surgery as a profession. Stoker, who matriculated as an undergraduate at Trinity College Dublin on 2 November 1864, did not, however, read medicine. Despite his own claim that he 'had got Honours in pure Mathematics', he was awarded an ordinary degree of Bachelor in Arts on 1 March 1870, and was admitted to the degree of Master in Arts without further study, as was customary at the University of Dublin, on 9 February 1875.[36] It is not the case, despite one twentieth-century biographer's insistence, that he graduated 'with a degree in science and stayed on for a Master's'.[37] Stoker's knowledge of science, as evidenced by his later fiction, is the result of enthusiasm and wide reading rather than guided, professional training.

Though academically unexceptional, Stoker's career at the University of Dublin was distinguished both by his prowess as a university athlete and by his ability in the debating chamber. He played competitive rugby football, and was awarded 'numerous silver cups' for both athletics and competitive weightlifting in the university gymnasium.[38] Stoker became President of the University's Philosophical Society in 1869, and was elected Auditor of the rival Historical Society, 'a post which corresponds to the Presidency of the Union in Oxford or Cambridge', in 1872.[39] He delivered papers at both societies, and was awarded certificates and medals for oratory. More subtly, though, he gained access to the main debates and many of the more important Irish intellectual figures of the day, many of whom were honorary members of the societies, or addressed their gatherings as honoured guests. Among his associates at this time were the future Irish historian

Standish O'Grady (1832–1915), the pioneering professor of English, Edward Dowden (1843–1913), and the family of Oscar Wilde (1854–1900). No evidence exists, however, that he was associated with J. Sheridan Le Fanu, author of both the influential *Uncle Silas* (1864) and the short vampire story 'Carmilla' (1871).

After his graduation Stoker maintained a connection with both university organisations, attending meetings and delivering occasional papers or responses. In 1870 he was appointed to a Civil Service post in Dublin Castle, an easy walk, for a fit man, from Trinity College. Though it appears his Anglo-Irish origins may have inhibited his progress in an Ireland struggling to accommodate an educated and vocal Roman Catholic bourgeoisie, Stoker was appointed to the office of Inspector of Petty Sessions in 1877.[40] In this office he wrote and published, at his own expense, the legal work *Duties of Clerks of Petty Sessions in Ireland* (1879); became, from 1871, an unpaid theatre critic; and edited, on a part-time basis in 1873, a short-lived popular newspaper, *The Irish Echo*.

It was in the second of these part-time literary occupations that Stoker met the man who was to persuade him to leave both Dublin and the security of a salaried and pensioned government post. Henry Irving, on his visit to Dublin in 1867, was a rising English actor and stage manager with an established reputation in the provinces and a growing popularity in London. He was, though, variously ignored or decried for his 'stiff and constrained' acting by the Irish press on both this and his subsequent visits in 1871 and 1872.[41] On 3 December 1876, Irving, to whom Stoker had been earlier introduced, included him in a private recitation of the dramatic poem *The Dream of Eugene Aram* (1829) by Thomas Hood (1799–1845). Irving was exhausted by his efforts, but Stoker exhibited a collapse which can only be considered as a form of emotional seizure, 'something', in his own words, 'like a violent fit of hysterics'. Stoker's subsequent rationalisation of the encounter is, at once, as sentimentally eulogistic as it is perversely homoerotic. Depicting himself as 'a very strong man', a university athlete who emblematises the masculine standard of *mens sana in corpore sano* (a healthy mind in a healthy body), he yet exclaims, 'Soul had looked into soul! From that hour began a friendship as profound, as close, as lasting as can be between two men.'[42]

This friendship, as Stoker perceived it to be, developed in such a way that in 1878 Irving invited the young civil servant to join him in London as Acting Manager of the Lyceum Theatre in the Strand. Stoker brought forward his marriage to Florence Ann Lemon Balcombe (1858–1937), the daughter of an army officer, in order to facilitate his transfer to London, where the Stokers moved first to fashionable Chelsea, retreating to Pimlico in later years as their finances became more stretched.[43] A son, Irving Noel Thornley Stoker, whose first and third Christian names commemorate the actor and Stoker's elder brother, a successful surgeon, respectively, was born in December 1879. The author was to retain his position, which made him effectively Irving's accountant, secretary and public spokesman for 27 years, until the actor's death in 1905. During this time, Stoker drafted a vast amount of correspondence, ghost-wrote speeches and articles for his employer, and oversaw the logistics of eight theatrical tours by the Irving company in the United States. He also qualified as a barrister, but never practiced law.

The majority of Stoker's works were completed on a part-time basis during this arduous and often unsocial employment. His fictional output had begun in Dublin, with the publication of a short fantasy story, 'The Crystal Cup' in the English journal, *London Society*, in 1872. Three years later, he published three serials in an Irish periodical, *The Shamrock*, though his first book production was to come only in 1882 with *Under the Sunset*, a collection of somewhat macabre short stories for children, released to catch the lucrative Christmas market. The author's fiction prior to *Dracula*, barring one or two macabre shorter pieces, was romantic rather than Gothic in tone, and depended much on exotic or spectacular geographical locations: the west of Ireland in his first novel, *The Snake's Pass* (1882), Aberdeenshire in *The Watter's Mou'* (1894), and the locality of Mount Shasta in California in *The Shoulder of Shasta* (1895). *Dracula* (1897) appears to have been reviewed no more nor less than any of these novels, and its Gothicism does not seem to have eclipsed Stoker's undoubted taste for the heterosexual romance: *Miss Betty*, published a year later, is an eighteenth-century love story set near the author's then-home in Chelsea's Cheyne Walk. Only three subsequent novels were researched and written prior to Irving's death and, it has to be said, these do return to the balance of Gothic with romance displayed in *Dracula*. *The Mystery of the Sea* (1902) is a religiously sectarian tale of second sight, kidnap and treasure hunting on the Aberdeenshire coast; *The Jewel of Seven Stars* (1903) is a novel of ritual and resurrection, set in Egypt, London and Cornwall; and *The Man* (1905), which shifts location between the English shires, the colleges of Oxford and the Canadian wilderness, is a rather anachronistic Edwardian riposte to the Victorian feminism of the New Woman.

Though the Lyceum itself had passed beyond the control of its lessee, Irving, in 1899, the actor's popularity remained relatively buoyant even in the new century. Though Irving attracted the scorn of, amongst others, George Bernard Shaw (1856–1950), for his resistance to the 'problem' dramas of the Norwegian playwright and poet Henrik Ibsen (1828–1906), the provincial audience was more indulgent of an actor who continued to balance essentially Victorian melodramas with reputable Shakespearean productions. Irving's death whilst on tour in 1905 inevitably heralded a watershed in Stoker's own career. The author's regular, if diminished, income from his management of the actor ceased, and he was forced both to look for alternative work and to rely frequently on his pen as a source of funds.

This period, between 1905 and 1912, was a time of both physical debilitation and great literary productivity for Stoker. The author succumbed to a paralytic stroke in 1906, followed by a second in 1909, and had long suffered from both gout and Bright's Disease, a disorder particularly affecting the kidneys.[44] During the first of these illnesses, remarkably, he researched and wrote his biography of the late actor, *Personal Reminiscences of Henry Irving* (1906). It was a pattern of struggle and achievement that was to continue until his death. In these seven years, he wrote topical articles for London journals on the theatre, fiction and Irish industry. For *The Daily Chronicle*, Stoker published interviews with old associates such as the creator of Sherlock Holmes, Sir Arthur Conan Doyle (1859–1930); the librettist of the Savoy operas, W. S. Gilbert (1836–1911); and the future British Prime Minister, Winston Churchill (1874–1965). He also completed a volume of theatrically framed short stories, *Snowbound*, in 1908 and a non-fictional study of imposture, *Famous Impostors*, in 1910. Relatively little short fiction, beyond *Snowbound*, was published by Stoker in this period, though he researched and wrote a further three novels: *Lady Athlyne*, a romance alternatively farcical and erotic, in 1908; *The Lady of the Shroud*, a *faux* vampire novel embodying a Ruritanian politi-cal fantasy in 1909; and *The Lair of the White Worm*, an erratic and meandering novel of mesmerism and physical metamorphosis in 1911. A further collection of short stories, *Dracula's Guest and Other Weird Stories*, was issued posthumously by his widow in 1914. It is a critical commonplace that, as Peter Haining and Peter Tremayne put it, all of these works 'fall far short of the standards he had set in his vampire novel'.[45]

Bram Stoker died at his home, 26 St George's Square, Pimlico, London, on 20 April 1911. The author's estate, with a gross value of £4,723, according to the annotations made upon the officially archived copy of his will, was bequeathed to his wife, who survived him by 26 years. He was cremated following a short service at Golders Green, London, attended by, among others, the Manx novelist Hall Caine (1853–1931), dedicatee of *Dracula*, the novelist and editor Ford Madox Hueffer (later Ford; 1873–1939), and the actress Genevieve Ward (1837–1922).[46]

BIBLIOGRAPHICAL CRITICISM

Stoker's six major biographers express this raw data in widely different ways, a consequence in part of the historical periods in which their work was published and the disciplines out of which they were writing.

Hence, Harry Ludlam's pioneering *A Biography of Dracula* (1962) was, as its subtitle suggests, simply *The Life Story of Bram Stoker*, a non-controversial narrative for a 'fireside' readership distant from the cultural turmoil of the Swinging Sixties.[47] Its successor, *The Man Who Wrote Dracula* (1975), written by Stoker's great-nephew, Daniel Farson (1927–1997), was, in contrast, a product both of that era and of its author's connections with broadcasting. Farson, notably, introduced the theme of sexual guilt to Stoker's biography, though such speculations had already gained a place in academic criticism. The style of Barbara Belford's *Bram Stoker: A Biography of the Author of Dracula* (1996), again, owes much to its American author's background in journalism. Though this was the first biography of Stoker to support its assertions with anything approaching an academic standard of referencing and quotation, it is still marred by occasional inaccuracies, and, indeed, by a number of imaginative evocations of intimate scenes or unrecorded conversations in Stoker's private life, including the unspoken thoughts of his preoccupied mind.[48] The author's most recent biographers, Peter Haining and Peter Tremayne (*The Un-Dead: The Legend of Bram Stoker and Dracula*, 1997) and Paul Murray (*From the Shadow of Dracula: A Life of Bram Stoker*, 2004) have maintained both a high standard of scholarly research, and, for the most part, of referencing. Both biographies are particularly strong on the Irish contexts of Stoker's works, reflecting the gradual incorporation of Stoker into the Irish Studies canon from the 1990s. Murray's work, in particular, benefits from a sympathetic access to Stoker family papers not realised, particularly, in Belford's work.

As the titles and subtitles of their works betray, all of Stoker's biographers share an underlying commitment to the centrality of *Dracula* – to Stoker's authorial career, certainly, but also implicitly or explicitly, as some sort of key to his wider life. If the criticism of *Dracula*, though, has become characteristically dependent upon a limited range of scenes from the novel, so, too, has the author's life been distilled down to a number of specific incidents emphasised in biography and deployed frequently in criticism. These incidents are, chronologically, Stoker's youthful illness; his relationship with Irving; his apparently troubled marriage to Florence Balcombe; and his final illness and death. Other matters have, certainly, been utilised in biography – W. N. Osborough, for example, has chronicled Stoker's hitherto neglected civil service career, Leslie Shepard has briefly recounted some of the contents of the author's library, and other writers have accounted for his time at Whitby and in Scotland – though these have enjoyed none of the topical longevity of the four issues outlined above.[49]

Stoker's youthful illness is recalled without explanation in his *Personal Reminiscences of Henry Irving* (1906). 'In my babyhood', the author notes, 'I used, I understand to be, [*sic*] often at the point of death. Certainly till

I was about seven years old I never knew what it was to stand upright'.[50] This statement is accorded little significance in Ludlam's work, though speculation upon a likely psychological cause begins with Farson's account of his great-uncle.[51] Belford expands gleefully upon Stoker's undefined disorder, accentuating the illness as 'a pivotal turning point, forever marking his destiny', claiming that the author's reticence 'points to a secretive nature', and contending that his 'childhood fantasies bred adult nightmares'.[52]

Psychobiographical writers have taken even more advantage of the tantalising vagueness of Stoker's illness. Though, as he admits, no evidence exists that Stoker was ever hospitalised or subjected to surgical blood-letting, Seymour Shuster (1973) argues that the vampire 'basically represents a child's perception of the surgeon who operates upon him'.[53] More explicitly theoretical in nature are the two distinctive contributions to the debate forwarded, in 1972 and 1998 respectively, by Joseph Bierman. In 'Dracula: Prolonged Childhood Illness and the Oral Triad' (1972), Bierman draws on the concept of the Oral Triad – 'the wish to eat, to be eaten and to sleep' – developed by the psychoanalyst Bertram D. Lewin (1896–1971). Dracula, for Bierman, is a consequence of the author's youthful sibling rivalry, the desire to displace the child who has replaced him at the maternal breast being translated, because of his physical prostration, into oral expression rather than physical aggression. This psychological trauma was, Bierman argues, regenerated in adulthood through the knighthoods conferred in 1895 by Queen Victoria (1819–1901; reigned 1837–1901) upon Irving and the author's elder brother, William Thornley Stoker (1845–1912). Bram Stoker, it seems, never quite dissipated his childhood frustrations, and even in Dracula could express them, at best, only obliquely.[54]

Bierman returned to Lewin's Oral Triad 16 years later in 'A Crucial Stage in the Writing of Dracula' (1998). In this study, the novel is still a working through of childhood insecurities, where the empty graves of the Whitby churchyard and the port's enclosed harbour reflect an enclosed space or claustrum, 'the interior of the mother's body, an orally regressive safe haven from anxieties, especially sexual anxieties'. Whitby, for Bierman, represents a regression to a childhood fantasy of the prenatal state as a place of safety: to be eaten is to be taken, in fantasy, from the breast into the womb, where one may sleep without fear. The perverse implication of Lewin's theory, though, is neglected by Bierman: it is the vampire that gains entry to both the harbour and the tomb, and it is the vampire which represents a phallic father eternally producing siblings to displace their forbears. Surely, it might be suggested, if this is the case, the novel cannot truly be said to represent a retreat to a pre-sexual space that is both 'safe and satisfying'.[55] The problem with psychobiographical accounts such as those by Shuster and

Bierman is their dependence upon, on the one hand, classic universal scenarios – orality, sibling rivalry, oedipality – and on the other a quantum of data which is far from comprehensive. The balance between biography, speculative biography and fictional-text-as-biography is a difficult one to maintain with absolute conviction in a modern age which is as fixated upon 'facts – bare, meagre facts, verified by books and figures' as that of the fictional Jonathan Harker (35).

Stoker's relationship with Henry Irving is, similarly, subject to myth and speculation. Irving was undoubtedly a charismatic actor, and Stoker was a willing participant in the media's love affair with the first professional stage player to be knighted by a British monarch. Irving's popularity brought, in turn, publicity for Stoker himself, in his capacity as the public face of the Lyceum Theatre. He was depicted beside Irving in affectionate cartoons published by the stage press, gently mocked as the actor's 'Faithful Bram' or more seriously recognised as the faithful companion or '*fidus achates* to a great personality'.[56] This relationship has, however, not always been regarded in such an idealised light by those intimate to the two participants. The actor's grandson, writing in 1951, suggested that Stoker 'worshipped Irving with all the sentimental idolatry of which an Irishman is capable'. More tellingly, according to the Stoker's granddaughter, the author's own son, himself named after the actor, 'seemed to dislike Irving' and 'thought that Irving had worn Bram out'.[57] Noel Stoker never willingly used his first name, Irving, and his attributed opinion arguably supports the contention of those critics and biographers who see in Irving a prototype for the vampire Count. '*Dracula* is all about Irving as the vampire', Barbara Belford suggests. Likewise, for Maurice Hindle, the writing of *Dracula* signals the start of 'a programme of (unconscious) fictional revenge upon his adored Master [...] Henry Irving.'[58]

All of this dovetails nicely with those Freudian interpretations of *Dracula* which see in the novel an autobiographical expression of ambivalence towards a father-figure who is both admired and feared for his strength, and who currently retains a particular level of control over a desired female entourage. This is not as crudely oedipal as one might expect. For Belford, such unconscious drives are manifested in *Dracula* through a scripting of Irving as the Count and Ellen Terry (1847–1928), the actor's leading lady and reputed lover, as 'the unattainable good woman', Mina.[59] Elsewhere, Royce MacGillivray, clearly influenced by Maurice Richardson's insistence upon Stoker's 'unusually strong father fixation' and his references to Freud's *Totem and Taboo* (1913), detects a theme of parricide in the novel. This is a counterpart, it has to be said, to an equally speculative Cain-and-Abel fratricide, specifically associated with Irving, raised in Joseph Bierman's evocation of the Oral Triad in the same year.[60] Stoker's own father, whom he seems to have admired and respected, scarcely enters into the equation at all. If there is a 'father fixation' in Stoker's character, then his taste was certainly for the exceptional rather than the homely; this would seem to be supported by his documented admiration of a variety of older male figures, including Benjamin Disraeli (1804–1881), Conservative Prime Minister in 1868 and 1874–80; W. E. Gladstone (1809–1891), Liberal Prime Minister in 1864–74, 1880–85, 1886 and 1892–94; Alfred, Lord Tennyson (1809–1892), Poet Laureate from 1850; the pioneering American poet Walt Whitman (1819–1892), author of *Leaves of Grass* (1855); and the explorer, diplomat and translator, Sir Richard Burton (1821–1890). Stoker, depicted as isolated and an outsider in many biographical readings, might well be regarded as one who displaced and dissipated his own sense of mundane isolation – as a sick child in Clontarf, as an Irishman in London – by way of the more spectacular Otherness exhibited by those regarded as exceptional in political, physical or artistic stature.[61] His fantasies, quite possibly, were not those of parricide, but rather of a reflected glory, similar to that which he enjoyed in the shadow of Irving. Stoker, it could easily be argued, lacked confidence in his own ability.

An alternative to the 'father-fixation' hypothesis, inevitably, is the popular interpretation of Stoker as a repressed homosexual, and *Dracula* as a scarcely concealed mobilisation of homoerotic desire. John D'Addario, for example, discerns a probably unconsummated homosexual attraction between Stoker and Irving, though surprisingly stops short of projecting the actor into the vampire as earlier critics had done.[62] D'Addario supports his contention by quoting some of the admittedly fulsome prose with which the author eulogised his late employer in *Personal Reminiscences of Henry Irving*. Stoker's rhetoric in his biography of Irving, though, pales somewhat when laid beside the letters which he sent to the American poet Walt Whitman whilst still an undergraduate at Trinity College Dublin. Stoker is discreet about these in his biography of Irving, and quotes only Whitman's affectionate reply.[63] Stoker's earliest letter to the poet, dated 18 February 1872, which did not come into the public domain until some 40 years after its writer's death, is somewhat more revealing, though. It is not so much the way in which Stoker draws attention to his own physique – 'I am six feet two inches high and twelve stone weight naked', 'a mighty graphic picture', according to the elderly Whitman – but rather the manner in which he projects his future relationship with the poet that is striking. His emphasised candour concludes with the statement: 'How sweet a thing it is for a strong healthy man with a woman's eyes and a child's wishes to feel that he can speak so to a man who can be if he wishes father, and brother and wife to his soul.'[64] Stoker's words, the emotional and probably spontaneous outpourings of a young man, were never meant for public consumption. Though much might be made of them in criticism, it is as well to remember that the context of these is again one of isolation – Stoker, the defender of Whitman's verse against moral censure, Stoker the underachieving second son seeking the reflected glory of patrician over-achievers, Stoker the struggling writer addressing a distant role model.[65]

Oscar Wilde, a contemporary of the author in both Dublin and London, has inevitably become another focus of the speculation surrounding Stoker's sexuality. Stoker, notably, avoids any acknowledgement of the disgraced Wilde in his biography of Irving, though the dramatist was an occasional visitor to both the Stoker house and the Lyceum. Talia Schaffer's identification of 'codes for the closet' in *Dracula*, and her suggestion that the author was conscious of an unspeakable 'secret affinity with Wilde' which he somehow exorcised in the novel is ingenious, but marginalises possibly the central premise for the perceived coolness between the two Dubliners. Florence Stoker had previously been courted by Wilde, who had drawn a portrait of her and presented her with a gold cross, which she returned on her engagement to Stoker at Wilde's request.[66] Barbara Belford suggests that both Stoker and Wilde perversely eroticised Balcombe as a paragon of 'chaste womanhood', though more provocative female figures, beguiling though cold as death, are to be found in their major published works from Wilde's *Salomé* (1891, in French; English trans. 1894) to *Dracula*.[67]

Florence Stoker, in the eyes of some critics, is intimate to both the misogyny of *Dracula* and the sexually assertive female vampires who people its pages. Daniel Farson, writing in 1975, casually reported Stoker's granddaughter's opinion that 'Florence refused to have sex with Bram after her father was born'. This may well have been the case, given the absence of reliable contraception. Whether this might evidence what Farson terms 'Bram's sexual frustration', and his recourse to prostitutes in London and Paris, cannot, however, be proved.[68] Equally impossible to prove is the assertion by Penelope Shuttle and Peter Redgrove 'that a woman with an unsatisfactory sex life will have very bad menstrual disturbances'. Shuttle and Redgrove further query 'Was it some image of these that gave Stoker's subliminal mind the hint that formulated a myth of formidable power, out of the ferocity of a frustrated bleeding woman, crackling with energy and unacknowledged sexuality?' 'It is certainly possible', as they suggest, though it is hardly provable. *Dracula* may indeed be read as 'a menstrual narrative', as Marie Mulvey-Roberts contends, but its status as an autobiography of Stoker's sexual frustration, and a biography of his wife's gynaecological health, remains somewhat less certain.[69]

The sexual health of the Stoker marriage, however, in turn informs the debate surrounding the author's death in 1912. According to the certifying physician, the cause of death was 'locomotor ataxy 6 months, granular contracted kidney, exhaustion'.[70] Harry Ludlam, mindful no doubt of Edwardian eulogies which depicted Stoker as a 'big, breath-less, impetuous hurricane of a man', stressed the concluding word, 'exhaustion'.[71] This lay diagnosis was challenged, however, by Daniel Farson who, apparently under the guidance of a medical practitioner, interpreted the symptoms tabulated on the Certificate as indicative of a death caused by tertiary syphilis. Farson's explanation for this was, inevitably, Stoker's alleged marital celibacy – 'his wife's frigidity drove him to other women, probably prostitutes among them'. This is all very convenient, given the depiction of sexual vampires and 'suddenly sexual women', to borrow a phrase from Phyllis Roth, in *Dracula*. Stoker's adultery, apparently, 'created a sense of guilt', so much so that, follow-ing his alleged and undated infection, 'Bram's writing showed signs of sexual guilt and frustration'.[72] Farson's certainty has been disputed by subsequent biographers, Shepard and Belford among them. Haining and Tremayne, and Paul Murray, Stoker's most recent biographer, are more equivocal.[73] It has to be said, though, that the syphilis hypothesis derives much of its longevity from the critical sexualisation of the vampiric act in the novel, and the convenient association of both illicit sexuality and vampirism with progressive personal exhaustion and eventual demise. The twentieth and twenty-first centuries, it would appear, still need reassurance of the repressed sexualities of their Victorian ancestors.

CRITICISING *DRACULA* IN THE TWENTY-FIRST CENTURY

This Guide is, at its heart, a survey of almost 50 years of academic criticism of *Dracula*. In this context, it considers both the predominant orthodoxies of thought and the various challenges to their primacy. The risk associated with a volume of this type is, inevitably, that a further orthodoxy of critical readings might be exemplified, or an existing one concretised, within its pages. That risk, though, is offset by the con-tinually developing field of criticism in which *Dracula* plays variously a central or an important role. This Guide will equip the reader with the essential critical contexts upon which the ongoing debate is founded. Thus, the tendencies, and indeed the critics, discussed in the five chap-ters that follow can – and ought to be – supplemented, compared and contextualised through reference to works published progressively from the first decade of the twenty-first century. There is a further impera-tive, though, that ought rightly to be imposed upon those who write about *Dracula* at all levels, from the undergraduate essay to the academic monograph. The critical response to *Dracula* has historically been too dependent upon a limited range of admittedly spectacular episodes extracted from the novel, whilst certain aspects of Stoker's work remain under-explored and thus still ripe for exploitation. Much, for example, has been written upon Lucy Westenra's fantasy of marrying all three of her suitors, and even more upon her despatch – alternately ritualised or sexualised – at the hands of her fiancé in a London churchyard, yet there has been relatively little consideration of the lunatic Renfield's meeting with Mina Harker, or indeed the pathology, subject in the novel to a post-mortem, of the former's physical demise at the hands of the Count. The possibilities for expansion into new readings of *Dracula*, in other words, remain very much open. It is to be hoped that criticism in the twenty-first century is emboldened to move beyond the limits unwittingly imposed by the twentieth.

The current volume thus represents a starting point for further criticism based upon an understanding of the critical field as it is constituted in the first decade of the twenty-first century: it does not represent a closure. Its overviews anticipate the future as well as assessing the past. The thematic organisation of this Guide has been suggested by the manner in which the novel is most likely to be utilised, particularly by the undergraduate reader. It is not a linear critical history of *Dracula*, for such a work would be of little use to the majority of academic readers. Rather, it is an index to 48 years of research in a field where older work is at times referenced as frequently as more recent publications. The thematic structure further facilitates reader access to relevant issues without inhibiting cross-referencing and comparison. The division is not strictly along the lines of theory, as significant critical concerns such as sexuality and gender are, inevitably, subject to the scrutiny of diverse analytical tools. Rather, the five significant and recurrent focuses of *Dracula* criticism identified in this volume – psychoanalysis and the unconscious, the corporeal body, the imperial and domestic politics of the novel, Irish Studies and gender – all embody a breadth of theoretical perspectives. Though the chapters may, of course, be read independently of each other, a judicious use of both the detailed summaries provided on the Contents pages and of the Index is strongly advised. Just as the juxtaposition of two or more fictional texts may add depth to an argument so, too, does the acknowledgement of methodological confluence or dissent. It is all too easy to stay rigidly within a single, easily identified theoretical area – though this is thankfully something which many critics of *Dracula* have historically resisted. *Dracula*, a novel which is both thematically rich and critically well supported, remains an ideal subject for analysis. The critical possibilities of *Dracula*, and the range of theories that might well be applied to it, are far from exhausted.

★   ★   ★

The psychological theories developed by Sigmund Freud (1856–1939) are central to the earliest published academic responses to *Dracula*.

It is appropriate, therefore, that this Guide begins with a survey of psychoanalytical criticism between 1959 and 2002. The opening chapter will consider not merely the critical interplay between the relatively orthodox Freudian analyses of Maurice Richardson, Phyllis Roth and others, but will examine also how subsequent theories of repression and taboo have been successfully applied to *Dracula*. This chapter represents essential reading even for critics who deliberately distance themselves from the assumptions and conclusions of Richardson and his successors: psychoanalysis remains, for many *Dracula* critics, the theoretical standard against which their own methodological originality may be most graphically demonstrated. A knowledge of the landmarks of the psychoanalytical commentary upon *Dracula* thus remains crucial for those who would appreciate the contextual richness of both the novel *and* its criticism.

CHAPTER ONE

Psychoanalysis and Psychobiography: The Troubled Unconsciousness of *Dracula*

Psychoanalysis has, for better or for worse, undoubtedly shaped academic criticism of *Dracula*. This statement is not an exaggeration. Certain commonly held assumptions regarding Stoker's novel might be said to be the consequence of the rhetoric and evidencing of the earliest, psychoanalytical accounts of *Dracula*. These include, for example, the assumptions that the novel embodies a coded sexual content; that it has what may be loosely termed 'an unconscious'; and that it somehow projects a fantasy or fulfils a wish on the part of its author. Psychoanalytic criticism has, equally, influenced the selection of representative or significant scenes from *Dracula* by critics in all theoretical disciplines: thus, the critical reader finds many interpretations of Harker's ambivalent response to his vampiric temptresses, and is repeatedly invited to consider the staking of Lucy Westenra. That reader, though, will find much less written regarding Harker's vulnerability to Brain Fever, or on the hypnotic practice deployed in the name of Freud's mentor, Jean-Martin Charcot (1825–1893), by the brain-specialist, Van Helsing. It is effectively impossible to ignore the abiding and implicit presence of psychoanalysis in the ongoing criticism of *Dracula* – a presence which is, indeed, frequently evoked to signal the novelty of critical positions antipathetic to the theories of Freud and his successors.[1]

Dracula is an ideal text upon which to map a psychoanalytical analysis. Its generic Gothicism aligns it with a popular genre characteristically dismissed as subcultural and unworthy of study by an Anglo-American critical establishment preoccupied with a rarefied and elitist 'Great Tradition'. If this assumed cultural ephemerality were not enough to align the novel with those telling moments in Freudian psychodrama – dreams, jokes, slips of the tongue – then its presentation of dream-like experiences, trance and recurrent oral and penetrative symbolism recalls in itself the central symbolism employed in psychoanalysis. The popularity of Stoker's novel as the basis for cinematic adaptations – adaptations that made free use of the potential sexual symbolics of the vampire's bite – also arguably prepared the ground for the ready circulation of radical analyses by critics and readers keen to liberate themselves from the restrictive post-war canon represented most popularly by the work of the influential Cambridge academic F. R. Leavis (1895–1978).[2] Psychoanalysis, with its consideration not only of the closely read text but also of the psychologically coded individual or cultural unconscious, represented a serious challenge both to critical methodology and to the formulation of canon.

SEXUAL GUILT, TABOO AND THE OEDIPAL

Freud, it must be noted, did not write about vampires. His followers did, however, and possibly the most influential of these was Ernest Jones, whose *On the Nightmare* inspired two of the earliest psychoanalytical studies of Stoker's novel.[3] Jones argues that attitudes towards the dead may function as an index of the troubled psychology of the living. The living, as it were, unconsciously desire the return of the dead, but cannot directly voice that desire because of psychological repression and the cultural taboos surrounding contact with the dead. Thus,

■ the wish for re-union is often ascribed to the dead by the mechanism of projection. It is then believed that they feel an overpowering impulse to return to the loved ones whom they had left. The deepest source of this projection is doubtless to be found in the wish that those who have departed should not forget us, a wish that ultimately springs from childhood memories of being left alone by the loved parent.[4] □

The presence here of the psychoanalytical process of projection – where an individual's psychological states are associated not with the self, but with an object in the outside world – suggests that these emotions are somehow taboo. Jones argues that this projection is a response to an unconscious 'sexual guilt', a desire within the self which can only be voiced by being projected onto another. The memory of the 'loved parent' is crucial here, whether or not the departed has ever actually fulfilled that role. Jones continues:

■ We are, of course, speaking of an unconscious guiltiness, which, paradoxically enough, is most acute in the presence of what is socially and legally the most permitted love object, the married partner [...] Psychoanalysis has shown unequivocally that this unconscious guiltiness owes its origin to infantile incestuous wishes that have been only imperfectly overcome in the course of development.[5] □

Implicitly, the vampire, whether partner, parent, child or stranger is psychoanalytically the victim's relative, a figure invested with the imperfectly dissipated desires of Oedipality. The vampire desires to visit the victim because, unconsciously, the victim *wants* to be visited not merely by *this* vampire (who may, indeed, be a husband or a wife, the repository of conventional and sanctioned desire), but potentially by a whole range of unacknowledged and unacknowledgeable taboo figures whose shadowy common ancestor is the desired parent. The very practice of vampirism, indeed, recalls both the infantile state and more adult erotic practices. As Jones asserts, 'The act of sucking has a sexual significance from earliest infancy which is maintained throughout life in the form of kissing; in certain perversions it can actually replace the vagina itself.'[6] It goes without saying that 'In the unconscious mind blood is commonly an equivalent for semen.'[7]

Jones's assertions explicitly underpin Maurice Richardson's 1959 article, 'The Psychoanalysis of Ghost Stories', an essay that must be considered the first published application of Freudian theory to Stoker's novel.[8] Richardson's argument may appear crude – obvious even – when placed beside the subtleties of subsequent considerations of *Dracula* which draw upon the post-Freudian thought of Jacques Lacan or Julia Kristeva. The article's rhetoric, again, has been sporadically ridiculed for its hyperbole, its invocation, among other things, of 'a vast polymorph perverse bisexual oral-anal-genital sado-masochistic orgy' finding few stylistic imitators either in criticism or psychology.[9] It is, though, a pivotal work in that it significantly develops the perceived motif of incest in *Dracula* through the application of Freud's *Totem and Taboo*.

Richardson identifies an 'endogamous motif' in *Dracula*, whereby characters not actually related by blood maintain a network of relationships which permit them to be identified psychoanalytically 'as members of one family'.[10] In contrast to the isolated widows who characteristically fall victim to the vampire in Jones's psychoanalytical anthropology, Stoker's women are caught up in a network of desires realised, frustrated and redirected.[11] In an obvious inversion of the Count's feudal world, the bourgeois heroines of Stoker's romantic England may *choose* their partners, safe in the knowledge that a rejected suitor will not become a threat, but instead be voluntarily retained thereafter as a chivalric and devoted defender. The novel is highly explicit in this respect; both Seward and Morris promise Lucy their friendship after their marriage proposals are rejected (58, 60).[12] Richardson, curiously, fails either to quote or reference these two important scenes which establish a powerful tie between these three members of the coalition against Count Dracula. His conclusion, though, that the novel is 'a quite blatant demonstration of the Oedipus complex' invites a further consideration of both the psychoanalytical family constructed by the vampire hunters, and the boundary that separates the Count from his opponents-cum-victims.[13] There is more at stake here than Lucy's transformation into an Oedipal focus for the frustrated desires of Seward and Morris.

The Count's antiquity, and his control over the women he inducts into vampirism, permits him to be identified by Richardson as 'a father-figure of huge potency'.[14] Thus, taking on board the Count's boast that 'Your girls that you all love are mine already' (267), Richardson is emboldened to assert that:

■ Apart from Van Helsing, who represents the good father-figure, the set-up reminds one rather of the primal horde as pictured somewhat fantastically perhaps by Freud in *Totem and Taboo*, with the brothers banding together against the father who has tried to keep all the females to himself. □

Richardson's argument is coherent, if somewhat sparsely evidenced – 'several more passages' of evidence are offered but never specified.[15] The argument might well have been taken further by an attempt to address how, in the act of communal patricide, the defenders of Mina resemble the cannibalistic perpetrators of the primal crime in *Totem and Taboo*. The most notable omission is their lack of horror or remorse at their act – a state of emotion that distances them explicitly from Freud's savages.[16] David Punter, most notably, was to develop the application of taboo to *Dracula* beyond the Primal Crime of psychoanalysis, in an influential consideration of borders and demarcations within his *The Literature of Terror* (1980).[17] The role of Van Helsing as a paternal alternative to the Count is also worthy of further consideration – though this issue was eventually addressed in a 1980 article by Richard Astle on the totemic implications of *Dracula*.[18]

Richardson's suggestion that the Oedipal might be regarded as an effective key to *Dracula* did not, however, go unchallenged by other Freudian critics. Phyllis Roth, in *Bram Stoker*, a work which surveys the breadth of Stoker's fiction, argues that the ambivalences and fantasies of *Dracula* are pre-Oedipal rather than conventionally Oedipal, their focus shifting between the 'morbid dread' identified by Richardson and a 'lustful anticipation of an oral fusion with the mother'.[19] Whilst freely admitting that '*Dracula* does appear to enact the Oedipal rivalry among sons and between the son and the father for the affections of the mother', Roth tempers her argument with the suggestion that the novel effectively duplicates its characters, facilitating their perverse identification with the Count and expressing an occluded 'fantasy of matricide underlying the more obvious patricidal wishes'.[20] Thus,

■ the split between the sexual vampire family and the asexual Van Helsing group is not at all clear-cut: Jonathan, Van Helsing, Seward and Holmwood are all overwhelmingly attracted to the vampires, to sexuality. Fearing this, they employ two defenses, projection and denial: it is not we who want the vampires, it is they who want us (to eat us, to seduce us, to kill us).[21] □

The coalition against the Count, Roth subsequently notes, enacts the majority of the killings featured in the novel, and is responsible for all of those which are directly perceived by the reader – the spectacular and violent 'deaths', as it were, of Lucy and the Count. The vampires, in contrast, despatch their victims out of the gaze of both reader and character, whether these be an abducted child, a ship full of sailors or an inconvenient madman. The wish to kill, Roth argues, is projected onto the vampire but enacted, as wish fulfilment, by the mortals who demonise him.[22]

The vampire is demonised in part by his perceived opposition to Christian spirituality. Reference to *Totem and Taboo* enables Roth to associate Van Helsing's reasoned and ritualistic attempt to save Lucy's soul from eternal 'paths of flame' (183) with the violations and renunciations identified by Freud in the primitive religions he associates with the savage (or unconscious) mind. These rituals, arguably, both exorcise and celebrate the power of the despatched and dethroned father, and it is their compulsive nature that empowers Roth to suggest that, as the Count 'acts out the repressed fantasies of the other male characters', consequently 'we have no difficulty in recognizing an identification with the aggressor on the part of characters and reader alike'.[23]

How this male fantasy, which embraces both violence and seduction, the aggressor and the vengeful vigilante, becomes associated with the female reader of *Dracula*, however, remains unanswered, and, indeed, unacknowledged. Problematically, Roth is forced to admit that the frisson of identification with the potent figure of the vampire represents also 'the reader's identification with the aggressor's victimization of women'.[24] The seeming coincidence that brings the Count to predate upon two close friends is also explained through the contention that, psychoanalytically, they represent the same figure, the mother – a desirable figure who, never the less, finds herself in anti-maternal and sexualised situations of predation in *Dracula*.[25] Roth's linking of reader and male protagonist undermines somewhat the progressive project of post-1960s culture, intimating the lingering presence of both repression and misogyny beneath those modern, 'liberated' cultures which celebrate the rise of the 'suddenly sexual women' in Stoker's fiction.[26]

MENSTRUATION AND THE PSYCHOLOGICAL SIGNIFICANCE OF BLOOD

Equally indebted to the concept of taboo is C. F. Bentley's 'The Monster in the Bedroom: Sexual Symbolism in Bram Stoker's *Dracula*'. Bentley concurs with Richardson regarding the novel's 'symbolic presentation of human sexual relationships' and with Jones on the equation of blood and semen, and stresses the predominantly heterosexual orientation of vampire predation.[27] The article's novelty is vested in its appreciation of genital symbolics, and in particular its invocation of menstrual taboo. Recalling how the bitten Mina proclaims herself 'Unclean! Unclean!' (259) following the Count's attack, Bentley states:

> ■ Mina's description of herself while 'the thin stream of blood' trickles from her recalls ancient primitive fears of menstruation. The mention of a 'thin open wound' is especially noteworthy: in *Dracula* the mark of the vampire's bite is usually described as two round punctures caused by the elongated canine teeth, whereas this phrase suggests a cut or slit similar to the vaginal orifice.[28] □

Blood, variously arterial and menstrual, 'has multiple meanings in *Dracula*'.[29] Bentley's work, though, reads the novel rather than the psychobiography of the author, and thus makes no abiding connection between Stoker's private life and his fiction. Admittedly, Daniel Farson's *The Man Who Wrote Dracula*, with its assertion that Florence Stoker had discontinued the couple's sexual relations following the birth of their only son, was not then available. Subsequent critics, though, were able to take the argument further by citing Farson's controversial claims of sexual frigidity, guilty infidelity and debilitative venereal disease within the Stoker family.[30] Drawing, in 1978, on a considerably more enhanced critical and biographical field than had been available in 1972 to Bentley, Penelope Shuttle and Peter Redgrove were finally able to reconcile both the vampire and the 'unclean' menstruating woman in the biography of Stoker's reputedly 'frigid' wife, Florence:

> ■ It is likely that a woman with an unsatisfactory sex life will have very bad menstrual disturbances. Was it some image of these that gave Stoker's subliminal mind the hint that formulated a myth of formidable power, out of the ferocity of a frustrated bleeding woman, crackling with energy and unacknowledged sexuality? It is certainly possible.[31] □

The brevity of Shuttle and Redgrove's analysis makes it anecdotal rather than truly analytical, though it was to influence a considerably more extensive review of the menstrual taboo published some 26 years later.

In '*Dracula* and the Doctors: Bad Blood, Menstrual Taboo and the New Woman' (1998), Marie Mulvey-Roberts advances a substantial, understated analysis of Stoker's novel through taboo, the concept of which is laudably rendered with reference to *The Golden Bough* (1890–1915) by Sir James Frazer (1854–1941) as well as Freud's 'The Taboo of Virginity' (1918). Though Mulvey-Roberts's article might most appropriately be addressed as a contribution to the interrogation of *Dracula* via Queer Theory, its relevance to the psychoanalytical debate ought not to be dismissed out of hand. Mulvey-Roberts argues that 'Reading *Dracula* as a menstrual narrative has its starting point with the menarche [the first occurrence of menstruation] and moves on to the pathologies associated with the menses to end with the menopause represented by the death of the vampire.'[32] Besides constructing the Count as a menstruating, feminised man, who is ultimately disposed of by being 'penetrated like a woman or homosexual', Mulvey-Roberts exposes a number of quite surprising *fin-de-siècle* writings upon the seemingly pathological nature of conventional menstruation.[33] Menstruation, in these medical and quasi-medical accounts, is not natural, it seems, but a consequence of a male sexual desire too frequently gratified and thus excessive.[34] Perversely, though male lust 'resembles the blood lust of the vampire, which is represented as an insatiable and addictive thirst', the menstruating woman is the one who is condemned because her periodic loss 'suggested that women were becoming less feminine in having appropriated the sexual appetites of men'.[35] Stoker's novel, according to Mulvey-Roberts, is imbricated with multiple *fin-de-siècle* sexual anxieties, from repressed and active homosexuality to the rise of an assertive feminism represented by the evocative New Woman. Thus, 'Stoker's reinforcement of the dominant power relations is expressed through the misogyny directed towards menstruating women represented by his fictional vampires, who are defeated by his triumphant doctor-hero.'[36] The adult sexualities of the *fin de siècle*, it would appear, require a surgical rather than psychological 'cure', in order to return those under affliction to the 'sweetness and purity' (192) of perceived well-being.

PSYCHOBIOGRAPHY

Shuttle and Redgrove – and, indeed, Mulvey-Roberts – argue that the preoccupations and practices of the fictional Count Dracula are a consequence of the allegedly frustrated sexuality of Stoker and his wife.[37] A more conventional focus for psychobiography, though, is the apparent reproduction of repressed or residual infantile neuroses in adult life. Given this theoretical preoccupation, it is not surprising that a significant proportion of psychoanalytical studies of *Dracula* have focused upon its author's youth. Though the details of Stoker's early life are at best vague and at worst ambivalent, certain biographical details have become effectively established as being intimate to specific scenes within *Dracula*. These, in turn, are often further contextualised through reference to recurrent images within Stoker's other writings, in such a way as rhetorically to suggest the involuntary expression of authorial preoccupations, obsessions or neuroses throughout his fiction. Arguably, the most frequently referenced of these assumed infantile crises is Stoker's early, debilitating illness, which the author himself acknowledged in his 1906 biography of Henry Irving:

> ■ It is true that I had known weakness. In my babyhood I used, I understand to be [*sic*], often at the point of death. Certainly till I was about seven years old I never knew what it was to stand upright. I was naturally thoughtful and the leisure of long illness gave opportunity for many thoughts which were fruitful according to their kind in later years.[38] □

This illness, tantalisingly undefined, might well represent nothing more than a rhetorical flourish on Stoker's part, a foil to help accentuate his subsequent account of a recuperative *mens sana in corpore sano*, graced by academic Honours, silver cups and sportsman's caps.[39] Biography, though, has made much of Stoker's confession. Barbara Belford, for example, posits the onset of a fever, but then speculates as to whether his convalescence at home might have led to a residual fear of abandonment − the origin, she suggests, of the many scenes of rescue that appear across Stoker's fiction.[40] Other biographical explanations have included mental illness, rheumatic fever and, inevitably, a form of romantic malingering, though no definitive diagnosis can be gleaned from Stoker's reticent account.[41]

The vacuum of detail, though, has been readily filled by psychobiographical accounts which relate Stoker's illness to *Dracula*, for the most part through the assumption that the youthful author was routinely bled during his seven-year malady.[42] This would seemingly make for an obvious symbolic connection between the vampire and the physician, though in psychobiographical readings the association between the two is complicated by suggestions that the author both fears the figure who drains his blood, and yet aspires to the admirable and awful power which he holds over both the patient/victim specifically and life more generally. The sick child, in such readings, characteristically becomes a thoughtful child, preoccupied not merely with a painful therapeutic regime which he is too young to understand but also distressed by the arrival of further siblings, each one of which, he fears, implicitly diminishes his relative value in the eyes of his parents.[43]

In 'Dracula: Prolonged Childhood Illness and the Oral Triad', for example, Joseph S. Bierman sees repressed sibling rivalry as the motivation not merely for *Dracula* but also as the background to several of the short stories in Stoker's 1882 collection for children, *Under the Sunset*. In 'How 7 Went Mad', the fifth story in *Under the Sunset*, the eponymous number is driven insane by his difference from his sibling digits and is bled by an Alphabet Doctor. Bierman reads this incident not merely as a re-enactment of Stoker's own physical experience, but also as a form of wish-fulfilment in which the seven Stoker children are effectively recalculated in such a way that he, the fourth, becomes again the central focus of parental attention. Bierman's analysis of 'How 7 Went Mad' is ingenious, and relies upon a miscalculation – effectively, the equivalent of a slip of the tongue – in the mathematics of the story. This, Bierman assumes, is as psychologically significant as the order in which four further siblings followed the bedridden author within his family. Its overall premise is that the short story memorialises the author's desire to move from number 3 to number 7, and to regain the parental love that had been taken from him by George (1855–1920), his youngest brother.[44] Bierman's thesis, though, is unconvincing in its mathematical complexity, and under-evidenced with regard to how each number might relate specifically to an individual sibling.

Taken in this context, *Dracula* becomes a second fictional exorcising of an unconscious aggression directed towards Stoker's younger brothers, Tom (1849–1925) and George, the recipients of the author's conscious affection.[45] Bierman suggests that *Dracula* came about because its author's repressed sibling rivalry was re-energised in 1895, when both Irving (whom Stoker associated with theatrical and poetic fratricide) and William Thornley Stoker were knighted by Queen Victoria.[46] The evidence Bierman finds for this in *Dracula*, however, seems contrived, to say the least:

■ The death wishes toward his baby brothers may be found in *Dracula* in the form of three instances of infanticide by eating and sucking and the frequent usage of the names Tom and George for different minor characters. For example, Harker arrives at Dracula's castle on St George's Eve. Even the novel itself is dedicated to a Tommy – to Thomas Hall Caine, a novelist friend of Stoker's.[47] □

It is never made clear by Bierman why Stoker's rivalry was not directed towards his eldest brother in 1895 – indeed, William Thornley Stoker's status as a consultant surgeon may well have influenced the successful and patrician Van Helsing in *Dracula* as much as it certainly did the more dogmatic Sir James Frere in the author's later Gothic novel, *The Jewel of Seven Stars* (1903).[48] Ingenious though Bierman's thesis is, the rhetoric of his account fails to integrate satisfactorily the disparate elements of biography, short story and novel. As individual components they are provocative, though the rapid, almost episodic, progression between neurotic signifiers in the article undermines any pretence of coherence. Sadly, this is 'medical detection' without a convincing closure, a case study that is rich in example but deficient in conclusion.[49]

A more extensive treatment of Stoker's experience at the hands of medical professionals is provided by Seymour Shuster's '*Dracula* and Surgically Induced Trauma in Children', an article which discerns parallels between the novel and twentieth-century case histories of children traumatised by surgery. The emphasis here is not upon Stoker's relationship with his siblings during his childhood illness, but rather his interaction with authoritative medical professionals. In common with Bierman, Shuster considers it probable that, during part of his childhood, Stoker was present in his parents' bedroom whilst they were sexually active.[50] This experience is prototypically confusing for the child: sexual love may be confused with violence by the prepubescent viewer. It may also, though, distort the child's perception of how adults ought to relate to children – particularly, one assumes, in situations which involve pain or nudity. Arguing that Stoker was either bled or subjected to surgery in hospital, Shuster contends that the Count 'basically represents a child's perception of the surgeon who operates upon him', and that

■ when a child has been frightened by a doctor during an examination, inoculation or operation, an important part of that child's fear lies in his fantasy that the doctor has been a loser in the sexual-aggressive battles of the primal bedroom (i.e. he is empty or castrated), has become 'mad', and is seeking to alleviate his misery either by castrating the child or by emptying his body of its content.[51] □

Shuster argues that *Dracula* functions essentially as a psychological process through which the author disperses his childhood fears by turning the passive patient into the active participant. His evidence for this comes from twentieth-century empiricism:

■ many child psychiatrists know that when a child has been frightened during examination by a doctor, he will soon after suggest playing 'doctor' with a friend. Only now, he will reverse the role. He will be the doctor and try to make the other child feel the anxiety he had just suffered. Essentially, I believe Bram Stoker was doing just this when he wrote *Dracula*.[52] □

This seems credible, though Shuster fails to specify the focus of the all-important anxiety projected by the novel's vampire encounters. Is the anxiety to be suffered by the characters, several of which have come to be conventionally identified with Stoker? If so, then the cathartic function of the novel would seem to be at best only partially effective. Or, is the anxiety directed towards the reader? If this latter is the case, then the reader is faced with the task of discriminating between two competing surgical methodologies, both of which appear equally preoccupied with violence and bloodletting. Again, the cathartic value of the novel seems questionable.

Bierman and Shuster, though they concur upon Stoker's psychological intimacy with the vampire, hold strikingly divergent opinions regarding the psychological significance of the Count. For Bierman, the vampire expresses not merely anti-social desires against the author's male siblings, but also a need to recover the affections of a mother preoccupied with his younger brothers. This latter, though, would seem to be somewhat obliquely addressed by the fictionalisation in the novel of a vampire who 'could appropriate for his sucking pleasure the women of other men, and have them feel threatened with the loss instead of himself'. Stoker, perversely, would seem to be identifying with the lost mother here, though Bierman is silent with regard to what processes of displacement have caused this to take place.[53] Shuster, by contrast, sees the writer's identification with the vampire-as-doctor as an attempt to regain control, to be the physician rather than the patient, he who takes rather than he who is taken from. Stoker, though, is doing far more than merely 'playing doctors' in order to exorcise an infantile trauma. Shuster suggests that the novel is also an attempt to 'feel a sense of mastery over the terrifying doctor'. This is not, however, achieved through the final denouement and death of the vampire and the apparent succession of the 'good' doctor, Van Helsing, a man who has not been a loser in the primal bedroom. Rather, it is enacted at the very start of the novel, when the Count is observed making Harker's bed and acting as his butler (32). In a way, this menial service, this ministering to one's needs, disarms the spectre that haunted Stoker's infirm childhood:

■ Not only will the vampire not hurt him, but the vampire likes him so much that he waits on him hand and foot. So, who's afraid of the big, bad vampire? Not Bram Stoker![54] □

Problematically, though, Shuster fails to indicate clearly how Stoker can be both vampire-doctor and Harker-patient – and, indeed, overlooks the final detail of how the vampire-doctor abandons his guest-patient to the less-qualified hands of three female assistants. Though a more credible and more protracted assessment than Bierman's, Shuster's account remains problematic because psychoanalysis and its derivatives characteristically resist closure and singularity when associating biographical identities with fictional characters.

Bierman returned to Stoker's novel some 26 years later in 'A Crucial Stage in the Writing of *Dracula*'. Making use of the unpublished manuscript material which informed Bierman's earlier, non-psychoanalytical study 'The Genesis and Dating of *Dracula* from Bram Stoker's Working Notes' (1977), 'A Crucial Stage in the Writing of *Dracula*' first considers the author's last-minute relocation of the vampire's port of entry from Dover to Whitby.[55] Bierman regards the change of location as being of psychological significance, rather than as an innocent commemoration of a family holiday at Whitby in 1890.[56] Again, there is the insistence that *Under the Sunset* may function as a key to its author's childhood traumas and fantasies, and that, in *Dracula*, Whitby succeeded Dover 'because certain features of the town recalled to [Stoker] three stories, and the certain fantasy they contained'.[57] Though Bierman raises various issues that connect the two works – from lies to madness, through physical geography to the symbolic nature of gates and apertures – the central psychological focus of the article is, again, Stoker's infantile anxiety.

Recalling his earlier analysis, Bierman makes use of Bertram D. Lewin's *The Psychoanalysis of Elation* (1950), and in particular its evocation of the Oral Triad – 'the wish to eat, to be eaten, and to sleep'. In Bierman's earlier work, the Oral Triad was briefly deployed to support the conjectural existence of 'death wishes towards younger brothers, nursing at the breast, and primal scenes expressed in nursing terms'. The infant Stoker, as it were, desired exclusive access to the maternal breast and harboured hostility to anyone usurping his place thereon: sleep, coming after fulfilment, is desirable, yet is also associated with death, the punishment for fratricide.[58] In 'A Crucial Stage in the Writing of *Dracula*', Bierman develops Lewin's theory more extensively – and, it has to be said, more coherently and successfully – by recalling the association of the Oral Triad with infantile fantasies that embody a return to the womb. In the womb, it is conjectured by the child, one is either eating or sleeping. One's return to the womb is also associated with ingestion, the wish to eat: in his imagination, the regressive child is either swallowed or gnaws his way into the womb-substitute. The psychological motivation of these womb-fantasies is prototypically the desire for 'a flight from sexual, internally originating dangers to a pre-sexual state that is then safe and satisfying'.[59] Thus, the womb-space or *claustrum*, as Lewin terms it, 'represents the interior of the mother's body as an orally regressive safe haven from anxieties, especially sexual anxieties'.[60]

Bierman argues that Stoker replaced Dover with Whitby because the physical and human geography of the latter port recalled his childhood *claustrum* fantasies. The port is a haven, to stressed holidaymakers from London as much as to ships driven towards England's eastern coast by North-Sea storms. The twin piers of Whitby harbour recall, for Bierman, the portal which guards the fantasy kingdom of the Land Under the Sunset in Stoker's 1882 children's collection, *Under the Sunset*. Bierman therefore equates the piers with the entrance to the *claustrum* and uses them to mark the safety which that womb-like space prototypically provides. Further spaces of intimacy and safe retreat are provided by the empty tombs in the Whitby churchyard frequented by Mina and Lucy – though the innocence of these is contaminated by the lies that are inscribed upon them, and the epitaphs that bear no relation to the non-existences within their narrow confines (66–7).[61]

The *claustrum*, though, is not a place of inviolable isolation. It may be invaded, much as the Edenic Land Under the Sunset is invaded by the sinful, worldly Children of Death in Stoker's 1882 title story, 'Under the Sunset'. Bierman notes that if one retreats to the *claustrum* to escape anxiety, then any invasion of that space will inevitably herald the return of trauma. Specifically, the threat symbolised by invasion of the claustrum is both violent and sexual, the interposition of the adult upon the infantile:

> ■ The intrusion into the *claustrum* that causes the anxiety is the fantasised father's penis. Lucy fears the invasion of her tomb with the stake and the knife [...] Dracula has the gypsies fight for his life to prevent the closed box he is being transported in from being prized [*sic*] open and penetrated by the intruding thrusts of Harker's and Morris's knives [...] Dracula is another Child of Death who passes through the Portal of the Whitby Harbour mouth between its twin piers and lighthouses and enters a new port [...] to disturb the peaceful holiday land in the forms of a wolf and a bat.[62] □

Effectively, there appears to be no psychological escape from adult sexuality – or, at least, no escape from the anxiety that its presence will disrupt the safety and irresponsibility of the infantile, pre-sexual state. The suggestion, though, that the Count is both menaced by the phallic father in the *claustrum* of his coffin, and represents that phallic father invading the *claustrum* of Whitby itself, parallels Stoker's own variant psychological identity as vampire, vampire-hunter and imprisoned, infantilised solicitor. The resistance to any form of symbolic closure characteristic of psychobiography undoubtedly facilitates conclusions such as this – at the same time, perhaps, as it opens them up to question. Perhaps the most questionable absence in Bierman's consideration of a threatening, phallic patriarchy is the figure of the father himself, Abraham Stoker senior, the very man who possessed the desired woman before the author's birth, throughout his troubled infancy and into his, apparently sexually frustrated, adulthood.

CHILD SEXUAL ABUSE

Surprisingly, the question of Abraham Stoker senior's possible psychological influence upon the novel had not been discussed in any meaningful way until it became the focus of Daniel Lapin's *The Vampire, Dracula and Incest* in 1995. Lapin, a psychiatrist in private practice, regards the vampire myth, as exemplified in *Dracula*, 'as deriving unconsciously from vampiric sexual abuse rendered unconscious since childhood'.[63] Vampiric sexual abuse does not involve the ingestion of bodily fluids – this Lapin terms concrete vampirism – though it is a form of psychic predation, a slow degradation of the mental faculties.[64] Vampiric sexual abuse frequently leads to depression on the part of the victim, and often prompts in that individual the extremes of either frigidity or involuntary sexual submission. When undertaken by a close relative, as vampiric incest, it is particularly debilitating and demoralizing.[65] Much of Lapin's book makes reference to the case histories of his clients in the 1980s and 1990s, though Stoker's protagonists, exemplified as psychopathological specimens, punctuate the work's speculations upon the abused psyche. The first three chapters, however, which read Stoker's novel in conjunction with Lapin's vision of the author's life, are likely to be of most interest to the critical reader of *Dracula*.

Lapin's thesis stands at the problematic intersection of relatively orthodox psychology and a more speculative, and almost New Age, appreciation of vampirism as a spiritual phenomenon. Some of Lapin's psychological conclusions are relatively uncontroversial. Lucy and Mina, for example, are marked out as potential victims by their submissive psychology prior to the Count's arrival in England. Lapin, uniquely in criticism, recalls a minor scene in *Dracula*, in which Lucy's mother invites a clergyman to supper and the two girls politely entertain him, despite their quite reasonable desire for sleep. Mina recalls:

■ Lucy was really tired and we intended to creep off to bed as soon as we could. The young curate came in, however, and Mrs Westenra asked him to stay for supper. Lucy and I both had a fight for it with the dusty miller; I knew it was a hard fight on my part, and I am quite heroic. I think that some day the bishops must get together and see about breeding up a new class of curates, who don't take supper, no matter how they may be pressed to, and who will know when girls are tired. (86) □

The two, Lapin suggests, find it hard to refuse the demands or requests of men. He sees Lucy and Mina as:

■ two women who not only cannot set limits and will override their own conscious needs/desires/preferences to please a man, but who imagine solving this problem by having the male 'know' what the woman prefers so she needn't say so.[66] □

If they cannot refuse a mild, youthful curate, how can they hope to spurn the advances of an aged, feudal aristocrat? It is not that they are incapable of refusing male demands. Rather, it is that even refusals are somehow compromises. 'Lucy, at 19, can't stand to cause a man heartache', Lapin insists, and so where a refusal is tendered, care is characteristically taken to offer or concede something in compensation – Lucy, most notably, grants her two unsuccessful suitors a promise of friendship and a kiss (58, 60).

Lapin sees the tendency to submit to debilitating psychic vampirism by an adult not as an unprecedented act, but rather as a re-enactment of abuse endured during childhood. The powerful child-abuser, who invades the body and who may be implicated with bodily fluids, effectively prepares the victim for the subsequent vampiric abuser. The fluids, in a neat, New Age symbolism, thus become spiritual as well as literal, opening psychic channels that recall the Count's telepathic intimacy with Mina, mobilised by her ingestion of his fluids (252). The psychological repression and loss of memory characteristic of childhood abuse, in addition, leaves the adult vulnerable to subsequent attack. This, when begun, facilitates the resurfacing of earlier emotions of powerlessness or of the need to please the abuser in the form of submissive behaviour.

Lapin's assertion of the presence of a repressed act of abuse perpetrated upon the characters of Stoker's novel is, at first sight, credible. It is evidenced with behaviours associated with infantile sexuality since the time of Freud, Lucy's sleepwalking is linked with hysteria by Lapin, and so, following the vampire's first attack, 'Lucy's re-enactment with an abusive male begins in her distinctly hysterical style'.[67] Lapin, further, sees Lucy's recollection of the event itself, with its 'vague memory of something long and dark', and images of flying and drowning (94), as a recognisable 'defensive dissociative phenomenon frequently reported by sexual abuse survivors', and her reluctance to sleep (116) as 'a common complaint of incest survivors'.[68] In the manner of psychologies which recover repressed memory, no textual evidence is advanced for the existence of this infantile abuse, nor any perpetrator named at this juncture other than the Count, who re-enacts rather than initiates the abuse. The symptom is, in effect, the evidence, the supporting evidence being drawn not from the novel, but from empirical work with incest survivors.

Lapin's work becomes potentially problematic, both on a critical and a psychological level, in its definition of blood. The rhetoric of Lapin's account of vampirism suggests that the act of draining blood is not simply a coded or symbolic device which a survivor may use to represent an event which cannot be vocalised in public. Curiously, he posits the existence of an immaterial life-essence, 'the blood of the psyche', and argues that 'vampiric abuse poisons the victim's psychic blood'.[69] Lapin, in his application of this theory to *Dracula*, makes rhetorical use of Sister Agatha's words regarding Jonathan Harker's delirium, where the solicitor raved 'of wolves and poison and blood' (95). Lapin further reconfigures the Christian concept of the soul by suggesting that, rather than a theological concept, it is 'a substructure distinguishable within the psyche, inseparable from and interpenetrative with the rest of the psyche, and inseparable from and interpenetrative with the Divine'. Thus, 'By damaging the Soul, a part of the psyche crucial in accessing the Divine, vampiric incest leaves the victim spiritually compromised, distanced from the Divine.'[70] This is a challenging viewpoint, whether its focus is *Dracula* or the spiritual-psychological well-being of one of Lapin's twentieth-century clients. This Guide is certainly not the place to debate the veracity of Lapin's empiricism or, indeed, to assess the relative merits of theological as opposed to psychoanalytical definitions of the intangible soul. Suffice it to say, though, that literary criticism ought to be mindful of the fruitful opportunities that may be presented by the soul as envisioned by Stoker through, variously, Renfield and Van Helsing, and the adaptation of this as projected by Lapin's psychology. The two, certainly, are worthy of a more protracted consideration – though this would necessitate a degree of awareness regarding Victorian conceptions of death and the afterlife.

Lapin's *The Vampire, Dracula and Incest* functions on two levels. The first of these, as has already been suggested, is a form of fictional psychobiography, where the behaviour of the female protagonists, in particular, is regarded as a psychopathological indicator of their early, unwritten, lives. Lapin, though, parallels this reading by attempting a psychobiography of Stoker himself – though his reading of the author is, to say the least, speculative, if not independent of the known facts of the author's early life. For Lapin, Jonathan Harker is a representative of Stoker's unconscious. If this is the case, then, logically, the neurotic behaviour of the character represents that of the author, and 'As each aspect of Jonathan's experience is reviewed, [the reader] will once again recognize, in Jonathan as in Lucy, an adult compelled to re-enact unconscious childhood abuse.' In the combat of that abuse, re-enacted in the novel, 'Stoker consciously identifies with Van Helsing and is unconsciously identified with Jonathan'.[71]

This is, again, an attractive hypothesis, and there is certainly credibility in Lapin's suggestion that the Count's immense strength, deployed against the menaced Harker in Transylvania, reflects how a vulnerable child might view the power of an adult. When the Count disperses the wolves outside his castle, leaving Harker with 'a dreadful fear' and 'afraid to speak or move' (20), Lapin queries: 'Can you hear the child, on his way home to Daddy's Castle, knowing that abuse is inevitable?'[72] Jonathan, in the castle, resembles the abused child placed totally at the mercy of a proprietary or parental adult: 'The castle is a veritable prison', Harker admits, 'and I am a prisoner!' (32), and even when the Count offers the solicitor his freedom, it is only to make him realise that, perversely, he is safer within the home of the abuser than out in the wolfish world beyond. Harker's 'tears of bitter disappointment' (52) are tears that reflect his resignation to an ongoing fate, his acceptance that escape from the man who holds him is impossible. As Lapin concludes:

> ■ If a child *were* to exit Daddy's Castle, he wouldn't know where to go, and he would have no money. Derivatively, we find Jonathan without information regarding railways and travel, without his letter of credit, lacking 'all that might be useful to me were I once outside the castle' [46]. So many adults abused as children tell of the occasion when they threatened to run away, to which their parent(s) responded by opening the door, saying 'You wanna go? Go!' [...] Just as the child does not exit, realizing that he/she is being cast to the wolves, so Jonathan selects to stay.[73] (original italics) □

The Count, seemingly, is not merely the bad father of psychoanalytical theory, but Stoker's abusive father specifically. That may be so, but Lapin has to admit that the Count (and, indeed, his three female protégées) never suck the blood or otherwise abuse the imprisoned solicitor. At this point, he is forced to equivocate:

> ■ Jonathan escapes Castle Dracula before the Count ever actually sucks his blood. Technically speaking, Jonathan was never vamped. I would be foolish, however, to insist that Bram, as a child, was as fortunate as Jonathan, especially since [...] the *impact* on Jonathan was clearly traumatic.[74] (original italics) □

Intention, it seems, is as good as action, though, to drive his point home, Lapin argues that Lucy and Mina are fictionalised representations of Stoker's own sisters, whom he claims were also the victims of a sexually voracious Victorian parent. Jonathan, who wakes to find his wife vampirised by the Count, thus becomes 'the brother who witnessed his sister Mina's rape by their father'. Further, the group's defence of the solicitor's wife is motivated by a consciousness of the sexual degradation of Lucy, again depicted psychologically not as a friend but a sister: 'Derivatively speaking, once *one* of your sisters has been molested, and you barely escaped yourself, you are quite naturally going to be pretty worried about another sister whom the vampiric father seems to fancy' (original italics).[75]

Lapin's analysis alternates between projecting the psychobiographies of the Count's victims and linking these with those of the Stoker family. The latter, though, as Lapin admits, have no documentary basis, and the psychobiographer's honesty here plainly illustrates the brittle nature of speculative biographies projected in this way. Stoker, Lapin suggests, may have consciously 'selected not to mention events which he remembered'. That said,

■ the absence of any documented evidence of vampiric incest in Stoker's childhood would prove nothing because he may have rendered unconscious any such experiences. In fact, I don't believe he could have written *Dracula* if he remembered childhood incest. It is precisely the unconsciousness of such experience which fuels such novels. At the same time, writing the novel is itself a defense against consciousness of the events from which the novel derives.[76] □

Whichever way one turns, it seems, the theory is sufficiently robust to stand in the place of any credible, documented evidence. If consciously recorded, the evidence 'proves' the psychobiographical hypothesis. If not documented, or if allegedly rendered in coded or oblique form, the act of repression again 'proves' that something traumatic has motivated the omission or encoding. 'Stoker', Lapin intimates, 'was well aware the vampire myth was not his private property'. But, if, as Lapin suggests, the vampire 'is *our* myth, and each of us who needs it to tell his/her story uses it as best as he/she unconsciously can' (original italics), then it is not, by his own admission, exclusively the unconscious property of the patient, but is implicated also in the conscious discourse of the analyst.[77] In the hands of the analyst, the therapist or the psychoanalytical critic, the vampire persists as a consciously deployed device whose function is to contain or explain the troubled, occluded psychology of the text or the patient. Thus, there are effectively two vampires – the vampire that fictionalises a trauma for the patient; and that which facilitates the diagnosis of a trauma for the psychoanalyst. The liminal nature of the vampire, its status as a being poised between two states, may thus be seen not merely in its location between the living and the dead but also in its ability to function for the unconscious or the conscious, for the patient or writer, as well as for the analyst or critic. Paradoxically, the vampire marks, as well as transcends, a boundary.

DIVIDED PSYCHES AND ABJECTED BODIES

The resolution of psychological division, rather than the uncovering of repressed or residual trauma, informs Elisabeth Bronfen's critique of *Dracula* in her influential study, *Over Her Dead Body: Death, Femininity and the Aesthetic* (1992). Unlike Lapin and many of his psychoanalytical predecessors, Bronfen eschews the psychobiography of Stoker as author, drawing attention instead to the text and its languages. Inevitably, given this strategy, the influence of Lacan as much as of Freud is evident in *Over Her Dead Body*. Bronfen's analysis, indeed, arguably belongs as much to psycholinguistics as it does to the psychology of desire.

In her reading of *Dracula*, Bronfen's focus is not the male vampire, but rather his two female victims, both in their apparent function as doubles of each other and as divided women in their own right.[78] This is, however, no simple gendered reading, no critical rediscovery of an occluded primal crime or Electra Complex – the female equivalent of the male Oedipus complex. Bronfen, rather, undermines the primacy of sexuality in psychoanalytical discourse by contextualising *eros* with *thanatos*, the life instinct with the death drive. Sex and death are close companions in psychology, though it is the former that has come to dominate the psychoanalytical criticism of *Dracula* from the 1960s. Bronfen, laudably, accommodates *both* within the myth of the vampire, a myth she claims as her own in a manner markedly different from that of Daniel Lapin. Bronfen argues that 'vampire lore [...] serves as a central trope for western attitudes towards death, so that Stoker's text represents not only an ambivalent desire for/fear of sexuality but also the same ambivalence toward mortality with the theme of sexuality put forward to veil that of death.'[79]

Death is certainly something fearful. Taken outside of the comforting immortalities associated with theology, it is a place of non-being or of non-thinking, a state of existence (or non-existence) which – as the pickled shark exhibited by Damien Hirst (born 1965) teasingly reminded the art world in 1992 – is impossible for the living mind to contemplate accurately or adequately.[80] Thus, for Bronfen:

■ The disruption that death incites must be resolved in a semiotic as well as a physical sense; the deceased and her story must receive a stable meaning even as the grave is closed to assure that the process of mourning is complete.[81] □

To leave mourning incomplete is to retain desire, to resist both closure and the withdrawing of a libidinal investment in one no longer sexually available or acceptable.[82] To mourn incompletely is to invite the breaking of taboo: Van Helsing's whole staging of the ritual disposal of Lucy is arguably for the grieving Arthur's benefit, 'to put closure on any necrophiliac desire'.[83]

If death in itself is troubling, then the vampire's transitional position is even more provocative. Turning to *Dracula*, Bronfen observes:

■ Stoker illustrates that after death the body can return in a fascinatingly dangerous or a soothingly safe form: the former a material somatic return, the vampire as body double, the latter an immaterial semiotic return, with documents, headstone inscriptions and memory images standing in for the absent body, doubling it not in an iconic/indexic but rather a symbolic mode.[84] □

The inescapably physical return of the vampiric Lucy in *Dracula* thus disrupts Arthur's necessary and healthy process of mourning and closure.

His romantic and erotic conception of his fiancée is disturbed when he encounters her outside her tomb, but he suffers also an epistemological shock, a rupturing, as it were, of his previous certainty regarding the nature of corporeal death. Death and the maiden, it would seem, are both surfaces that hide meaning, and when Death *is* the maiden, as in *Dracula*, the tension becomes particularly acute:

> ■ The revenant, occupying the interstice between two forms of existence – a celebration and a triumph over death – calls forth two forms of anxiety, i.e., the anxiety that death is finitude and the anxiety that death may not be the end. Because the heroines are revenants of sorts, because their appearance deceives, they function as living tropes for the notion that a secret, a truth, lies hidden beneath the surface of the body.[85] □

The cure for vampirism is thus not merely physical and vested in the ritual staking of Lucy, with all its potential for phallic symbolism. It is, in addition, an anticipation of the 'talking cure' popularised by psychoanalysis, and its linguistic and semiotic practice might be said to be enacted by the novel's entire collection of documents, testimonies and interpretations. When Bronfen argues that 'Throughout the novel, the danger of an unhinged mind, of the unconscious desires triumphing is apotropaically soothed by accurate documentation', she links proto-psychoanalytic practice to the occult exorcism (apotropaic meaning, literally, 'turning away') of ill fortune.[86] Bronfen, curiously, elsewhere explains the novel's information-gathering through the motif of the detective or detection plot.[87] The outcome, though, is surely more that sought by the analyst.

In a sense, the 'project' of *Dracula*, if such there is, is one of reconciling the divided psyche of Lucy (and of attempting to regulate and restrict the dividing psyche of Mina). It matters not that Lucy does not receive the benefit of her talking cure in her lifetime, as the novel projects a conventional theological destiny for her as one of 'God's true dead, whose soul is with Him' (193). What *does* matter is that her deviance has been not merely contained but understood, thus facilitating the later 'cure' of Mina, and her return to a singular rather than divided selfhood:

> ■ A corpse spurs on the urge to detect missing facts with death explained by virtue of a reconstruction of the events – the doubled narrative imitating the uncanny position of the dead/remaining woman. Once her death has been explained the corpse can lie peacefully, the end of the narrative double plot equal to the end of her revenant position. The divided woman poses questions which are resolved as her division is undone, as the uncanny double is transformed into the canny division between buried corpse and transmitted emblem.[88] □

Lucy, it seems, may be regarded as collateral damage, a necessary sacrifice in the psychological drive towards epistemological certainty. The novel is explicit regarding how the ritual staking expels ambiguity and doubleness from the victim-patient, and restores in its place, 'Lucy as we had seen her in her life' (192). For Bronfen, though,

> ■ This staking fixes semantic instability which the vampire Lucy enacted in two ways – as a dead body mocking a living woman, and as a woman who is superlatively beautiful while sleeping yet who mocks this beauty by exhibiting violent feminine wantonness while awake. Her semantic duplicity is arrested as she is resurrected as an angel and a holy image.[89] □

Mina, of course, goes through a broadly similar pattern of predation and a consequent (though temporary) deterioration into ambiguity and division. As Bronfen makes clear, though, Mina is more clearly aligned with the obsessional male discourse of the vampire hunters than with the hysterical discourse that typifies the vampirised Lucy. She is not silent, but tells of her experiences – and, though Bronfen fails to note it, of the experience of her significant, ambiguous Other, the Count.[90] Lucy, it seems, was prepared for an ambiguous and troubling association with death because of her liminal social and sexual position as bride-to-be: Mina, in contrast, as wife 'accepts her fixture within the symbolic order and resists the call of death'.[91]

Bronfen concludes this section of her analysis of Lucy and Mina with the short statement that 'The transparency and purity of women's bodies serves in both cases as the proof that the abject, toward which they are shown to incline more than men, has been expelled'.[92] Bronfen's passing reference to Julia Kristeva's *Powers of Horror* (1980, translated 1982) here is noteworthy, in that it is one of very few applications of the theory of abjection to the criticism of *Dracula*. The muted use of abjection in *Over Her Dead Body*, and its relative absence elsewhere in *Dracula* criticism, is curious to say the least. Abjection, as defined by Kristeva, has obvious relevance to a novel preoccupied not merely with transitional states but also with the biological excrescences of the body – blood, literally, but also, by association in psychoanalytical terms, semen and excrement.

Powers of Horror is a difficult and, at times, linguistically frustrating book, but its focus upon the psychological response to certain substances is both cogent and compulsive. Popularly, abject substances are those which are intimate to, or produced by, the body, yet which have been expelled or amputated from its wholeness, either by the routine of bodily function or by the intervention of surgery or physical accident. Blood, obviously, is abject, as are urine, excrement, pus, mucus and semen, as well as extracted organs, severed limbs and, by association, the prosthetic substitutes which replace the latter. Part of the psychological fear of these things is arguably bound up with their relationship to disease – to retain many of these substances is to invite infection or pain, where others carry inside their physicality the biology of transmissible infection.

These substances and organs, though, are not abject in their own right. Appropriately, in the context of Bronfen's argument:

> ■ It is [...] not lack of cleanliness or health that causes abjection but what disturbs identity, system, order. What does not respect borders, positions, rules. The in-between, the ambiguous, the composite.[93] □

Abject objects or substances draw attention to the illusion of the body's unity, breaking up its integrity and identity through excessive or disruptive presence. The corpse, prototypically, is taboo because it is dead and potentially disease- or corruption-ridden; it is abject because it *was* life but is no longer, because it looks like a person but has been expelled from humanity by death. The abject, as it were, marks borders, among other things – as well as reminding us of the origins of those borders in the self and its past.[94]

Abjection, then, is clearly more than bodily fluids and corpses, though this is often as far as many readers of *Powers of Horror* are prepared to comprehend. There is more to be said, however. Pioneering work on the possible connections between the abject and *Dracula* were undertaken as early as 1995 by Anne Williams, whose subtle evocation of both vampirism and motherhood as states which disturb the boundaries of 'the clean and proper self' has surprisingly passed with almost no comment.[95] At greater length than Williams's reading, and with laudably greater clarity than Kristeva's theoretical prose, Jerrold E. Hogle further develops the application of abjection to the Gothic generally, and to *Dracula* specifically though briefly, in the introduction to his *Cambridge Companion to Gothic Fiction* (2002). Hogle pointedly reminds the reader that Kristeva's concept has its origins, literally, in *ab-ject*, effectively a throwing off of what Kristeva terms 'the fundamental inconsistencies that prevent us from declaring a coherent and independent identity to ourselves and others'.[96] Thus, in Hogle's reading of *Powers of Horror*,

> ■ Whatever threatens us with anything like this betwixt-and-between, even dead-and-alive condition, Kristeva concludes, is what we throw off or 'abject' into defamiliarized manifestations, which we henceforth fear and desire because they both threaten to reengulf us and promise to return us to our primal origins. Those othered figures reveal this deeply familiar foundation while 'throwing it under' the cover of an outcast monster more vaguely archaic and filled with contradictions than supposedly normal human beings. □

Hogle's reading of Kristeva emphatically deflects the potential of abjection away from the individual ego and towards a credible form of social psychology. Hogle continues:

> ■ By these means all that is abjected is thrown under in another fashion: cast off into a figure or figures criminalized or condemned by people in authority and thus subjected to (again, thrown under) their gaze and the patterns of social normalcy they enforce. The process of *abjection*, then, is as thoroughly social and cultural as it is personal. It encourages middle-class people in the west, as we see in many of the lead characters in Gothic fictions, to deal with the tangled contradictions fundamental to their existence by throwing them off onto ghostly or monstrous counterparts that then seem 'uncanny' in their unfamiliar familiarity while also conveying overtones of the archaic and the alien in their grotesque mixture of elements viewed as incompatible by established standards of normality. (original italics) [97] □

This, certainly, accords with Hogle's own subsequent definition of the Gothic as being preoccupied with 'opposed conditions' such as 'life/death, natural/supernatural, ancient/modern, realistic/artificial and unconscious/conscious'. Equally, it confirms his suggestion that the Gothic is committed to their abjection into Others which simultaneously attract and terrify both bourgeois characters and readers.[98]

Hogle's short application of the abject may function primarily as a stimulus to future work rather than as a closure or conclusion in its own right – as, indeed, all good scholarship should. There is certainly a great deal that remains unsaid but which is implicit in Hogle's thesis, where the vampire is a nemesis for both the individual and the culture. These things have, of course, been voiced before under the terminologies of a variety of critical preoccupations – but not in the theoretical context of Kristevan abjection. Other questions, too, remain unasked and thus unanswered. Abjection, after all, need not concern itself exclusively with the evocative vampire, his intimacy with bodily fluids, his transitional status between life and death or East and West, and his demonic personification of bourgeois fears and fetishes. Renfield, too, has his place in an abject gaze, and not merely in his position of one who initially consumes blood (70) and then successively vomits (71) and haemorrhages it (240). Renfield, of course, attempts to position himself *between* captivity and freedom through his appeal to the reason of his physician's associates (215–18) on the night they enter the vampire's English residence. He is, equally, a fearful vision of what might lie within a sane man – a potential which Seward himself acknowledges on the day when he claims to understand his patient's *idée fixe* and imposes a theoretical, linguistic and conceptual closure upon the lunatic by defining him 'a zoophagous (life-eating) maniac' (71). Certainly, abjection remains an underused and eminently adaptable tool to be taken up at length in future *Dracula* scholarship.

★   ★   ★

The psychoanalytical debate on *Dracula* has arguably entered upon a relative decline, a consequence of the rise of other theoretical approaches. Its historical and contemporary importance, though, should not be dismissed lightly. If only because of its contentious theoretical claim to a unique insight, its allegation of repressed truth, or its assertion of an atemporal connection that may parallel the desires of the text with those of the reader, psychoanalysis is likely to maintain a presence in *Dracula* criticism for the foreseeable future. Psychoanalysis, though, is not the sole theoretical discipline critically concerned with the depiction of mental health in *Dracula*. Cultural materialism, too, in the form of analyses drawing upon the traditions of medical history, has made significant statements regarding the perceived symptomatologies of Stoker's novel. In this context, the mind is not a psychological but a physiological concept: it is intimate with the body, and responsive to pathological, rather than merely psychopathological, trauma. Chapter 2 discusses this particularly vibrant aspect of modern *Dracula* criticism, outlining not merely the Victorian medical theories that have informed the novel but also placing these within a cultural consciousness that has implications for the novel's oft-quoted pronouncements upon race and national identity.

CHAPTER TWO

Medicine, Mind and Body: The Physiological Study of *Dracula*

The successful imposition of psychoanalytical criticism on to *Dracula* (or, for that matter, any other pre-Freudian text) is dependent upon the conceit that unconscious phenomena can be both theorised in the present *and* discerned in texts produced prior to the explication of the theory. Psychoanalytical criticism is thus, paradoxically, both timeless and anachronistic: it assumes a continuity of unconscious motivations which, though historically expressed unknowingly, have been but comparatively recently theorised. That theorisation, however, transforms the unconscious into a rhetorical tool, deployed consciously in the act of criticism in such a way as to impose the order of a commentating present upon the textuality of an earlier period. Twentieth-century psychologies have, in this way, obscured their nineteenth-century counterparts, and the unconscious has gained a priority over those things which have been, arguably, consciously and rhetorically deployed in the pre-Freudian text. The rise of historicism, and the progressive referencing of *Dracula* in studies of the explicitly *conscious* manners and culture of the *fin de siècle*, have successfully challenged this emphasis. In the twenty-first century, *Dracula* has arguably become a novel as much associated with the psychology of the nineteenth century as it is with that of the twentieth.

THE PHYSIOLOGY OF THE MIND

The psychological contexts of *Dracula* are emphatically pre-Freudian. Though the novel's publication in 1897 appears tantalisingly close to Freud's earliest proto-psychoanalytic output, the *Studies on Hysteria* of 1893 and 1895, there is no internal evidence to suggest that Stoker was influenced by what was then a little-known, untranslated and highly speculative venture in mental science.[1] The psychology of *Dracula*, rather, is one whose origins may be traced not merely to the work of the three European theoreticians of the mind, Jean-Martin Charcot, Cesare Lombroso and Max Nordau, whom Stoker names in passing (171, 296), but also to a more general, and distinctively physiological, model of mental activity, popular from the mid-nineteenth century, and recalled both explicitly and implicitly throughout the novel.[2] *Dracula*, indeed, is arguably as influenced by established British theories of the body as much as it is by fashionable Continental models of the mind.

Stoker's grasp of such things is that of a layman rather than of a practitioner. Medicine and psychology, rendered accessible in relatively non-technical language, were popular topics in the educated periodicals of the day. Stoker, in addition, came from a family with substantial medical connections. His brothers Richard (1851–?), George and William Thornley all qualified as medical practitioners, the latter gaining distinction as President of, successively, the Royal College of Medicine and the Royal Academy of Medicine in Ireland.[3] William and George were published authors within their specialist clinical fields, with George publishing, in addition, *With 'The Unspeakables'* (1878), an autobiographical account of his medical service in the Russo-Turkish War of 1877–78. The four brothers shared William Thornley Stoker's house in Dublin in 1874, and the author was also a Dublin acquaintance of John Todhunter (1839–1916), physician and playwright, and Sir William Wilde (1815–1876), ophthalmic specialist and father of Oscar.[4] Stoker was thus ideally placed to observe the medical debates of the late nineteenth century, and to apply both the language of medicine and the symptomatology of mental and physical disorder to the protagonists of his undeniably pathological novel.

The corpus of critical works which read *Dracula* through the discourses of nineteenth-century medicine should be viewed as being quite discrete from those biographical and psychobiographical readings which associate the novel with the author's illnesses and death. These latter readings are intimate not merely to a number of conventional critical assumptions with regard to the author's mental and physical health, but are dependent, additionally, upon the convention that certain disorders invariably generate guilt, or inculcate repression, on a psychological level. This guilt, as the Introduction to this Guide suggests, is arguably expressed involuntarily, and possibly exorcised and discharged, through certain significant scenes in the novel. The central issue for non-biographical medical readings, however, is verisimilitude: the text embodies identifiable clinical discourses, expressed through both the incorporation of specialist languages and by the representation of symptomatologies and pathologies which may be recognised by non-medical readers. These readily identifiable disorders, which impact upon both the fictionalised body and mind, in turn carry with them cultural implications which further condition how a character may be read, or how his or her actions and motivations ought to be interpreted. A seemingly systematic reproduction of identifiable medical disorder, however, need not necessarily lead to a conventional pathological outcome in *Dracula*. However accurate their fictional portrayal might first appear, symptoms in the novel are almost invariably overdetermined. In effect, they signify both a conventional medical interpretation to the physician initially ignorant of Count Dracula *and* an alternative pathology, based upon the victim's encounter with the vampire, accessible throughout by the reader. Misdiagnosis is always a risk where a symptom may signify in both a conventional (that is, human) and an occult (or vampiric) pathology. Misdiagnosis, indeed, is the central human error that facilitates the vampire's progressive debilitation of both Lucy Westenra and Mina Harker.

The diagnostic procedures of *Dracula*, as critical consensus now acknowledges, are premised upon a layman's understanding of the physiologically centred practice that dominated both British medicine and psychology for much of the nineteenth century. Under this diagnostic regime, the mind, conscious and unconscious, was customarily viewed not as a psychological abstract, but rather as the reflex output of a physiological organ, the brain. Mental health is thus intimately associated with bodily well-being, the brain enjoying a reciprocal relationship with the other organs and vital functions of the body. A brain either damaged in itself, or imperilled by disorder or contamination elsewhere within the body, was thus regarded as the likely matrix of delusion or even madness.

The presence of this pervasive medical discourse within *Dracula* is signalled explicitly through the novel's sporadic references to unconscious cerebration, a model of mental function popularised by the British physician William Carpenter (1813–1885) through his *Principles of Mental Physiology* (1874) and other works, many of them written for a non-professional audience. Unconscious cerebration, according to Carpenter, is the production of sound and logical conclusions '*below the plane* of consciousness either during profound sleep, or while the attention is wholly engrossed by some entirely different train of thought' (original italics).[5] The mind, in effect, uses the same processes which it utilises in conscious reasoning – these are deployed successfully because they have become an habitual action of the brain. The brain, according to Carpenter's theory, manages its mental processes in much the same way as other bodily organs 'learn' to perform actions without conscious direction – just as walking is a physical action that may take place whilst the brain is otherwise engaged, so logical reasoning, too, may become an habitual and unperceived process. The phrase 'Unconscious cerebration' was recognised as a specialist medical term as early as 1975 by the American critic Leonard Wolf, but the implications of Stoker's incorporation of Carpenter's work remained oddly unexplored in

Dracula criticism until the mid-1990s when it emerged as a central issue in two separate projects independently researched and subsequently published by David Glover and William Hughes.[6]

The physician John Seward is the primary embodiment of Carpenter's work in *Dracula*, and it is he who introduces the concept of unconscious cerebration in his observation of the lunatic Renfield. Renfield, as Seward rapidly appreciates, consumes life-forms not in a random fashion, but systematically, totalising the cumulative lives of flies eaten by spiders, and spiders ingested by sparrows, as they are in turn added to his own bodily economy. Seward observes:

> ■ There is a method in his madness, and the rudimentary idea in my mind is growing. It will be a whole idea soon, and then, oh, unconscious cerebration! you will have to give the wall to your conscious brother. (69–70) □

Patient and physician alike display the same mental processes. For Renfield, a 'deep problem in his mind' finds conscious expression in a notebook's tabulated columns and rows of figures (69). For Seward, empirical data is digested by unconscious cerebration until the moment that its nascent theory is developed enough to find conscious expression, presumably in the drafting of a scholarly paper. Both outcomes, reached through analogous processes of unconscious cerebration, are logical within the frame of mind of their creators. The demarcation between sanity and insanity, it would seem, is one of outcome rather than of process.[7]

Hughes's analysis of the relationship between Seward and Renfield in '"So unlike the normal lunatic": Abnormal Psychology in Bram Stoker's *Dracula*' (1993–95) emphasises the orthodoxy of the physician's Carpenterian clinical practice, even where it is deployed for unethical ends. Renfield's disorder is read as being more of a physiological than a psychological problem. The delusion becomes an *idée fixe* – a psychologically concretised idea – not because of the impersonal inevitability of an abstract psychological complex, such as might be imposed upon it by Freud or Carl Jung (1875–1961). Rather, it concretises as a direct consequence of Seward's decision not to distract the lunatic, but instead to 'keep him to the point of his madness' (61). In effect, Renfield is habituated into furthering his own delusion, his unconscious cerebration being trained by repetition and encouragement just as his limbs might be familiarised with some complex physical task. Such actions, such thoughts, become involuntary and, indeed, unconscious – or 'automatic', as Carpenter terms them.[8]

This argument underpins a further reading of 'automatic' psychology in Hughes's *Beyond Dracula* (2000). The focus in this later work is Lucy Westenra, whose customary daytime journeys from her holiday residence to the Whitby churchyard are replicated during her nocturnal sleepwalking. Lucy's somnambulistic mind, as Carpenter's psychology suggests, replicates the behaviour of her wakeful self because both are underpinned by habituation. It is not an occult agency that summons her to the fatal encounter in the churchyard, therefore, but force of habit.[9] It is only when the unprecedented pathology of vampirism, with its spiritual as well as physiological consequences, is interposed upon Lucy that the broad Carpenterian theory which lies behind unconscious cerebration is called momentarily into question. Eventually, though, the novel suggests that even the slow mental development of the vampire's reasoning, from 'child-brain' (264) to 'man's stature' (263), is based on a model of unconscious cerebration and empirical habituation reminiscent of that associated with mortal humanity. *Dracula*, in Hughes's reading, would thus appear to affirm the validity of conventional physiological medicine in its mental application. The crisis of diagnosis, as it were, does not enjoin any debate beyond the novel: the novel's speculation is thus bounded not by medical controversy but by the need to contain vampirism within a fictionalised, though ostensibly conventional, clinical discourse.

In contrast to Hughes's reading, David Glover locates Carpenter, and thus by implication *Dracula* also, within a broad *fin-de-siècle* debate regarding the development of human character. Unconscious cerebration is considered in Glover's *Vampires, Mummies, and Liberals* not as a concept within a primarily medical discourse, but rather as a point of intersection between medicine and the human sciences. *Dracula*, indeed, enjoys a somewhat muted presence in Glover's argument, as his analysis turns to a detailed reading of Carpenter's uneasy relationship with materialist and spiritualised views of free will and determinism. These are, further, issues which underpin Glover's thesis that a number of central questions regarding race, nation and self, expressed in late-Victorian ethnology, sexology and the 'scientific' determinisms proposed by physiognomy, physiology and psychology, characterise the breadth of Stoker's fiction.[10]

Glover argues that the fictionalisation in *Dracula* of mental conditions such as 'Hypnotism, somnambulism, trances, [and] unconscious cerebration' acknowledged both Victorian attempts to 'put the idea of character [...] on a scientific footing', and the 'difficult questions of voluntarism and determinism' which arose in consequence.[11] Stoker's *Dracula* thus becomes characteristic of the writer's greater oeuvre, with its alternation between what Glover identifies as 'the expressive man of sensibility and the strong, steadfast man of action'.[12] Both masculine types are ostensibly present within the novel, though never in an absolute or pure form. The man of action, as it were, ensheathes the man of feeling, and the man of feeling, when provoked or stimulated, may reveal the man of action.

Stoker's consistent characterisation of alternating sensibility and action encodes, for Glover, a crisis in the late-Victorian 'scientific' conceptualisation of human character. Appearing as they do during moments of trauma, such transitions in character signal the interface of the conscious and unconscious mind as theorised by Carpenter and his contemporaries. Harker, selected by Glover as a representative example, collapses into a state of apparent hysteria upon comprehending, successively, his imprisonment in the Count's castle and his apparently 'sexual' passivity in the hands of the three female vampires. Carpenter's model of the mind, as Glover correctly identifies, has no theory of repression, so the unconscious that emerges in such circumstances represents the resurgence of matter once learned but now forgotten, a discarded but still habituated state of mind that preceded the conscious self-determination of the adult, masculine self. Harker's passivity, as more than one critic has contended, may thus represent childish helplessness or a feminisation of the identity.[13] The subject, as Glover argues, is always vulnerable to forces within the self which are capable of temporarily disengaging rational free will.[14] If Harker and his associates do not ultimately become creatures of irresponsible appetite like the Count, then they do find their characters rendered deviant through an unconsciousness which eclipses the will, and which renders the self subject to automatic actions as compulsive as the vampire's primitive drive towards the absorption of nutritive matter.

Though written apparently without knowledge of *Vampires, Mummies, and Liberals*, John Greenway's '"Unconscious Cerebration" and the Happy Ending of *Dracula*' (2002) might be successfully deployed as a critical counterpart to Glover's reading of the Carpenterian script of Stoker's novel. Greenway here, and in his earlier and better known work 'Seward's Folly: *Dracula* as a Critique of "Normal" Science' (1986), notes the fallibility of Seward's own unconscious cerebration, and the alienist's characteristic inability to reach the logical conclusions that ought to be intimated by his recollection of his thought processes. Seward's mental vivisection of Renfield, Greenway argues, ought to lead the alienist to the conclusion that Count Dracula, rather than mortal humanity, is the apex of the food chain. Seward, though, is unwilling (or possibly unable) to 'complete the thought'.[15] To do so, would be to challenge the cultural, philosophical, religious and medical conventions that celebrate humanity over all other forms of life. Indeed, it would be a presumption, Greenway argues, likely to destabilise the essential relationships within which the characters live. Seward's mental impasse is not an evasion or a displacement such as might be envisioned by more recent psychoanalytical models of the unconscious. Rather, it appears to be a *conscious* determination to control or halt the inevitable advancement of unconscious cerebration – though such a thing would appear to be utterly pointless, given Carpenter's model of thought continually produced by a mind consciously engaged. Greenway's contention, which he also evidences through other characters in *Dracula*, is on the surface a valid one – but remains problematic when viewed in the context of Carpenter's continually evolving unconscious problem-solving process. Stoker's characters might be in denial, as Greenway suggests, but their unconscious minds will continue to pursue a logical course, none the less.

Glover's emphasis, in contrast, remains very much upon the unconscious mind, and its capability temporarily to disrupt the processes and beliefs of conscious rationality. Glover argues for an effective containment of the disorder proposed by the eruption of the Carpenterian unconscious by suggesting that Stoker's fiction associates a redemptive function with moments of crisis such as those suffered by Harker. The mortal sufferer, as it were, endures the crisis and returns, eventually, to his customary volitional self, a stronger and a wiser man. A night's sleep, the reassertion of a familiar world-view, appears to dispel the delusion, a process of distraction which echoes the moral management which Seward ought prototypically to apply to Renfield.[16] It is notable, though, that in *Dracula* volition or right-mindedness seems to be as easily restored by the passage of time as by the conscious exercise of will. Glover concludes, rather oddly in context, that 'though the male unconscious seems to possess a self-regulating capacity to return the psyche to a state of balance or equilibrium, its workings remain mysterious'. This mystery, Glover suggests, reflects the imprecision of Stoker's use of both medical and social science: the author's later novels, and possibly *Dracula* also, exhibit not a coherent script but 'a kind of muddled pastiche of Carpenter's own scientific language'.[17] There is, though, a cohesion in Stoker's use of both medical terminology and systematic physiology that Glover appears to overlook. The 'muddle', if it is there at all, seems to occur in criticism when the physiology of the text is extruded into social science and the debate regarding free will and determinism. When Carpenterian mental physiology is read primarily as a medical system underpinning the novel, however, the depicted mental processes arguably appear both systematic and logical.

THE MULTIPLE MEANINGS OF BLOOD

As Victor Sage argues, 'Stoker's *Dracula* is an extended play on various senses of "blood"'.[18] Inevitably, criticism regards the majority of these 'senses' as being figurative or symbolic: as David Punter suggests, 'the blood which gives Dracula his life is, as usual in vampire legendry, not merely literal'.[19] Blood embodies an obvious theological resonance. Acknowledging Stoker's Irish Protestant origins, Sage envisions the consumption of blood in the novel as 'an imaginative inversion of the Roman

Doctrine of the Eucharist', a 'Real Presence' (98), as it were, of the human rather than of the divine.[20] Intriguingly, Sage's argument implicitly draws its force not from the New Testament, but from the Pentateuch, and Renfield's insistent quotation from Deuteronomy 12:23, '[For] The blood is the life!' (130, 206). Though twentieth-century critics might associate Renfield's consumption of the forbidden substance here with psychoanalytical models which equate blood to semen, or which are premised upon Kristeva's theory of abjection, the explicit taboo in the novel is Judaeo-Christian rather than Freudian. To take Sage's argument a little further, *Dracula* embodies not merely a commentary upon the literalism of the Roman Catholic doctrine of Transubstantiation, in which the consecrated Host and wine become the Real Presence, the body and blood of Christ. The novel mobilises, equally, an encounter between the spirituality of the Old Testament and the secularity expressed by late-Victorian professionals such as Seward.

That secularity finds itself expressed in other meanings associated with the overdetermined signifier that is blood. It is a central cultural icon of common identity: one is 'of the same blood', to quote Foucault.[21] Thus, 'The sense of national identity', as Sage suggests, 'is defined by blood', and blood may function also as a signifier of familial as well as racial consanguinity: 'blood relations' may connect nations much as they bind the loyalties of families.[22] Blood is, equally, a signifier associated with lineage, and with qualities passed down figuratively in the bloodstream – a more acceptable metaphor of descent than the literal, seminal fluid of conventional conception. This much the bourgeois Harker should recognise when his host raises his own arms to proclaim 'What devil or what witch was ever so great as Attila, whose blood is in these veins?' (34). The Count here voices the conventional language of a nobility based upon bloodlines, yet with an irony that Harker is yet to perceive: the warlike blood of Attila, as it were, already circulates uneasily alongside that of fearful Transylvanian peasants, and will later conjoin with the intimate secretions of a rabble of superstitious Russian sailors, a flighty English heiress and a bourgeois schoolmistress.

The relationships vested in blood are thus perilously fragile when it is recognised that their cultural meaning derives not merely from the evocative substance that is blood but also from the physiological processes by which it is secreted, depleted and circulated. As Foucault suggests, the meanings of blood are precarious because the substance is 'easily spilled, subject to drying up, too readily mixed, capable of being quickly corrupted'.[23] A change in the quality of blood, a dilution or a diminution of its substance affects its meaning. Likewise, the vessel in which that evocative blood is enclosed, whether it be an individual or a race, finds its own signification, its own place in the order of signs, affected by the perceived quality of the substance which circulates within it. Blood is a synecdoche, a part which may signify the qualities of a greater whole. The health of the blood stands in semiotic relation to the health of the associated body; likewise, that body stands in synecdochal relationship to the race, family or nation with which it is associated. Thus, the vampire's attack, as Punter suggests, 'blurs the lines' between the demarcations of species, of spirituality and of gender that stabilise late-Victorian society.[24] That blurring, though, is dependent upon a symbolic conception of blood underpinned by medical convention.

To adapt a phrase from Foucault, blood functions in *Dracula* as '*a reality with a symbolic function*' (original italics).[25] The literal value of blood, and its place in the Carpenterian bodily economies of *Dracula*, ought thus to be fully acknowledged in criticism. In a manner which parallels the figurative debilitation of racial or familial bloods 'contaminated' or 'diluted' by miscegenation, Carpenter notes that the introduction of impurities such as alcohol or poisons into the bloodstream will impair or pervert the customary processes of cerebration.[26] The men whom David Glover identifies as being engaged in an apparently confused battle between volitional will and unconscious mental processes suffer no such circulatory contamination beyond that which might ordinarily be occasioned by an unexceptional Western diet. They drink and they smoke, but this appears to affect them little, if at all. The two central female characters in the novel, however, do find themselves exhibiting abnormal mental states – trance in particular – and their condition is clearly a result of the integrity of their blood being compromised.

David Hume Flood, in a surprisingly under-read 1989 analysis of the implications of transfusion in *Dracula*, takes up this point when considering the evident prioritisation of certain bloods above others in the novel. He suggests that

■ Stoker's understanding of blood itself in the novel harkens back to the seventeenth and eighteenth century idea of a substance that contains the personal characteristics of its original possessor. When it comes to selecting a donor to replace the blood that Lucy has lost to the vampire, for example, Van Helsing establishes the following criteria. First, a young donor is better than an old one, not because of the quicker recovery that a young person might have but because of the youthful vitality that can thus be transmitted. Similarly, a person of physical activity is to be preferred to one of mental pursuits because of the robustness the former's blood will contain. □

Flood emphasises, further, 'Van Helsing's chauvinistic insistence of the superiority of a man's to a woman's blood'.[27] Yet, though he notes the youthful vigour of Arthur Holmwood, Lucy's fiancé, selected by

Van Helsing as the first donor, Flood underplays the evident marital symbolism that is acknowledged in the novel both by Holmwood (157) and his close friend and fellow donor Quincey Morris (138). The sexual symbolism of transferred or transfused blood is arguably far less sublimated in the novel, as C. F. Bentley, acknowledged by Flood as an influential commentator upon the novel's sexual symbolism, would have it.[28] Holmwood's blood is not merely strong, it is appropriate – appropriate in terms of the specific social and sexual relationship between the donor and the recipient, and appropriate also in its medical qualities. Van Helsing's clinical remark to Seward – 'He is so young and strong and of blood so pure that we need not defibrinate it' (114) – further indicates not merely the physical value of his blood but the fluid, non-coagulative nature, that makes it eminently suitable for circulation both within and between bodies: fibrin is the clotting agent in human blood. Unfortunately, the purity and fluidity of Holmwood's blood ensures its easy transfer not merely between his own and his fiancée's bodies but also between her circulation and the Count's.

One might note, also, how the receipt of strong, mortal, male blood rejuvenates or regenerates Lucy, as testified by Seward's observation that 'something like life seemed to come back to poor Lucy's cheeks' (114) during the first transfusion.[29] Arthur's pallor, which Seward also notes, is a consequence of this. The blood of the Count, though, which Mina drinks, and which both Lucy and Mina are apparently exposed to through the vampire's bite, is far less beneficial.[30] This latter encounter suggests the presence of a form of osmosis or cellular absorption, a sanguine exchange more subtle than Mina's active ingestion of the Count's blood. The vampire does not merely take substance out, it would seem, but injects his own 'poison' (286) into the victim's circulation simultaneously. It is this contamination of the physiological circulation that motivates Lucy's erratic behaviour on her deathbed, her alternation between the 'softness' of her mortal self and the 'dull and hard' and 'voluptuous' (146) qualities of the vampire identity which is eclipsing that self. The Count's presence within Lucy's circulation drives, equally, his ability to command her behaviour from a distance, as is demonstrated when she attempts to destroy the letter (139) which obliquely records his visit to her room on the night of her mother's death (130–2). Mina, who ingests the Count's blood, as well as being exposed to the intimacies associated with his bite, exhibits exaggerated, rather than different, phenomena of progressive, personal change and mental control. Though Flood does not acknowledge it, the Count's occult blood is an economic substance whose value at times negates, at other times modifies, the values of both energy and implication encoded into the mortal circulations of the men who come to oppose him.

For all its occult implications, Lucy's demise at the hands of the vampire is, however, the result of a quite conventional anaemia. Seward's assessment of the cause of her death – 'nervous prostration following on great loss or waste of blood' (170) – is logical, if lacking any explanation as to how that blood was drained. Criticism, however, has been quick to associate the pale woman with a danger that is as moral as it is pathological. 'The pallid woman is the sexually active, sexually exciting one', claims Victor Sage, though, historically, criticism has relied not upon medicine, but rather Lucy's own words and behaviour to enforce that association.[31] Lucy is, after all, the flirtatious virgin who wishes to marry all of her suitors, a social as well as religious 'heresy' (60), and who may (apparently) innocently trade *double entendres* about being 'broken to harness' (59) with a virile Texan horseman.[32]

The blood shed from Lucy's wound need not, however, be unequivocally that of a symbolic virginity lost to the predatory vampire. Marie Mulvey-Roberts's '*Dracula* and the Doctors: Bad Blood, Menstrual Taboo and the New Woman' argues that Lucy is an encoding of the signifiers and consequences of abnormal menstruation. Mulvey-Roberts views Lucy's immediately pre-mortem pallor as being characteristic of amenorrhea, an abnormal absence or suspension of the menses. As she admits, the veracity of this conclusion is undermined by Seward's establishing that she is not anaemic (105).[33] Mulvey-Roberts's contention is, indeed, difficult to accept without further qualification: Lucy's complexion, after all, more obviously suggests menorrhagia, an excessive and debilitating menstrual discharge, leading unsurprisingly to pallor. Lucy's symptoms thus appear far less clear-cut in their association than Mulvey-Roberts's rhetoric suggests, though her contention that Lucy's pallor is underpinned by the Count's intervention is certainly credible. Whatever the case, her argument is convincing when she suggests that, whatever its origins, Lucy's 'revitalisation is brought about only when she embarks upon her career as a blood-drinker' and, indeed, that the blood stains that mar 'the purity of her lawn death-robe' (187) signify an 'excess menstrual flow', a menorrhagia that, perplexingly, does not make her pale because she has maintained an adequate input of blood in anticipation.[34]

After death, Lucy is seemingly the demonstrative and *active* succubus of the churchyard, though her sexually provocative invitation to Arthur – 'Come, and we can rest together. Come, my husband, come!' (188) – expresses a desire not for semen, but for blood. Mulvey-Roberts links this aspect of vampiric behaviour to a woman's apparently prototypical economic need to replace lost menstrual blood with male 'life-blood' absorbed through sexual intercourse.[35] Lucy, however, is not literally *sexually* dangerous here, though she is using the conventional languages of sexuality and of seduction in order to satisfy her new desires. Again, she is no longer pale, for as Van Helsing observes, she is physically 'more rose and more beautiful' (180) a week after her interment. Perversely, and on a number of levels therefore:

> ■ The signs of health have been reworked into the indicators of danger. Conventional medical logic testifies that the corpse of Lucy cannot of itself secrete the blood whose presence, as in her lifetime, is manifested through her complexion. The laws of internal circulation still seemingly apply after Lucy's apparent death, although their edges have become undeniably permeable.[36] □

For the first time, Lucy excites the revulsion, rather than the desire, of those who have loved her (189). Lucy's archly erotic teasing has seemingly become more than an acceptably flirtatious provocation, though its presence here is inappropriate to an unblushing corpse as much as it ought to be to a blushing virgin. Paradoxically, Lucy is never so well as when she is displaying the symptoms of illness, for these are the only reliable guarantors of her conventional mortality.

When mortality succumbs to immortality, the institutions of *Dracula* criticism seem far more inclined to celebrate the revelation of an apparent sexual liberation on Lucy's part. Phyllis Roth's influential 1982 account of Lucy's post-mortem state is indicative of the way in which many subsequent critics have come to associate immortality with immorality in *Dracula*:

> ■ Only when Lucy becomes a vampire is she allowed to be 'voluptuous', yet she must have been so long before, judging from her effect on men and from Mina's description of her [...] Thus, vampirism is associated not only with death, immortality, and orality, but also with sexuality. □

Almost ten years later, for example, Elaine Showalter echoed Roth's words with the suggestion that 'Lucy is the first to be sexually aroused in monstrosity by Dracula's bite'. Showalter, though, tempers a critically conventional sexual symbolism with an awareness of *fin-de-siècle* medicine. When she states unequivocally that 'The female vampire represented the nymphomaniac or oversexed wife who threatened her husband's life with her insatiable erotic demands', she is drawing explicitly on a contextual gynaecological account of the apparent need for the female body to replenish the quantum of blood lost through menstruation.[37] Showalter considers the various daytime transfusions into Lucy's circulation to be such a replenishment of her nocturnal losses. One might note here, though, another context not drawn upon by Showalter: the cultural and medical convention of the spermatic economy, a discourse on the body which proclaimed semen as a derivative of blood. Though the bias of this particular vision of bodily economics is apparently towards the pathology of the male – characteristically, a masturbator displayed pale skin because his blood had been consumed by the excessive production and 'spending' of semen – its potential application to the study of both sexes in *Dracula* must not be overlooked.[38] Both men and women in *Dracula* lose blood, grow pale and find their vitality sapped in consequence. The connections between semen and blood should be regarded as chemical and physiological as well as a focus of psychoanalytic symbolism. Sexuality is, after all, a matter of physiology as much as it is of psychology.

SEXUALITY, INFECTION AND THE OBSESSIVE CONSUMER

That is not to say that the pallid woman does not represent a literal sexual threat, or a danger consequent upon incautious or promiscuous sexuality. In a provocative comparison between *Dracula* and the anonymous erotic novella *Lady Pockingham* (1879), Diane Mason reads the languid pallor displayed by Stoker's declining heroine not as a quantitative anaemia, but rather as the overdetermined signifier of a debilitative malady associated, both culturally and medically, with sexual excess. Mason draws a comparison between the explicit symptomatology of tuberculosis in *Lady Pockingham*, and the ambiguities which permit Lucy to be read as a masturbator in *Dracula*, configuring both women as simultaneously alluring and infectiously fatal to those who seek their intimate favours. For Mason, Lucy is a eugenic case study: though her verbal sexual precocity is duly noted, it is the unfortunate heroine's parentage, a somnambulistic father and a valetudinarian mother, that provide a key to her pathological inheritance, her susceptibility to what might be seen, variously, as a disorder or a vice.

If this in itself were not enough, Mason's reading of Lucy's education challenges the somewhat conventional view of the heroine's sentimental sister-like relationship to the unmarried Mina. Reading against the seemingly innocent grain of an early letter from Lucy to Mina in which the former confesses that 'we have told all our secrets to each other since we were *children*; we have slept together and eaten together, and laughed and cried together' (57, original italics), Mason elaborates that Lucy's lubricious potential may well have been exploited at a relatively tender age. The passive recipient may in turn become the active distributor of the vice. Given that contemporary medical writers were inclined to view boarding establishments as 'the very hot-beds of this destructive vice' – masturbation – Mason concludes that, as Lucy and Mina have 'secrets', then 'why not a secret vice?'.

Indeed, Mason suggests that Lucy's pallor, with its erotic association, is one of the very things that attracts the Count to her:

> ■ It could be argued here that Count Dracula – like Lucy's other admirers – is similarly drawn to Lucy precisely because she exhibits the erotic symptoms of masturbation, and therefore, according to medical discourse, is both morally depraved and sexually insatiable. □

The Count and his opponents may be far closer in terms of their fictionalised psychology of attraction than either might be prepared to admit. However, one must consider here also the perceptible change in the attractive value of Lucy occasioned by her conventional bodily death. For all but the momentarily bewitched (188) fiancé, Arthur Holmwood, the Lucy of the cemetery represents the fatal without the erotic. For the Count, similarly, Lucy is no longer a source of food, but rather, in his own words, nothing more than one of 'my creatures, to do my bidding and to be my jackals when I want to feed' (267). Once taken to the logical conclusion of a lingering death, the erotic seemingly loses its allure. It becomes a finite consummation rather than the promise of infinite seduction or foreplay. 'Masturbators and consumptives are', Mason asserts, ' "dying" but are, equally, "un-dead" and infectious.' The same is arguably true of vampires. The attraction of such states is that of the liminal: to enjoy the erotic or eroticised pleasures of masturbation or vampirism is to participate in an irresponsible state of enjoyment without responsibility, where any consequential damage to the body or the soul is overlooked for a time. To react with revulsion is, therefore, to take up the reality of consequence, to see the dangerous consequences that await not merely the alluring other, but also the self which is attracted to that infectious being.[39]

The mingling of bloods, healthy and contaminated is not, however, the sole threat to the integrity of the body in *Dracula*. Leila S. May in her 1998 article, ' "Foul things of the night": Dread in the Victorian Body' suggests, more broadly, that:

> ■ *Dracula* embodies a seemingly boundless array of Victorian anxieties, nearly all of which revolve around the bourgeois subject's obsession with the maintaining of clear and distinct boundaries: boundaries which, despite all efforts to preserve them, are incessantly in danger of collapsing entirely, and worse, in danger of being corroded from some internal disease.[40] □

May's distinctive achievement in this relatively under-read article is to discard the customary critical approach to the issue of cross-contamination and consequent deterioration, which is based upon the ingestion and circulation of blood. This model of infection is replaced in her argument with the equally Victorian fear of contamination through the inhalation of, in the words of the social explorer, Henry Mayhew (1812–1887), 'atmospherical granite, dung and refuse dust'.[41] Paralleling the foul-breathed vampire with the characteristically odorous prostitute, May suggests that contiguity and coexistence with the infected Other may be as dangerous to the victim as actual, invasive, bodily contact. To breathe in the elemental dust of the vampire or the flocculent air of his explicitly dusty residences in London (220, 262) or Transylvania (40, 50) is potentially as dangerous as passing by the harlot's door or inhaling her own characteristic odour. The physiological pathology of both figures, inevitably, gains a further figurative association: physical putrefaction equates easily to moral decay. Hence, to absorb their emanations is passively to absorb also their moral fibre, to compromise the self with that of the Other, the substance of the living with that of the dead. If the waxing and waning complexion of the vampire constitutes one visible sign of his difference from mortal humanity, then his odour is a further embodiment of his association with things marginalised and conventionally pathological. As the sanitary reformer Edwin Chadwick (1800–1890) suggests, 'offensive smells are true warnings of sanitary evils to the population': 'sanitary evils', needless to say, are associated with deficient hygiene, and, cleanliness conventionally being next to Godliness in the bourgeois mind, with backsliding morality also.[42] If it is perilous, as Diane Mason suggests, to sleep next to a masturbator, it is as subtly dangerous to breathe the noxious air that emanates from the body of one condemned to another physiological disorder, be it conventional or occult.

It is significant that so much critical attention has been lavished upon the bodies of the vampire's victims. These bodies – which are variously seduced, raped, liberated, contaminated or invaded, in accordance with the critical preoccupation of the perceiver – are endowed with a symbolic significance reciprocal to the cultural investment, Victorian and post-Victorian, in the mythology of the vampire. The vampire may be regarded not simply as an embodiment of external disease or disorder threatening, from outside, both the healthy self and the integrated nation which is based upon a collection of such selves. It is, equally, a symptom of those undesirable qualities, physical or moral, latent within the self though not necessarily readily visible through the façades of social existence. 'Sin', as Oscar Wilde suggests, conventionally 'writes itself across a man's face'.[43] Such graphic visualisations of things considered forbidden, secret or merely deviant do not confine themselves, however, to the physiognomies of men, nor indeed to the face alone. Sin, or the lurking capability for committing sin, may be exhibited on the faces and the bodies of men and women, may be expressed in the most innocuous of casual remarks, betrayed in the most fleeting of gestures or grimaces.

In criticism, every gesture is fraught with meaning, betraying (and not necessarily in a Freudian sense) hidden things that testify against the conscious actions and conventional words of the victim-in-waiting, potentials the more destructive because they are unacknowledged, even unsuspected, by the self and others.

Lucy's desire to marry all of her three suitors (60), much recalled in criticism, comes to stand for a certain type of sexual self-possession, at best flighty, at worst actively promiscuous, which is perceived by the critical reader but never openly vocalised by the characters in the novel. Lucy's remark, however light-hearted and ironic it might be, may be a symptom of the mental promiscuity of masturbation, as Diane Mason suggests, or equally the vocalisation of a virginal sexual curiosity fuelling conventional clinical hysteria.[44] Whatever it may be, it indicates a pre-existent condition upon which the vampire predates, rather than a novel departure in her personal pathology initiated by the Count. Medical criticism here concurs with other, more conventionally gendered, readings of the same scene, such as that advanced by Alan P. Johnson.[45] In these, Lucy is characteristically not changed but awakened, an innate but denied (or unsuspected) sexual identity becoming not merely active but assertive. Lucy is not the object, but the embodiment of desire in such readings. Desire, coded as immodesty, may still be regarded as a pathological condition, and one requiring both cure and containment.

Likewise, Mina Harker, though sexually monogamous to her mortal partner, might still be an appropriate victim of the pathological vampire-as-catalyst. Unlike that of the provocative Lucy, Mina's curiosity is not immediately sexual in its focus – indeed, she strikingly exhibits 'repulsion' (317) at the alluring voluptuousness displayed by her vampiric 'sisters' in Transylvania. Rather, her curiosity, if not her desire, is intellectual, her knowledge embracing not merely the detail of railway timetables (293) and the applications of technology such as stenography (72), typing and the phonograph (197) but also the traditionally male discourse of medicine, albeit in its speculative branches of criminal anthropology and non-therapeutic hypnotism (296, 271). Mina's single-mindedness, evident from her earliest correspondence with Lucy, signals her as exceptional amongst the few women portrayed in *Dracula*. Van Helsing's dismissively sexist praise of Mina as having a 'man's brain' and a 'woman's heart' (207) proclaims her deviance from the perceived norm for her sex at the same time as it grants her conditional (and limited) membership in the otherwise exclusively male club of gentlemen-adventurers. Mina's intellectual independence and organisational abilities teasingly link her also to the New Woman, whom she is so vocal in decrying (86–7). Though an asset in troubled times, the presence of Mina's acute mental abilities may suggest that, like the New Women, Girls of the Period, Wild Women and other proto-feminists of her generation, she has, in the words of one *fin-de-siècle* commentator, 'not "bred true" – not according to the general lines on which the normal woman is constructed'.[46] The vampire, in other words, may be as attracted to Mina's mental precocity as much as he apparently was to Lucy's somewhat intense pre-marital sexuality.

It is thus critical interpretation that delineates whether the eventual outcome of the Count's predation is rendered as a liberation or an enslavement of the victim. The imperative of twentieth- and twenty-first-century criticism to read against the grain of the novel's overt attitude towards vampirism, to reject the horror expressed by the proprietary males in favour of the apparent freedoms granted to the vampirised females, characteristically codes the vampiric encounter as a sexualised awakening rather than the exploitation of a pathological predisposition. Though it is convenient – indeed, expedient for some exponents of feminist sexual politics – to express the tie between vampire and victim as an act liberating a repressed sexuality, it must still be recalled that *Dracula* is a novel whose origins are not Freudian but Carpenterian. Though there is a consistent insistence upon psychological repression in the criticism of the novel, Carpenter's model of the mind, upon which so much of the psychology of *Dracula* depends, admits to no repression in the Freudian sense, no drive to vocalise or enact the forbidden.[47] If he chooses them at all, the Count arguably selects his associates on the grounds of their generalised mental deviance, rather than their specific sexual predilections: Lucy is sexual, though Mina – along with Jonathan Harker and Renfield, who are compromised though not bitten – is an obsessive consumer of data. The Count, too, is obsessed with such detail, as his vast library of Anglocentric trivia testifies: it includes books of 'history, geography, politics, political economy, botany, geology, law', 'the London Directory, the "Red" and "Blue" books, Whitaker's Almanack, the Army and Navy Lists [...] the Law List' (25) and even 'an English Bradshaw's Guide' (28), this latter the cumulative railway timetable of its day. Arguably, obsession, irrespective of focus, rather than specific and singular sexuality, motivates and mobilises the intimate connections between the vampire and his victim. There is an undoubted resemblance, therefore, between predator and prey. The difference is one of degree, the Count exhibiting a more developed form of the disorder. Vampires, customarily subjected to the discourses of theology or of folk-lore, are thus in *Dracula* brought, surprisingly, within the compass of conventional human mental pathology.

SCIENTIFIC CRIMINOLOGY

There is in the novel, though, a further striking resemblance between the un-dead body of the vampire and those of his conventionally mortal victims. The well-being of both the occult and the mortal bodies within *Dracula* is based upon broadly similar economies of secretion (or accretion) and depletion. Like the obsessive mental processes that link the Count and his victims, the symptoms associated with the presence and absence of blood within the body are exaggerated in the descriptions of the vampire. Lucy suffers, as has been noted, a quite conventional pallor as a consequence of what Seward terms his patient's 'great loss or waste of blood' (170). This distinctive complexion is temporarily relieved, again quite conventionally, by the interventive act of transfusion – a process which brings, simultaneously, a corresponding pallor to the donor:

■ As the transfusion went on something like life seemed to come back to poor Lucy's cheeks, and through Arthur's growing pallor the joy of his face seemed absolutely to shine. After a bit I began to grow anxious, for the loss of blood was telling on Arthur, strong man as he was. It gave me an idea of what terrible strain Lucy's system must have undergone that what weakened Arthur only partially restored her. (114) □

The Count, likewise, exhibits an 'extraordinary pallor' (24) when Harker first encounters him in Transylvania. On a later occasion, though, when Harker's host has implicitly fed prior to his journey to England, his 'cheeks were fuller, and the white skin seemed ruby-red underneath' (53). Lucy, as a vampire, similarly exhibits a 'delicate bloom' (178) upon her cheeks. The Count, though, gains more than a ruddy complexion from the unconventional transfusion of blood into his circulation represented by vampirism. Harker records, in addition, how his host now looks 'as if his youth had been half-renewed, for the white hair and the moustache were changed to dark iron-grey' (53). Later, as Mina notes, the Count sports an emphatically 'black moustache' (155), an indication, though she does not know it, of the success of his cumulative campaign in London. Harker is only too aware of the implications of the Count's darkening hair: 'he has grown young', he says, and 'if this be so' (155), then the 'teeming millions' of London, himself included, are now the vulnerable prey of the vampire's 'lust for blood' (53).

Conventional medical logic is thus both upheld and extended in the occult body of the vampire. The Count is subject to laws of circulation and health analogous to those governing humanity, and this facilitates his continued encounter with the mortal species from which, Van Helsing insists, he is descended (212). That said, 'this man-that-was' (212) is somehow an amplification, a culmination even, of that species. The vampire extends the interim, mortal corporeality of the human body to regenerative, immortal possibilities not known to current science. These, in a parody of logic and empiricism, are extruded from 'nature's laws' (211). Though, as Van Helsing admits, the Count represents the 'father or furtherer of a new order of beings' (263), he is not, however, celebrated in the novel as a *progressive* development of his original species.[48] He is, rather, something akin to both a disease and the host infected by that disease: he represents humanity in superficial form, but a humanity rendered both degraded and infectious by the degenerative condition which he carries within him.

Given the frequency with which the vampire hunters comment upon the foul odours associated with both the Count's body and the places he inhabits, however temporarily, it thus seems extraordinary that no great heed appears to have been taken of his presence by anybody other than the well-informed Van Helsing circle. The question therefore arises as to how the Count, an aged, malodorous Eastern aristocrat, might successfully pass unseen, unrecognised even as a stranger, for at least a month in what is arguably the most bourgeois of Western cities. The Count's ambition is, in his own words, to be 'like the rest, so that no man stops if he see me' (26). It is not necessarily his ambition, though, to be simply bourgeois in his apparent manners, which he seeks to learn from Jonathan Harker, or unexceptional in his tailoring.[49] Indeed, perversely, it is the Count's supposedly distinctive physiology and physiognomy that makes him invisible amongst the 'teeming millions' (53) of the capital, that allows him to be both mundane and yet still one of the contextual demons of the educated consciousness of the British *fin de siècle*.

The 'very marked physiognomy' (23) of the Count is painstakingly described at the inception of the novel, the density of detail in the description being quite characteristic of Harker's obsessive recording of local colour. Seated with his host, and fortified by 'some cheese and a salad and a bottle of old Tokay', the young solicitor recalls:

> ■ His face was a strong – a very strong – aquiline, with high bridge of the thin nose and peculiarly arched nostrils; with lofty domed forehead, and hair growing scantily round the temples, but profusely elsewhere. His eyebrows were very massive, almost meeting over the nose, and with bushy hair that seemed to curl in its own profusion. The mouth [...] was fixed and rather cruel-looking, with peculiarly sharp white teeth; these protruded over the lips, whose remarkable ruddiness showed astonishing vitality in a man of his years. For the rest, his ears were pale and at the tops extremely pointed; the chin was broad and strong, and the cheeks firm though thin. The general effect was one of extraordinary pallor. (23–4) □

There is more to this scene, though, than yet another reminder of the Englishman's alternately endearing and irritating obsession with minutiae. The Count's face, and even his hands – a masturbator's hands, with 'hairs in the centre of the palm' (24) – are thoroughly saturated with the signifiers of a medical discourse preoccupied not so much with individual health and accumulation as with a *fin-de-siècle* debate upon deterioration and wastage across a broader section of humanity. In this debate, medicine, and medical signifiers, become implicated in a cultural crisis bound up with social class and, to some extent, with immigration and race also.[50] The context here is less that of the clinical and more of the popular, the references and allusions advanced by the novel having a currency among those not specifically trained in medicine but educated enough to appreciate the social implications of medical science when embodied in the topical pages of *The Nineteenth Century*, *The Fortnightly Review* or *Blackwood's Magazine*. The Count is invisible in London quite simply because he resembles the demons – dissolute aristocrats, criminally minded proletarians, insidious foreigners – of a bourgeois age conscious of the fragility of its own recent ascendancy. Dissolute, criminal and foreign himself, the Count may move unseen amongst the commonly encountered degenerates of the streets, may fraternise, even, with them in much the same way as he has always been wont to 'command all the meaner things: the rat, and the owl, and the bat – the moth, the fox, and the wolf' (209).

As Leonard Wolf tantalisingly suggests in his notes to *The Annotated Dracula* (1975), Harker's description of the Count should be regarded as being intimate to Mina's subsequent account of the vampire's mental condition and the behaviour that condition motivates.[51] Prompted by Van Helsing's own depiction of the Count as a criminal 'predestinate to crime' (296), and fresh from her own telepathic contact with the vampire, she concludes:

> ■ The Count is a criminal and of criminal type. Nordau and Lombroso would so classify him, and *qua* criminal he is of imperfectly formed mind. Thus, in a difficulty, he has to seek resource in habit. His past is a clue (296) □

For many years the critical possibilities presented by this explicit reference to Max Nordau and his mentor Cesare Lombroso, key thinkers within the *fin-de-siècle* disciplines of medicine, anthropology and sociology, were ignored in *Dracula* criticism. Whether such an omission was prompted by ignorance, or betrayed a fashionable disdain either for materialist criticism or for the whole period of the *fin de siècle*, is irrelevant here. Suffice it to say that the potential of Wolf's observation that, in Harker's description, 'Lombroso is being closely followed', was not taken up for nine years, when it became the fulcrum of 'Lombroso's Criminal Man and Stoker's Dracula' (1984), an agenda-setting article by Ernest Fontana.[52] Since this time, the work of

Lombroso in particular has influenced the writings of critics as varied as Victor Sage, Daniel Pick, Robert Mighall and John Greenway. Less attention, oddly, has been paid to the more culturally orientated writings of Nordau who, like the similarly under-explored experimental physicians Sir David Ferrier (1843–1928) and Sir John Scott Burdon-Sanderson (1828–1905) (71) and the medical hypnotist Jean-Martin Charcot (171), all named in *Dracula*, represents a still-unexplored medical context ripe for scholarly consideration in the future.[53]

The basic premise for each of these critics has not been merely to tabulate the points of resemblance between Lombroso's view of deviant humanity and the body and behaviour of Stoker's Count, but also to project the implications of the vampire's perceived deviance onto those who are victims to, or opponents of, Dracula's regime of predation, infection and replication. Lauded by lay as well as professional people in the nineteenth century as a creditable model of human behaviour, the 'scientific criminology' of Lombroso and his contemporaries is now regarded as a questionable pseudoscience. Its determinism has become dismissed, at best as a grotesque parody of the idealised relationship between truth and beauty, and at worst as a precursor to twentieth-century eugenics, selective sterilisation and the European cultural attitudes that underwrote the Nazi Final Solution.

For Lombroso in particular, the born criminal – one 'predestinate to crime', as Van Helsing twice affirms (296) – may be readily detected and his likely temperament similarly predicted in the distinctive features of his physiology and especially in the conformation of his skull. Mina's suggestion that the Count's 'past is a clue' (296) is a teasing reference not merely to how she has predicted his current retreat as a repetition of his behaviour following an earlier defeat in his mortal life. It is, equally, a reminder that the Count retains the qualities of his distant ancestry as much as those of a more recent past. As Lombroso suggests in *Criminal Man* (1875), criminal degenerates constitute an exceptional embodiment of qualities appropriate to less evolved times, being a visible throwback to the savage ancestors whose physical characteristics are either absent or muted in the acceptable citizens of modernity. The nineteenth-century criminal is, for Lombroso:

■ An atavistic being who reproduces in his person the ferocious instincts of primitive humanity and the inferior animals. Thus were explained anatomically the enormous jaws, high cheek-bones, prominent superciliary arches [...] extreme size of the orbits, handle-shaped or sessile ears [and] the desire not only to extinguish life in the victim, but to mutilate the corpse, tear its flesh, and drink its blood.[54] □

So, too, as Fontana asserts, the Count himself involuntarily signals his criminality, his status as a man out of time, dangerously at large in a more civilised world, by those facial tokens that bespeak behaviours unacceptable in the present:

■ Dracula's 'aquiline nose', 'massive eyebrows', and 'pointed ears' correspond to characteristics identified by Lombroso: 'the nose is often aquiline like the beak of a bird of prey'; 'the eyebrows are generally bushy in murderers and violators of women' and 'tend to meet across the nose'; and there is 'a protuberance on the upper part of the posterior margin' of the ear, 'a relic of the pointed ear characteristic of apes'.[55] □

Needless to say, such atavistic figures, who possess strength and resourcefulness without restraint and discretion, are emblematic also of the fragility of the present, civilised, commentating age, and portentously indicate how such virile figures might shape and dominate the future if left uncontrolled and uncontained.[56]

Taking this on board, Stoker's Count, with his nose, forehead, teeth and ears all so emphatically recorded by an observant Harker, who is apparently ignorant of their degenerative import, represents a somewhat dualistic threat to modernity.[57] As a vampire the Count is, as Stoker's contemporary reviewers pointed out, an anachronistic threat to a modern and increasingly secular age. An occult power not recognised by modernity, the un-dead may be as easily dismissed by *the fin-de-siècle* readership as those 'new beliefs, which think themselves new; and which are yet but the old' – 'corporeal transference [...] materialization [...] astral bodies [...] the reading of thought' (171) – so glibly passed over by the empiricist physician, Seward. Simultaneously, though, the Count is encoded as a thoroughly *modern* threat, cast in the mould of the apparent cutting-edge of Victorian medical and social science. The degenerate, like the vampire Count, is rooted in the past, and ought to have no place in the progressive present. The Count is, admittedly, a literal survival of his own past rather than a genetically predetermined atavist, the product of somebody else's past, but enjoys with the latter the fearful reputation of one whose resilience and reproductive capacity defy both time and the progressive doctrines of evolution. The vampire is Other, but he is not wholly alien to the present race. Van Helsing's 'man-that-was' (212) is still identifiably, and in terms of his origins, a man.

The critical debate upon the 'scientific criminology' of *Dracula* characteristically couples the portentous warnings encoded into the vampire's physiognomy with the reproductive nature of vampirism itself. As Ernest Fontana argues:

■ Dracula is a threat to societies of predominantly morally and socially evolved humanity, because there survives within these societies, even in England, a minority of potentially 'diseased' individuals who are driven, subconsciously, to a reversion back to the atavistic, pre-civilized world from which Dracula survives □

Thus,

■ Dracula's practice of vampirism is a defiance of the evolutionary cycle. By resisting his personal death, and by infecting others into the condition of the 'Nosferatu', Dracula threatens to conquer not merely the civilized world, as his ancestor Attila did, but the entire race of evolved and evolving humanity.[58] □

Evolution, even in the cosmology of a Protestant Christian such as Stoker, represents unquestionable advance, inevitable betterment. The past, however superficially attractive it might seem, cannot be placed rhetorically in anything other than an unfavourable light in such a context – unless, of course, the present is seen as being subsumed by a more distant, atavistic, past. The coalition against the vampire, therefore, represents an assertive policing of the borders of modernity, a scrutiny not merely of the threat from without – the vampire who comes in from the east – but that which is also perceived within, even where the exemplars of Western evolved civilisation are inclined to betray their recidivism more subtly than the aquiline Count. The past is, literally, always with us, threatening to erupt through the veneers of collective civilisation and personal self-control.[59]

Fontana ranges across the Count's English victims, proclaiming Renfield, first, as 'obviously a Lombrosian criminal type, who comes under Dracula's power because of their biological and psychological kinship'. Indeed,

■ Neither his education, nor his acquired sentiments, which he manifests when he attempts to warn Dr Seward of the approaching menace to Mina, are strong enough to overcome his innate criminality, which is, in Lombrosian terms, an incurable disease.[60] □

Fontana is too rapid in his dismissal of Renfield as incurable here. The scene to which Fontana refers, Renfield's encounter with the coalition against Dracula on the night during which they first enter the Count's London dwelling, is ambiguous to say the least (215–18). On the one hand, the lunatic may well be warning Seward's associates of the impending threat to Mina posed by the Count's counter-attack. On the other, his desire – to be removed from the asylum – is selfish: either he fears the Count's wrath, or he is aware of his own inability to resist the temptation with which the Count seeks to gain his ingress to the building, through Renfield's invitation (244, 245). Renfield, though, later attacks the Count, in part because he is angry at the vampire's not having sent food for him to consume, but more emphatically because he has come to regard Mina Harker with the reverence associated with a civilised, chivalric modern gentleman. It is, indeed, a cumulative process, one which brings him progressively out of his supposedly atavistic demeanour: 'when she went away I began to think, and it made me mad to know that He had been taking the life out of her' (245). Renfield is, in a sense, cured on his very deathbed by his determination to stand effectively outside of his lunacy, and 'to use my power', the 'unnatural strength' (245) that he has heard is appropriate to lunatics, because 'I didn't mean him to take any more of her life' (246).

Arguably, the Count merely adapts Renfield's 'zoophagous (life-eating)' (71) *idée fixe* to his own zoopotous (life-drinking) practice, the lunatic's obviously antisocial cumulative obsession signalling his congruence to the vampire's own perceived mission. Fontana, though, is careful to script corresponding patterns of deviance in the vampire's two female victims, Lucy and Mina, neither of whom is depicted in the novel as being in any way a danger to their social circle. Indeed, both, even when infected with vampirism, are permitted to move freely in society, to enjoy the intimate company of friends, family and servants. Lucy's predisposition to vampiric attack, according to Fontana, is not vested in her precocious sexuality, as is often asserted in criticism,[61] but rather stems from 'her somnambulism, which, according to Lombroso, is a frequent characteristic of epileptics'.[62] It has to be said, though, that Lucy never unequivocally displays the customary symptoms of an epileptic in *Dracula*.[63] For Fontana, though, 'the vulnerable Lucy' is 'an epileptic atavistic reversion', the epileptic being yet another version of the degenerate, and thus, with the Count in the vicinity of Whitby, 'she is drawn to him as he approaches and, subconsciously, she seeks him out, bidding him to come to her the night after his disembarcation.'[64]

Fontana's contention that 'Lucy's latent criminal nature "bids" Dracula to come to her, despite her acquired morality and her betrothal to Arthur' stands somewhat in opposition to Van Helsing's own assessment of the relationship between the vampire and his victim. Where Fontana considers Lucy's trance to be an expression of the 'biological and psychological kinship' that links vampire and victim, Van Helsing sees evidence of a 'dual life' (179) in her sleepwalking condition. In this 'dual life' the essential Lucy is innocent, and the 'guilty' Lucy is not Lucy at all but rather her illness, her condition rather than her self. The trance-persona, in other words, is a discrete entity rather than a phase of the self. The difference between the opinion of the fictional Van Helsing and the critical Fontana is one of essence: for Fontana, the somnambulistic or epileptic Lucy is the true or essential Lucy.

Fontana's opinion as to what constitutes the truer (or truest) Mina, though, is less clear. Rather than identify explicitly the 'potential of savage reversion' which attracts the vampire to Mina, Fontana merely contends that it is after she is attacked that she exhibits the symptoms of hysteria, which for Lombroso is identified with both epilepsy and a susceptibility to suggestion, implicitly by hypnotism. One might counter the vagueness of Fontana's argument with the suggestion that the Count's annexation of Mina represents a strategic move on his part, rather than an opportune encounter with a fellow degenerate, and that her access to the very normality of her trusted position is the point of his action. She becomes not an active vampire, but rather a passive conduit of information, first between the group and the Count, and, latterly, in the reverse direction. If anything, her symptoms are not an exaggeration of qualities already present, as they would seem to be in the vampirised Lucy, but rather stem from her literal ingestion of the Count's own substance, as depicted in the scene in which the group encounters the vampire within the Harkers' bedchamber (247, 252). She is arguably not, as Fontana insists, 'a diseased reversion' in the manner of Lucy.[65]

For all this, Fontana is correct in assigning Mina a significant place in the Lombrosian world of reverse evolution depicted in *Dracula*. Her empowerment is not to a rebellious sexuality such as that associated with the 'voluptuous' (188) post-mortem Lucy, but to a more conventional role in mortal reproduction and the advancement of the species. As Fontana argues:

> ■ The hysterical [Mina] by feeding upon the blood of him who feeds upon the blood of others is empowered to bear the man-child whose birth is celebrated in the coda of the book. Caught between the poles of civilization and Lombrosian criminal atavism, Mina is shocked into becoming a vessel of evolution rather than a victim of reversion.[66] □

Mina's child bears the names of those who have opposed the vampire (326), yet arguably carries within his own veins only the mortal blood of his two biological parents, a schoolmistress and a solicitor. Unlike Lucy, Mina is never the recipient of the blood of the noble and professional men whose contributions vainly extended the vitality of her friend. She is bourgeois, through and through. Harker has, himself, been debilitated by brain fever, and in addition begins the novel as a man of words rather than of action.[67] He has achieved professional status through book work rather than inheritance or physical adventurousness (21). On such mundane foundations are the future generations of *Dracula* seemingly reared. However, 'There is a poison in my blood' (286), as Mina admits, and this addition to her bodily economy is not necessarily discharged from her upon the vampire's demise, when her facial scar is erased (326). As Fontana concludes, 'traces of Draculian atavistic blood survive commingled in the blood of future life'.[68] There is more to be said here, though. This circulatory presence might well be viewed in evolutionary rather than degenerate terms. It is, in effect, an injection of the adventurous and aggressive blood of Attila into the tired, inglorious, unadventurous world of the domesticated, Western middle classes.

Stoker's Count may therefore be a social and racial menace cast in the mould of one of Lombroso's degenerates, though his degenerate status is arguably equivocal. Indeed, as Victor Sage suggests, the Count's highly evocative physiognomy presents the observant reader with something of a conundrum. As Sage notes, the Count's bushy eyebrows are a classic signifier of the degenerate. The problem is, though, that Van Helsing, too, shares this facial characteristic. As Mina recalls of Van Helsing:

■ The poise of the head strikes one at once as indicative of thought and power; the head is noble, well-sized, broad, and large behind the ears. The face, clean shaven, shows a hard, square chin, a large, resolute, mobile mouth, a good-sized nose, rather straight, but with quick, sensitive nostrils, that seem to broaden as the big, bushy brows come down and the mouth tightens. The forehead is broad and fine, rising at first almost straight and then sloping back above two bumps or ridges wide apart; such a forehead that the reddish hair cannot possibly tumble over it, but falls naturally back and to the sides. (163) □

The intimacy between the vampire and the vampire hunter, under-written by the specific attention paid to their eyebrows, chins, nostrils, hair and foreheads, is emphasised in considerably more detail than that which is created between the Count and his apparently degenerate victims.[69] Evading the easy suggestion that Van Helsing is nothing more than a parody of the Count, the positive half of a divided double, Sage instead revisits the vampire hunter through Lombroso's other, and lesser-known, study of degeneration, *The Man of Genius* (1891), in which the writer suggests that genius is 'one of the teratologic [monstrous] forms of humanity, a variety of insanity'.[70] As Sage suggests:

■ Genius, according to theory [*sic*], is a form of degeneracy; it, too, is a throwback. Van Helsing is thus a mirror-image of Dracula, a genius in this sense. They are the only people in the novel who do not make records and keep diaries. They are perceived, but not presented as directly perceiving agents to the reader.[71] □

The implication of Sage's contention is that *Dracula* is indeed a study in monstrosity: the novel, though, is as much a study of the deviant nature of Van Helsing as it is of that of the Count – and, acknowledging the central place of testimony and evidence in the argument of Sage's *Horror Fiction in the Protestant Tradition* (1988), it is also a study in how such deviant figures may be observed and written about.[72]

Sage, oddly, omits any reference to Seward's fear that Van Helsing's obsession may have driven him to stealing Lucy's body from the grave in order to furnish proof for his otherwise incredible hypothesis. As Seward suggests, Van Helsing is 'so abnormally clever that if he went off his head he would carry out his intent with regard to some fixed idea in a wonderful way' (182). The pointed use of 'abnormally' here would seem to bear out Sage's contention that Stoker was familiar with the import of Lombroso's work beyond *Criminal Man*, and was as diligent in applying the thesis of *The Man of Genius* to Van Helsing as he had applied the earlier work to the Count. One might note also the manner in which Seward clothes his own mediocrity by proclaiming his personal devotion to a cause, the very selflessness of which associates him with the degenerate Renfield and the genius Van Helsing, both of whom are preoccupied with explicitly 'fixed' ideas or points (62, 182). Ambition, for Seward, is an obsessive pursuit whose drives might lead to unethical behaviour, if not psychological imbalance:

> ■ If only there were a sufficient cause! I must not think too much of this, or I may be tempted: a good cause might turn the scale with me, for may not I too be of an exceptional brain, congenitally? (71) □

Madness, perversely, is to be celebrated when it may be connected with visionary genius. As Sage, though, is careful to emphasise, Seward is unimaginative and resistant to epistemologically unconventional ideas, a 'purblind empiricist' rather than a visionary.[73] In some respects, Seward – stolid, empiricist, materialist – represents the mundane and unexceptional future as much as does the bourgeois child of Jonathan and Mina Harker.

VAMPIRES AND THE DEFINITION OF DEVIANCE

The vampire, therefore, is apparently as replete with anthropological, sociological and criminological symbolism as he is with his victims' blood. His physiology and physiognomy underline his degeneracy, and his practice, poised as it is between the figurative representation of seduction and the literal practicalities of infection and transmission, enforces the notion of his representing a whole range of contextual fears and perceived evils. Yet, for all this, he is still a vampire – a mythological being, an opportunist consumer of blood, albeit one strikingly adapted to, and available for, appropriation by those who deploy and manipulate both discourse and public opinion.

Robert Mighall, in an essay in the 1998 collection *Bram Stoker: History, Psychoanalysis and the Gothic*, and later in his *A Geography of Victorian Gothic Fiction: Mapping History's Nightmares* (1999), is acutely aware of this very duality. Mighall's analysis of *Dracula* is informed not by the criminological theories of Lombroso, but rather by way of the sexology of Richard von Krafft-Ebing (1840–1902), author of the medico-legal study *Psychopathia Sexualis* (1886). The specialist nature of Krafft-Ebing's work, with its limited currency beyond the medical and legal professions, and its more emphatic interrogation of the question of specifically sexual perversions, makes this an analysis far less dependent upon the conceit that Stoker knew at least something about the (for the most part accessible) medical and anthropological theories discernable in *Dracula*. For the most part, these are identifiable through the presence of their terminology in the novel, or by a passing reference to the name of a well-known theorist – but it is clear that Krafft-Ebing's name does not appear alongside those of Ferrier, Burdon-Sanderson, Charcot, Lombroso or Nordau, nor does his research seem to be clearly signalled in the manner of Carpenter's physiology.

For Mighall, arguably, the influence of Krafft-Ebing upon *Dracula* does not come through *specific* quotation or even systematic paraphrasing. Rather, the influence is more subtly discursive, *Psychopathia Sexualis* being intimate to a range of other works, clinical and popular, which have effectively structured the way in which medical and sexual deviance have come to be conveyed through images of monstrosity. 'Such practices', as Mighall intimates, 'do not reflect "fear" but power'. Mighall is at odds here with the conventional view of the deviant or degenerate as a source of general social unease. Anxiety is, admittedly, present in the structuring of such threats to a culture, though Mighall suggests that the medical and legal professions themselves verbally 'nurtured' deviance and deviants through the imposition of terminologies derived from 'zoology, folklore, and ancient history'. This right to define, if not to contain, both deviance and threat in turn proclaimed the professional and the specialist as powerful and indeed separate from the lay-person, for whom such monstrosities 'may well have struck a very fearful chord'.[74] There is a difference, in other words, between popular (or bourgeois) anxiety and the more contained and rhetorical anxiety expressed by the professional.

The cliché of Victorian bourgeois anxiety finds a parallel in the cliché of twentieth-century academic criticism. As Mighall sees it, criticism is prone to insisting 'that vampirism is erotic; that it embodies some form of sexual threat or "subversive" sexuality; and that the (male) characters in the text, being "typical" Victorians, fear vampires because of the threat they pose to orthodox sexuality'.[75] Hence, 'The critical consensus is that either Stoker, the text, its characters or its readers – collectively "Victorian culture" – did not fear vampires so much as what these figures masked, disguised or embodied.'[76] As Mighall argues, such an opinion is only tenable if sexology is viewed as being part of a fearful response to deviance in general, and to sexual deviance in particular. His critical innovation, though, is to question this assumed fearfulness, and to restructure sexology as a more assertive practice that appropriates imagery from outside of clinical practice and medical jurisprudence. By doing this, sexology brings not merely empirically *observed* human deviance but also the *portrayed* deviance embodied within 'mythology, folklore, and fiction' under the gaze of science.[77] Hence:

> ■ The impetus is to eroticize monsters and vampires; turning them *into* sexual beings, *into* perverts. Sex and its dysfunctions is used to explain these monsters scientifically, replacing evil with sickness, and mystery with perversion. The status of 'sexual pervert' provides a scientific alternative to the folkloric, mythical, Gothic or sensational identities that these figures would retain if medicine did not intervene and reinterpret them. (original italics) □

Van Helsing, strikingly, first prefigures and then concurs with Mina's lay diagnosis of the Count as a Lombrosian degenerate (295–7), though neither character speaks openly regarding the sexual rapacity that is often associated with such figures across the breadth of medico-anthropological writings upon degeneracy. Though sexuality is not mentioned, the effect is the same: the Count's occult practice is channelled through more conventionally human models of congenitally damaged, childish or insane personal psychologies, just as his genesis, first associated with a folkloric pact with the Devil (212) latterly becomes the outcome of 'something magnetic or electric' that lies behind (and explains) 'these combinations of occult forces' (278). There is a subtle difference between the Van Helsing who queries, 'A year ago which of us would have received such a possibility [as vampires], in the midst of our scientific, matter-of-fact nineteenth century?' (210), and the later vampire hunter who predicts the retreat of his foe back to his homeland through an empirical use of legend and history as evidence (296). As Mighall suggests, from this evidence, 'It could be argued that if these Victorian commentators "feared" anything it was superstition, and it was this that they used sexuality to counter in their writings.'[78]

Mighall's revisionist reading of *Dracula* climaxes with a consideration of the ritual staking of Lucy. In this ambiguous scene, the heroine is penetrated by a stake, which embodies both a folkloric rusticity and a more contemporary suggestion of phallic symbolism. The setting, moreover, is a modern tomb, temporarily transformed into a surgical theatre through the inclusion of Van Helsing's 'operating knives' and the meticulous practice of 'a doctor's preparations for work' (190). Thus, the exorcist-vampire hunter becomes a consultant surgeon demonstrating a novel curative procedure, and instructing a new (and reluctant) professional initiate in 'this bloody work' (179). If the vampire, as Mighall argues, has his occult significance overwritten through the imposition of sexuality, then so too does the whole occult process of exorcism find itself occluded by the familiar reassurance of professional surgery in the age of Ferrier and Burdon-Sanderson.[79] The only problem is that the subject of the operation looks like a mortal woman, but is an immortal vampire.

Inevitably, though, the veneer of sexuality associated with the scientific adoption of vampirism returns to the forefront in the enacting of that operation, most notably in the phallic symbolism apparently encoded into the insertion of the stake, the appreciation and encouragement expressed by the other men in attendance, and the consequent exhaustion of Arthur. The whole group – Van Helsing, Holmwood, Seward and Morris – are in an ambiguous position, as Mighall is quick to point out:

■ The 'gang rape' reading of the scene relies upon a symbolic hermeneutic which equates a sharpened piece of wood with a phallus. If this equation is denied then the stake is only a stake and the men are 'mutilating' Lucy's corpse. If this is what they are doing and the scene has a 'sexual' meaning which reflects an historical situation (Victorian sexual codes), then it must be concluded that these men are necro-sadists, sexual deviants, and therefore 'subversive' of Victorian morality.[80] □

The problem here, as Mighall bluntly notes, is that the righteous band of vampire hunters, had they been discovered at their work by one who did not share their discourse, might well have found themselves exemplified as deviants in just such a book as *Psychopathia Sexualis*. Thus, logically, 'It is essential in this instance that vampirism really *is* vampirism, and that "sexuality" does not enter the picture.' Mighall has, in essence, highlighted an implication that has been overlooked by critics keen to ascribe a sexual encoding to the vampiric act: the vampire hunters, virtuous and altruistic, commit acts which bring them within the discourses framing not merely illegality but equally those pertaining to perversion and deviancy. To preserve the totality of the vampire hunters' righteousness, Mighall argues, it would be as well to remember, once in a while, that 'a vampire was sometimes only a vampire and not a sexual menace'.[81]

Medicine, in its practice as a physiological discipline, embodies both a explorative and speculative mission as well as a containing and reassuring function. It is a powerful tool with which to predict and contain the unprecedented or deviant body within models premised upon the conventional, and yet a chilling indictment of the mundane nature of those who might not be deemed 'exceptional'. The same might be said of the incorporation of medical paradigms and medical knowledge within the criticism of fiction. The risk faced in criticism, though, if not mundanity, is certainly stagnation. Medically informed criticism of *Dracula* is characteristically aware of the most relevant of nineteenth-century contexts, though it has to be said that it has come to depend upon a relatively small number of medical texts and paradigms. More, certainly, might be done to consider the influence of non-clinical para-phrases of, and extracts from, medical works in the popular journals likely to be enjoyed by Stoker and his educated, metropolitan circle. There are, similarly, neglected possibilities to be found in those medically informed works researched by Stoker, though not mentioned in *Dracula* other than in his research notes. These include *On Superstitions Connected with the History and Practice of Medicine and Surgery* (1844) by Thomas Pettigrew (1791–1865), *The Natural and the Supernatural: Or, Man – Physical, Apparitional and Spiritual* (1861) by John Jones (dates not known), as well as the two-volume study, *The Theory of Dreams* (1808) by F. C. and J. Rivington (dates not known).[82] Finally, nothing substantial has yet been said with regard to the trepanning of Renfield in *Dracula*, an operation which Stoker researched and recorded in his manuscript notes. Given the potential of the material yet to be discussed in detail, it appears likely that medically informed criticism of *Dracula* will continue to develop for the foreseeable future.

★ ★ ★

Scientific criminology was one of the discourses which underpinned the late-Victorian debate upon race. The association between the degenerate and 'savage' working-class inhabitants of the nation's cities was heavily influenced by writings about the empire, and by the institutional racisms which justified the repression and control of non-civilised peoples. The fear, though, which lay behind the rhetoric of domestic degeneration had its parallel in the British contemplation of imperial possessions and continental neighbours. Chapter 3 extends many of the debates discussed in Chapter 2 in its consideration of the often perverse rhetorics of race, colonialism and invasion.

CHAPTER THREE

Invasion and Empire: The Racial and Colonial Politics of *Dracula*

Read on a superficial level, *Dracula* can all too easily appear to be a somewhat simplistic parable of invasion repulsed – a comforting and affirming reminder, even, of the irresistible power of the familiar over the alien, a power redoubled and rejuvenated by the very stress of adversity. There are obvious features of Stoker's novel which support this tempting, though ultimately misleading, viewpoint. In his association with money, implicitly deployed in 'usury, avarice, sharp practices, secret wealth, miserliness', the Count, further, recalls two central figures in clichéd Jewry: Shylock, the money-lender in the play *The Merchant of Venice* (1600) by William Shakespeare (1564–1616), and Fagin, the leader of a gang of young thieves in the novel *Oliver Twist* (1838) by Charles Dickens (1812–1870).[1]

The Count, explicitly, comes from the East, and from a superstitious, backward land characterised by racial miscegenation and feudal, rather than constitutional, governance. The Count's homeland is stagnant and inward-looking, and so betterment, for the ruler as much as for the populace, may only be achieved beyond inherited borders. Lacking the necessary force for a modern imperial adventure, invasion thus takes the form of immigration, a subtle and unseen crossing of borders by way of trade routes, in the holds of cargo vessels, and upon the very carts and railway trucks that distribute imported wares from the British east-coast ports to the metropolis. Invasions are not always effected by armies, but the Count is simultaneously a historical and a modern threat: he is a military commander and a civilian, a nobleman who yet wants to move unseen in a bourgeois world, a lone domestic consumer and an empire-builder.

THE CONQUEST OF THE WEST

The (specifically English) West, to which the vampire travels, is, in contrast to the vampire's East, meritocratically governed, enlightened by both science and Protestantism, and rejoices in punctual trains and a reliable postal service. When Van Helsing notes that the West enjoys the 'power of combination – a power denied to the vampire kind' (210), he implicitly acknowledges the racial and cultural basis of that unity, mobilised through Aryan and Anglo-American alliances, and expressed in the common moral standard of the chivalrous modern gentleman.[2] Alone and unassimilable to these identities, the vampire will always implicitly be at a disadvantage, and not merely because his grasp of both technology and his own capabilities (279) is at best rudimentary on his arrival in England. Though nominally the invader, the Count is rhetorically viewed under the gaze prototypically reserved for the invaded or the colonised. The vampire is always narrated rather than narrating, his apparent motivations inscribed upon his actions rather than vocalised exclusively in his own words.[3] As he physically invades, he is himself rhetorically invaded, subjected to scrutiny and, indeed, to the kind of hostility frequently reserved for unwelcome immigrants. In this rhetorical position, the Count cannot hope for a fair representation in the novel: few readers, it might be suggested, would willingly echo Van Helsing's admiration of the Count's enterprise (279), or Mina's pity for his damned soul (269). Even acknowledging these two concessions, the Count, it would appear, cannot avoid being structured as the polar opposite of the West he has come to invade.

The complex way in which *Dracula* apparently mobilises racial and national Othering has been progressively acknowledged in criticism, and the polarities characteristic of the earliest imperial studies of Stoker's novel have been overwritten by more fluid models of invader and invaded. The critical situation at the turn of the twenty-first century is, perhaps, most succinctly explored in the preface to Branka Arsić's 'On the Dark Side of the Twilight' (2001), a study not of *Dracula* but of the apparent spectralisation of contemporary Balkan culture. Arsić contends:

■ When Bram Stoker situated the dark, unarticulated, evil forces of the vampire in the Balkans, he projected the Balkans as a heterogeneous body of the Other, as the threat to the homogenous body of the Same, an evil eye of the East directed toward the goodwill of the West. Bram Stoker's *Dracula*, however, is only one instance of a wild fear that has obsessed the West since the Enlightenment; a fear that reason, perhaps, will never be enlightened enough, that it will forever remain in secret, invisible collusion with madness; that, also, it would not be possible to discipline the bodies of the West, and that the threat of rebellion of those undisciplined bodies was there to stay, that it would be forever and unpleasantly present in the very heart of the West.[4] □

At the core of Arsić's analysis is the contention that the Other (or a version of the Other) dwells within the Self (or Same, as Arsić phrases it).

Homogeneity is thus an illusion: the West is as disparate as the East. There is some commonality, of morals, of behaviour or of physicality, that links some sections of the beleaguered culture with the external forces that seek to invade it. Rhetorically, both the tendency within and the threat from without are liable to be regarded as degenerate in the interests of preserving the hegemony and homogeneity of the existing (and threatened) identity. The 'enemy within', in other words, is born out of cultural necessity.

Arsić's stress upon the undisciplined body may serve as a timely reminder of the functional relationship between sexuality and racial and national identities. Racial purity, as well as miscegenation, are promulgated through sexual activity. Discipline and self-control represent only one aspect of the policing of the potentially promiscuous individual body: national policies restricting immigration, as well as more draconian interventions into marriage and conception, all impact upon the reproduction of a homogenous racial and cultural identity. Sexual conquest, through rape or seduction, might well be said to represent an invasion or 'possession' (to use a traditional sexual term) of the individual body, and, in addition, an annexing of the race or the nation through the smallest integer of its identity.[5] As the Count boasts to his Western opponents, 'Your girls that you all love are mine already; and through them you and others shall yet be mine' (267): the taunt is specifically directed at a fiancé and a husband and their associates, but it may as well be a retort to the Anglo-American West more generally. The Count has, after all, not merely annexed a woman who *literally* embodies the West in her surname but has, through her, begun to annex the children of the West in a curious parody of motherhood and nurturance.[6]

Those children, significantly, are working class. It is worth noting at this juncture how the late-Victorian debates upon industrialisation, proletarian urban life and criminality frequently draw upon the discourses commonly associated with contemporaneous issues of immigration and foreignness. For example, the very title of In Darkest England and the Way Out (1890) by the temperance reformer William Booth (1829–1912), a study of working-class intemperance and irreligiosity, explicitly alludes to the colonial travelogue In Darkest Africa by H. M. Stanley (1841–1904), published the same year; elsewhere, social explorers such as Henry Mayhew freely identified the indigent poor with exotic and implicitly primitive 'wandering tribes' such as 'Bushmen', 'Fingoes' and 'Arabian Bedouins'.[7] Stoker, whether deploying these discourses consciously or not, may arguably be seen as part of a tradition that embraces the spectacular images of Gustave Doré (1832–1883) as much as it does the evocative prose of Blanchard Jerrold (1826–1884), Henry Mayhew and James Greenwood (184?–1929),

writers who deployed the exotic and the foreign as a means of expressing and explaining the prosaically proletarian.[8]

Stoker's dialect-speaking proletarians, whether domiciled in Whitby
or the East End of London, are, to bourgeois eyes, a strange people.
Rhetorically, their strangeness configures them as being not merely
different, but also as all too easily subject to the influence of outsiders
and invaders. In *Dracula*, British carters (231) and unemployed loaf-
ers (232) are seemingly as keen to assist the Count as Transylvanian
Szgany (45) and Black-Sea Jews (302–3).[9] Admittedly unknowingly,
these British citizens are complicit in an invasion and occupation of
their homeland. Recalling the close symbolic connection between
exchanges of blood and sexual intercourse, explicitly vocalised by both
Morris and Van Helsing in the novel (138, 158), it is inevitable that the
vampire's action will itself take on a sexual symbolism. The children
of working-class men such as Thomas Snelling, Joseph Smollet and
Sam Bloxam (229) thus represent a further development in the colonial politics of Stoker's writing. If the vampire *invades* through finance
and trade, he *occupies* and consolidates his occupation through sanguine
though sexualised conquest. Once bitten, these children display not
merely compromised behaviour but will also eventually exhibit the
physical characteristics of the invading, alien race. Their descendents,
too, will display those alien characteristics in succession to the more
familiar physiognomy of the home nation. The parallels to documented
British fears of immigration and miscegenation at the Victorian *fin de
siècle* are compulsive, if not convincing, if the symbolism of *Dracula* is
read in this way. Culturally, Self and Other do not simply equate to
British and non-British stereotypes. The Alien is not merely external, but enjoys a disturbing intimate relationship with the internal also.
Its geographical proximity and apparent resistance to control from the
cultural centre of identity further suggests that the alien is continually
expanding, colonising the fringes of 'us' and challenging the prior-
ities of identity which structure the alleged homogeneity of racial and
national identities. When reading the urban, proletarian landscape, the
common perception of cultural and physical degeneration may be taken
as the rhetorical twin of the externalised fear of immigration.

Dracula was almost certainly first identified in criticism as a form of
colonial Gothic in 1979 by Carol Senf, who suggested that Harker's
rage and terror during his final days in Transylvania indicate 'that he
fears a kind of reverse imperialism, the threat of the primitive trying
to colonize the civilized world'.[10] Judith Wilt, similarly, in *Ghosts of the
Gothic* (1980), considered the novel to be a fiction of colonial-domestic
'penetration and counterattack', and a pioneer in a sub-genre that was
to become (as 'weird tales') 'the spine of Gothic fiction in a century
of imperialism and world war'.[11] These assertions, though provocative,

were comparatively brief, and even though a more substantial reading of Imperial Gothic generally was advanced by Patrick Brantlinger in *Rule of Darkness* (1988), it was not until 1990 that a dedicated and detailed exploration of the invasion narrative of *Dracula* specifically was published by Stephen Arata.[12]

Arata's 'The Occidental Tourist: *Dracula* and the Anxiety of Reverse Colonization' (1990) effectively set the agenda for subsequent readings of the invasion motif in *Dracula* through its consideration of how imperial fantasies of this type may structure an introspection upon both domestic and colonial politics. Arata argues that, in common with the broader British culture of the *fin de siècle*, 'Late Victorian fiction [...] is saturated with the sense that the entire nation – as a race of people, as a political and imperial force, as a social and cultural power – was in irretrievable decline.'[13] Citing works by writers as diverse as H. Rider Haggard (1856–1925), Rudyard Kipling, Sir Arthur Conan Doyle and H. G. Wells (1866–1946), Arata asserts that

■ Versions of this story recur with remarkable frequency in both fiction and nonfiction texts throughout the last decades of the century. In whatever guise, this narrative expresses both fear and guilt. The fear is that what has been represented as the 'civilized' world is on the point of being colonized by 'primitive' forces [...] In each case, a terrifying reversal has occurred: the colonizer finds himself in the position of the colonized, the exploiter becomes exploited, the victimizer victimized. Such fears are linked to a perceived decline – racial, moral, spiritual – which makes the nation vulnerable to attack from more vigorous, 'primitive' peoples.[14] □

One needs to draw a distinction here between the 'reverse colonization narrative' proposed by Arata and popular fictions of national humiliation such as *The Battle of Dorking* (1871) by George Chesney (1830–1895). The latter genre, which Arata terms 'invasion scare' novels, are primarily polemical and propagandist works focused upon a technologically advanced (and, typically, Germanic) enemy whose gathering strength is being ignored by domestic politicians and population alike. Chesney's narrator, characteristically, chides his reader with the statement that his fictional Britain, invaded and occupied by Prussia, had 'had plenty of warnings, if we had only made use of them'.[15] Fictions such as these are, in a sense, consciously patriotic works, often tinged with nostalgia, though their sentiments may well be strikingly at odds with government policies or what is perceived as public opinion.

For Arata, rather than striving to awaken a complacent nation to the prospect of impending danger, 'reverse colonization narratives' embody an introspective function that implicitly appeals to a sleeping and potentially responsive imperial conscience. He states:

■ fantasies of reverse colonization are more than products of geopolitical fears. They are also responses to cultural guilt. In the marauding, invasive Other, British culture sees its own imperial practices mirrored back in monstrous forms [...] Reverse colonization narratives thus contain the potential for powerful critiques of imperialist ideologies, even if that potential usually remains unrealized. As fantasies, these narratives provide an opportunity to atone for imperial sins, since reverse colonization is often represented as deserved punishment.[16] □

This distinction works well with Arata's other chosen example, H. G. Wells's *The War of the Worlds* (1898), with its understated critique of British imperial policy towards indigenous peoples in Tasmania.[17] The valid application of the distinction to Stoker's work is arguably less certain, though, even when the author's explicit commitment to Gladstonian Liberalism is acknowledged. Stoker's fiction, with its racist disdain for black Africans and somewhat patronising view of the rural Irish, the provincial Scots and the English working classes, does not sit easily alongside Wells's socialist idealism. Indeed, if that were not enough, Arata's attempt to inscribe a symbolic version of Ireland's colonial relationship with England upon *Dracula* appears markedly unconvincing in the context of his more valid points about the novel's imperial scripts. Arata argues that

■ *Dracula* suggests two equations in relation to English-Irish politics: not just, Dracula is to England as Ireland is to England, but Dracula is to England as England is to Ireland. In Count Dracula, Victorian readers could recognise their culture's imperial ideology mirrored back as a kind of monstrosity, Dracula's journey from Transylvania to England could be read as a reversal of Britain's exploitations of 'weaker' races, including the Irish.[18] □

Stoker's nationalist credentials, as biographers and critics alike have frequently asserted, are far from convincing, even if his retention in London of an Irish accent and an Irish circle of friends is well documented.[19] Stoker's Gladstonian Liberalism, indeed, would arguably have caused him to view Home Rule as a quite different prospect from political independence. Stoker's vision in his earliest novel, *The Snake's Pass* (1890), of a Utopian Ireland, free of sectarianism and regenerated by paternalistic English intervention, is probably as close to a colonial model of Anglo-Irish relations as his personal politics would admit.[20]

The colonial analogy must, however, be applied with qualification to Arata's representative 'reverse colonization narratives', with the obvious exception of *The War of the Worlds*. Predominantly, in works such as Rider Haggard's *She* (1887), Conan Doyle's *The Sign of Four* (1890) and Kipling's 'The Mark of the Beast' (1890) – exemplars of the genre, for Arata – the colonising enemy is normally not gifted with superior technology nor strength of numbers. Indeed, the invasive force is often subtle or singular, and its target is more likely to be the individual as representative of the nation rather than the nation, as a geographical entity, itself. The invasion, as it were, need not be a conventional occupation of literal soil – to colonise the West, one may simply compromise the Westerner at home, or on occasions, whilst he or she is domiciled abroad; this is the fate, certainly, of Kipling's Fleete, and, but for his escape, would have been that of Stoker's Harker, also.[21] It should be noted that the Orientalist, cross-dressing fantasy, *The Beetle* (1897) by Richard Marsh (1857–1915) to which Arata does not refer, embraces both of these projected scenarios of an individual invaded at home and abroad, as Rhys Garnett convincingly argues.[22] The Occident and the Orient may be perceived as being as much opposing states of mind as they are cartographical conventions.

The War of the Worlds is thus atypical of Arata's 'reverse colonisation narratives'. For the most part these are characteristically 'obsessed with the spectacle of the primitive and the atavistic'.[23] The West, these narratives assert, is as unable to defend itself against the threat of the barbaric intruder as it is incapable of resisting the superior technologies of Wells's Martians. The threat is twofold. By itself, the threatening barbarianism is dangerous, though by no means assured of a victory over Western civilisation and technology. An element within that civilisation, though, which may be scripted variously as proletarian, female, mad or sexually deviant, is perceived as sharing qualities with the invader, so that a form of natural alliance is achieved, to the detriment of the home nation. The alien barbarian is thus a catalyst, literally a foreign body within the body politic, exploiting and accelerating the weakness and degeneration that an apprehensive bourgeois culture fears is already there.

Reading *Dracula* through this contention, Arata – possibly mistakenly – argues that the Count's racial and geographical origins function as a scarce-concealed index to the literal threat facing British culture at the *fin de siècle*. In *Dracula*, Arata insists, 'Stoker continues a Western tradition of seeing unrest in Eastern Europe primarily in terms of racial strife'.[24] That strife was widely reported in the British press at the time, though, as Ludmilla Kostova claims in 'Straining the Limits of Interpretation: Bram Stoker's *Dracula* and its Eastern European Contexts' (2007), Arata may have inadvertently confused Transylvania with another multiracial component of the Hapsburg Empire in his reading of Stoker's sources.[25] Whether or not Arata's historical vision is accurate, his interpretation evokes the vampire as being not merely a symbol of the Carpathians but one which also carries the germ of national instability into any territory which it visits:

■ Stoker thus transforms the materials of the vampire myth, making them bear the weight of the culture's fears over its declining status. The appearance of vampires becomes the sign of profound trouble. With vampirism marking the intersection of racial strife, political upheaval, and the fall of empire, Dracula's move to London indicates that Great Britain, rather than the Carpathians, is now the scene of these connected struggles.[26] □

The novel, in other words, is a parable against immigration, and its primary assumption is that 'Miscegenation leads, not to the mixing of races, but to the biological and political annihilation of the weaker race by the stronger.'[27] The fear is that, technological superiority notwithstanding, the domestic, Anglo-Saxon race is enervated and thus vulnerable to being subsumed within other, more physically virile, 'primitive' races. The vampire's scripted racial origins and the conquest encoded in his blood-drinking thus come, for Arata, to represent a twofold fear of racial decline and impending absorption. Quoting *The Land Beyond the Forest* (1888) by Emily Gerard (1849–1905) which he claims as a source for *Dracula*, Arata states:

■ The 'anticipated apprehension' of deracination – of seeing Britons 'ultimately dissolving into Roumanians' or vampires or savages – is at the heart of the reverse colonization narrative. For both Gerard and Stoker, the Roumanians' dominance can be traced to a kind of racial puissance that overwhelms its weaker victims. This racial context helps account for what critics routinely note about Dracula: that he is by his very nature vigorous, masterful, energetic, robust. Such attributes are conspicuously absent among the novel's British characters, particularly the men. All the novel's vampires are distinguished by their robust health and their equally robust fertility. The vampire serves, then, to highlight the alarming decline among the British, since the undead are, paradoxically, both 'healthier' and more 'fertile' than the living.[28] □

Arata is wise here to append 'vampires' and 'savages' to the perceived threat of 'Roumanians'. Romania, though no doubt troubled by racial strife and subject to depopulation through immigration, presented no substantial threat to *fin-de-siècle* Britain, far from its borders, in the West. Arata's rhetoric is much too racially specific here: 'Roumanians' really ought to be 'immigrants' generally, Romania functioning not as a literal location but as a form of shorthand for a broader East, one that embraces other nations in Eastern Europe, including Poland and Russia, multiracial and multi-faith cultures whose immigration patterns were frequently determined by racial (and racist) criteria.

ANTI-SEMITISM IN STOKER'S FICTION

The immigrant vampire must be seen as representing far more than a singular threat from Romania. The Count, it has to be said, may signify many races, many nations, and more than one religion, though his perceived threat is consistently Eastern and Other. It is curious that Arata fails to acknowledge what, for many in late-Victorian Britain, was arguably the most evocative face of the Othered, immigrant and unacceptable East – the Jew. Jewish immigration to the West increased substantially following the Russian pogroms of 1871 and 1881, and similar persecutions within the Austrian Empire: apparently, between 1881 and 1900 the number of foreign Jews within England increased by some 600 per cent, their European languages and often distinctive clothing making them highly visible amongst British Jews and gentiles alike.[29] Though the liberal ideologies of British culture were resistant to strident anti-Semitism, hostility to immigrant Jews could still be expressed not merely through polemic but also through incorporation into fiction and drama.[30] Stoker, certainly, displayed a consistent distaste for Jewry, both foreign and British, as is testified by a number of hostile characterisations from Mr Mendoza, the Hamburg moneylender in *The Watter's Mou'* (1894), to the Cockney supplier of bogus Scottish regalia, The MacCallum More, otherwise known as Joshua Sheeny Cohen Benjamin, in 'Crooken Sands' (1894), and the Anglicized and urbane usurer, 'Mr Cavendish, whose real name was Shadrach' in *The Man* (1905).[31]

Inevitably, the anti-Semitic content of *Dracula* is represented by considerably more than the grasping materialism of the Romanian merchant Immanuel Hildesheim, 'a Hebrew of rather the Adelphi Theatre type, with a nose like a sheep, and a fez' (302). As Jules Zanger argues in 'A Sympathetic Vibration: Dracula and the Jews' (1991), the Count himself exists in a symbolic and metaphoric relationship to British perceptions of Jewish activity and migration. Zanger's study is undoubtedly influenced by Nina Auerbach's *Woman and the Demon: The Life of a Victorian Myth* (1982), a work which linked Stoker's Count to both Svengali, the fictional Jewish mesmerist of the novel *Trilby* (1894) by George Du Maurier (1834–1896) and to Sigmund Freud, in the guise of a Continental Jewish doctor whose *fin-de-siècle* practice incorporated hypnotism. The central theme established by Auerbach's juxtaposition of the three Jews and their gentile female associates is the negation of the will.[32] Zanger appropriates this image in order to develop a racial, rather than sexual, reading of the Jew–gentile encounter: the Jew, in the guise of an alien, conquers and dominates, and yet is a parasite rather than a host. Count Dracula, in the novel, is explicitly not a Jew but a Christian, albeit one who has become an apostate and a student of Satan (34, 212). He may, however, be effectively 'read' as Jewish because of the complex of identities and Otherings that meet within his physiology, his practice, his foreignness and his perceived aspirations.

Frustratingly, and despite the promise of its title, much of Zanger's study is concerned with the general context of British anti-Semitism rather than with the detail of *Dracula*. A significant portion of the article concerns the English mythology of the so-called 'Blood Libel', in which the Jews, variously of Norwich and Lincoln, are alleged to have drained the blood of a Christian child (St William and St Hugh, respectively) in order to celebrate their Passover rites. Zanger does not satisfactorily link this mythology, which he considers to have 'a figurative dimension, depicting the Jewish community as parasitic, as draining the blood of the Christian host country, as "blood sucking"', directly to the plot of *Dracula*. Indeed, it is never suggested that the Irish author knew anything of this English myth, even in the form of its incorporation in Chaucer's 'The Prioress's Tale' in *The Canterbury Tales* (1387–92) by Geoffrey Chaucer (*c*.1343–1400).[33] Stoker's anti-Semitism is certainly as apparent in *Dracula* as it is elsewhere in his writings, and the author is no doubt a participant in the cultural hostility which Zanger identifies in 1890s Britain. 'A Sympathetic Vibration', though, is just that – a suggestion of likeness rather than a truly demonstrated congruence. Zanger's work should therefore be regarded as indicative, though it is influential in having established the greater symbolism vested in both the vampire and the Eastern European immigrant.

A more comprehensive and detailed reading of the Jewish script of *Dracula* is to be found in Carol Margaret Davison's *Anti-Semitism and British Gothic Literature* (2004). Davison's admirable analysis combines a number of complementary readings which crystallise around the vampire's condensation of domestic hostilities towards both resident and immigrant Jewry. In particular, she recounts the theme of a recurrent Jewish mythology within British culture not merely through the Blood Libel but also through the recurrent myth of the Wandering Jew. In considering the Blood Libel and its symbolisms, Davison is in general agreement with Zanger (and, indeed, with the broad argument propounded by Arata). She does, however, clarify the nature of the Count's parasitism in a way that extends the argument into a more 'scientific' conception of miscegenation and reproduction:

■ In keeping with established anti-Semitic stereotypes, Count Dracula is guilty of the Blood Libel, of desecrating the Host, and of endangering the national body politic, which was increasingly viewed as racialized. This desecration extends to the biological meaning of the term 'host' and

gestures towards the Count's ultimate role in Stoker's novel: he is a parasite from a racially alien nation who vigorously feeds off Britain, his Christian
host nation. In his figuration of vampirism as a type of blood disease, Stoker
both draws upon longstanding anti-Semitic stereotypes associating Jews
with plagues, and speaks to his era's syphilis epidemic and burgeoning
racial nationalist ideology.[34] □

The Wandering Jew, likewise, is linked firmly to Stoker's biography, via
conversations recorded in Ludlam's pioneering life of the author, and
through the inclusion of the errant and eternal Semite in Stoker's *Famous
Impostors* (1910).[35] Davison admits that 'Dracula's role as a Wandering
Jew figure may be nowhere explicitly expressed in Stoker's novel':
it is, however, 'frequently and variously suggested'. The Semitically
inflected Count of Stoker's novel represents not 'The ascetic, abste-
mious Wandering Jew of legend', but rather a parallel drawn from 'a
new racialized anti–Semitism in Britain that held the Jew to be nation-
ally unassimilable and morally irredeemable'.[36] The Count's desire to
pass unseen within London (26), if read in the light of Davison's analysis, sounds like a hollow reassurance advanced only to hoodwink the
unwary Christian, Harker.

Where Zanger passes quickly over the physical resemblance
between Stoker's Count and Svengali, the Jewish Mesmerist and sexual predator of George Du Maurier's *Trilby* and its 1895 dramatisa-
tion, Davison develops a lengthy and detailed paralleling of cliché
Jewish physiognomy and the fictional specificity of *Dracula*.[37] She
notes how,

■ Like Hildesheim, Dracula is Mammon-obsessed and has a stereotypical
Jewish physiognomy. Apart from his sinister 'pointed beard' – a signa-
ture feature of the devil's traditional physiognomy – a figure with whom
the Jews were traditionally associated – great care is taken to describe
Dracula's nose which is strongly aquiline, hooked, and beaky. A passage
from Stoker's *Personal Reminiscences of Henry Irving* illustrates that
Stoker associated this type of nose with Jewishness. In his description
of his employer, Henry Irving, as he applied his make-up for the part of
Shylock, Stoker notes that he 'could never really understand [...] how the
bridge of the nose under painting [make-up] rose into *the Jewish aquiline*'.
[Davison's ellipsis, interpolation and italics][38] □

Further, 'Dracula also has a distinct and pungent odour similar to the
foetor judaicus long attributed to the Jews'. Again, in Davison's argument,
the clichés of popular culture become associated with the more scientific
racism of the *fin de siècle*. Recalling Harker's impressions of the Count's
London crypt (251), domestic soil which has been literally saturated

with the foreign vampire's personal miasma, Davison concludes:

> ■ Dracula is essentially a social *polluter* who threatens to infect the British nation. He is often accompanied by rats, a longstanding symbol of the plague. Since at least the Middle Ages it was believed that Jews spread this and other infections while, as a result of demonic pacts made with the devil, they remained immune. [original italics][39] □

The Count, though not explicitly a Jew, represents in extreme concentration those qualities which exist only by implication and cliché in the person of the avaricious Hildesheim. The Count is truly, as Davison suggests, 'a *fin-de-siècle* Frankenstein monster borne of various established anti-Semitic stereotypes and contemporary anxieties relating to the Jewish question in Britain': in effect, he allows a freer expression of prejudice and hostility than might otherwise be acceptable if associated with an unequivocally constructed and explicitly acknowledged member of the Jewish race.[40] It has to be said, though, that, in Davison's conception of it, late-Victorian Britain appears far more openly anti-Semitic than the more liberal culture depicted by Zanger.[41]

Davison's most significant achievement, however, is to dispel the established myth, in *Dracula* criticism, of a unified and homogenous West besieged by a racially diverse East. Though she acknowledges the Protestant consensus of Christian Britain, Davison is careful to note the (often influential) presence of Anglicised though still practising Jews within the late-Victorian polity. This admission of division, which contrasts with the 'supra-national, monolithic "Occident"' which Cannon Schmitt proposes for *Dracula* in his *Alien Nation: Nineteenth-Century Gothic Fictions and English Nationality* (1997), draws the vampire even more perversely close to those who set themselves, as representatives of the West, in opposition to him.[42] Though conventionally associated with the aggrandisement and jingoism of the Victorian and Edwardian periods, imperialism, Davison asserts, was considered a 'widely unpopular foreign policy' in Britain. If this were not enough, Davison suggests that 'This policy was promoted, and even said to have been invented by, Benjamin Disraeli', a Prime Minister who 'Despite his conversion from Judaism to Christianity at the age of 12 [...] was nonetheless regarded as a crypto-Jew whose "doctrine of empire and interest" was subverting standard and stable British policy.'[43] Thus, 'Protestant Britain [...] continued to displace its anxieties about its tendencies by projecting them onto a Jewish *Doppelgänger*' or double. In a complex transfer of identities, imperial Britain becomes somehow Jewish because of the foreign policies of a racial Jew who has embraced both the Protestant faith and a national (as opposed to racially encoded) identity. The very actions of creating and maintaining empire thereby confirm that the home nation has itself already become changed by a form of imperialism enacted from within:

■ In true Gothic fashion, Dracula's greatest threat thus lies in the elimination of the secure boundary between the novel's British gentlemen and the alien, Judaizing vampire they resemble and enable [...] The vampire-gentleman equation is suggested early on in the novel during Harker's trip to Transylvania when he does not perceive Dracula's reflection in the mirror despite the fact that Dracula is standing immediately behind him. Dracula's perpetration of brutal acts in Transylvania while wearing Harker's clothes further blurs the boundary of identity between vampires and imperialists. Albeit perhaps unconsciously, Stoker intimates an unsettling point of contact between these two groups.[44] □

Count Dracula, a foreigner whose imperial aspirations are all too familiar, an outsider who may yet circulate unseen in the Anglo-Saxon public space that is Piccadilly, thus 'combines the joint threat of immigrant alien Eastern European Jews, and demonized, speculating capitalist Anglo-Jews'.[45] Indeed, his need to 'convert' his opponents to his own persuasion seems almost redundant: they are already arguably far closer to him than they could ever suspect.

TRANSYLVANIAN SUPERSTITIONS AND BALKAN POLITICS

Colonial readings of *Dracula* have been shaped by the assumption that British culture, at its imperial apogee, was preoccupied with the threats of both invasion and decline. The ready acceptance of that assumption has turned criticism's imperial gaze inwards, as it were, prioritising and privileging the British reader and his or her threatened, though undoubtedly familiar, milieu in the process. If this is inevitable in readings of those portions of the novel that take place on British shores, it is questionable when applied to the significant component of Stoker's work that depicts the journeys to Transylvania, and the time spent by both Harker and the Van Helsing circle in greater Romania, from the Black Sea Coast to the Borgo Pass and its environs. These components of the novel cannot be read in a simplistic critical gaze premised upon imperialism because Britain's interest in the Balkans was not, strictly speaking, colonial. British foreign policy in Eastern Europe was concerned with influence rather than settlement, and where it did touch upon the Empire, it was preoccupied with protecting existing interests in the region – Malta, Cyprus, the route to the Suez Canal – rather than appropriating territories from the declining Ottoman Empire. Where

British observers considered the racial and nationalistic issues of the Balkans it was, again, in a somewhat detached manner: emotions of sympathy or of revulsion might be periodically provoked by rumours or reports of massacres and pogroms, though there was arguably little real fear that such things might impact upon the equilibrium of the distant British homeland.

The Balkans, nevertheless, exerted a fascination for educated Britons from the declining years of the nineteenth century to the eve of the First World War. The region is associated with a rich heritage in British culture, and with an evolving attitude towards Europe's often tense interface with Ottoman power. On the one hand, the Classical Order of ancient Greece underpinned British public-school education across this period, though the poetic idealism evoked earlier in the nineteenth century by the struggle for independence from Turkish rule was no doubt dissipated by Victorian images of a nation that did not appear to have subsequently advanced out of poverty and technological backwardness. Ottoman Turkey, associated historically with advances in science and architecture as much as with hostile military might, is equally disabled in the Western gaze through characterisation as 'the Sick Man of Europe', its European possessions engaged in alternately covert or open revolt, their own aspirations to statehood being tempered by the interests of adjoining powers such as Russia and Austria-Hungary.

Most fascinating of all, the Balkans are *in* Europe though not necessarily *of* Europe, as Jonathan Harker observes when, after crossing the Danube at Budapest, he finds himself firmly 'among the traditions of Turkish rule' (9). This liminal identity, this oscillation between familiar-European and alien-Ottoman cultures endows the region with a rather *unheimlich* quality. At the heart of the *unheimlich* (or uncanny) experience, as Freud would have it, lies the *heimlich* or familiar: unease is provoked, in other words, by the ambivalent relationship with the known, so that '*Unheimlich* is in some ways or other a sub-species of *heimlich*'.[46] One may project the application of the *unheimlich* beyond its strictly psychoanalytical origins. In an 1885 review of Transylvanian superstitions, which Stoker read in his research for *Dracula*, Emily Gerard is moved so far as to claim for the region an essential European identity premised upon its apparent retention of historic folk memories. Gerard notes:

> ■ It would almost seem as though the whole species of demons, pixies, witches, and hobgoblins, driven from the rest of Europe by the wand of science, had taken refuge within this mountain rampart, well aware that here they would find secure lurking-places, whence they might defy their persecutors yet awhile.[47] □

The 'imaginative whirlpool' of Stoker's Transylvania seems somehow to draw Europe – and the European as traveller – into its vortex. Yet, as Vesna Goldsworthy suggests, the descent into that maelstrom might well be a return to a more primitive, even a more European, self: for Goldsworthy, Stoker's 'Transylvania is not the periphery of Europe but the continent's omphalos [navel]'.[48]

Goldsworthy's *Inventing Ruritania: The Imperialism of the Imagination* (1998) is admirable in its detailed reading of how Stoker's novel represents a late phase of 'The gradual move of the chosen Gothic locale eastwards into the Balkans'.[49] For Goldsworthy, Harker resembles the beleaguered traveller rather than the confident imperialist, his mental preoccupations being less a matter of reflection and introspection and more a constant confusion with novelty and difference. Indeed, for Goldsworthy:

■ Both in detail and in overall structure, the opening chapters of *Dracula* are organised as a typical Balkan travel narrative of the second half of the nineteenth century. The book starts with the *locus communis* [commonplace] of such literature, a 'farewell to the known world' (that is, Western Europe)[50] □

The traveller, it would appear, is overwhelmed by his impressions, though Goldsworthy insists that this is in itself a function of the defamiliarising effect of the travel-writing genre. As she suggests,

■ Jonathan Harker's entrance into the 'Eastern' world could never, in reality, have been so abrupt. Stoker creates an impression that the oriental world is almost sucking Harker in, as Munich, Vienna and Budapest flash by. While he gradually loses control over everything else, Harker desperately clings to the (very Victorian) obsession with train timetables, even as time itself appears to dissolve around him: 'It seems to me that the further East you go the more unpunctual are the trains. What ought they to be in China?' (11)[51] □

The import of Goldsworthy's reading of Harker's Transylvanian journal is that the Solicitor's record is fractured by internal tensions. On the one hand, the journal is a characteristically Western form whose purpose or effect is to impose order and linearity upon disparate data. Such a rhetorical position allows the commentating self to take an at-times patronising (and, at other times, a merely critical or derogatory) view of the inefficiency and difference of other cultures – witness Harker's obsession with railway punctuality, as singled out by Goldsworthy. Further, Harker's obsession with detail – which Goldsworthy considers appropriate to the 'didactic' drive and function of the Victorian travel narrative – emphasises his bourgeois purposefulness, as well as distinguishing his mission from the dilettante Grand Tour:

> ■ Train travel, which symbolises [...] progress, imposes occidental time on the Orient. Harker's exasperation with the lack of regard for time is thus a reaction typical of the Victorian traveller in the Balkans. While the Romantic traveller would have had no particular reason to hurry, the Victorian (male) traveller frequently visited the region on business – as a journalist, scientist, politician, army officer or – in Harker's case – as a solicitor sent to conclude a property deal.[52] □

As Goldsworthy states, 'A contrasting attitude towards time is supposed to be a *differentia specifica* [defining distinction] between the East and the West.'[53] Harker's utilitarian purposefulness, though, is a façade. Beyond its stated purpose in the formal completion of an exchange of property, it is as Romantic as any pre-Victorian voyage to the East. If Harker betrays his fascination with the Orient explicitly through his urge to collect, tabulate and distribute the regional recipes he experiences (9, 10, 13), he more subtly evokes what Goldsworthy terms 'a recurrent theme in [...] Romantic literature which perceives the East as a "free", ahistorical (timeless) realm of exotic pleasure'.[54] Goldsworthy might well have added that Jonathan Harker rapidly becomes subsumed within the chronological influence of the East, his indignation at irregular railway timetables notwithstanding. Once he neglects to wind his watch (44), he becomes dependent upon Eastern time, with all its imprecisions and variations, rather than upon the precise chronology he has transported with him from Exeter.

The timelessness and 'air of unreality' of Stoker's fictional Transylvania, underscored as it is by a resident who, in depicting distant historical events, 'spoke as if he had been present at them all' (33), is not wholly vested in the narrative of the overwhelmed tourist-solicitor.[55] Stoker's own grasp of Balkan history is markedly imprecise, despite his research at Whitby and, apparently, in the British Museum. Though Goldsworthy argues for a 'playfulness' in Stoker's deployment of historical events and contemporary geography, the confusion and conflation evident in the novel may equally be the outcome of hurried scholarship.[56] Whatever the cause of the novel's inconsistencies, the effect is to make spectacular regional and racial differences and, in so doing, to emphasise the marginality and isolation of Transylvania specifically, and Romania more generally.

For all his detailed exposition of history, Stoker's Count, as recorded by Jonathan Harker, is a hybrid that bears no absolute relation to the historical Vlad Ţepeş, more commonly known in the West as Vlad the Impaler.[57] Indeed, for Goldsworthy, the Vampire's construction is

dependent not upon biography but rather supports the novel's drive
to evoke 'an exotic, alien background, while preserving the essentially European identity of the Count'.[58] The acknowledgement of
these European origins is among the key developments that can be
attributed to *Inventing Ruritania*. The Count need not represent Arata's
specific threat of a Romanian race or nation – though, admittedly, his
European identity remains ambivalent. Goldsworthy is arguably the
first critic confidently to disregard the customary polarity of East and
West in *Dracula*. In so doing, she facilitates the development of critical
analysis of a perplexing relationship between the Count and his opponents recognised since the earliest days of *Dracula* criticism. The Count
resembles the English enemy when he aspires to move to the West. In
Transylvania, he reads their books (including, significantly, a Bradshaw's
railway timetable), and literally clothes himself in Harker's British tailoring (25, 28, 47): in London, he walks unnoticed in Piccadilly, and
speaks a more grammatically correct English than the working men
whom he employs (155, 267). Additionally, Harker – and, indeed, the
Van Helsing circle on their first incursion into Transylvania – equally
come to resemble the Count. 'Madam Mina, our poor, dear Madam
Mina is changing' (280), says Van Helsing at the inception of the group's
pursuit of the Count into his homeland. The Dutch physician ought
to note, though, how, as the journey progresses, his assistants so readily embrace violence and the absolute rule of strong over weak, how
the Western Lord Godalming issues bribes with the alacrity of the
Eastern Count De Ville. The Van Helsing circle need to be cautious in
Romania, for the murderous 'work of a Slovak' (303) might as easily
have been done by an Englishman caught up in the 'imaginative whirlpool' (10) that is Transylvania.

At this juncture, Goldsworthy seems curiously reticent, and an unwary
reader might all too easily come to anticipate her argument petering out
into the customary conclusion that *Dracula* is nothing more than a fantasy of 'reverse colonisation'.[59] Some support for Goldsworthy's subtle
distance from this conservative stance might perhaps be drawn from her
projection of the Van Helsing circle into a multinational force committed
to destroying a threat which is all the more terrible because its perceived
'Europeanness' undermines the polarities of self and Other, observer and
observed, West and East.[60] Just one passing remark hints of the further,
political, possibilities of *Dracula*, before Goldsworthy moves on to an analysis of the Balkan context of Stoker's 1909 *faux* vampire novel, *The Lady
of the Shroud*. Tellingly, Goldsworthy says of the Van Helsing circle:

■ Their mission to restore order in the Balkans represents a (subconscious?)
fictional expression of the attempts in the late nineteenth and twentieth
centuries by the Western powers to impose peace on the peninsula.[61] □

The challenge effectively and implicitly posed by Goldsworthy's final reflection on *Dracula* is to construct a convincing reading of Stoker's fictionalised Balkans which is dependent not upon 'reverse colonisation' but which addresses the issue of British foreign policy. This context, of international rather than domestic crisis, was considered at the turn of the twenty-first century and in 2006, respectively, by Eleni Coundouriotis and Matthew Gibson.

Coundouriotis, as Gibson acknowledges, is the first critic of *Dracula* to observe the novel primarily in relation to the Eastern Question – the complex interface of nationalisms and imperial interests that accompanied the decline of Ottoman power in Eastern Europe. Her work is, though, dependent upon the accepted perception of Stoker as a persistent, if not dogmatic, Gladstonian Liberal. In '*Dracula* and the Idea of Europe (1999–2000), Coundouriotis credits Stoker with a Gladstonian suspicion of Turkey, and a belief in the Ottoman Empire's inability to assimilate itself to a European political model. She extends this alleged authorial suspicion, however, to those Balkan nations struggling to assert their European rather than Ottoman credentials to the adjoining West. *Dracula*, it would appear, rhetorically opposes contemporary history: in what she terms the novel's 'deligitimation of history', the emerging Balkan nations are both denied European kinship and are regarded as being as incapable of assimilating to Europe as their Ottoman neighbour.[62]

Effectively, Coundouriotis asserts, to accept these nations into Europe is to destabilise, or even threaten, the whole concept of Europeanness. Their presence, in effect, poses a threat to Europe that is epistemological rather than military or migratory. Viewing the Count as a sort of synecdoche for his region, an 'Ottomanised European', Coundouriotis argues that he 'represents the irreconcilable aspects of history that do not fall neatly into a European narrative of progress and cannot be accommodated without forcing a significant change in that Western identity'.[63] This is somewhat different to the invasion theses advanced by Arata and other *Dracula* critics: Coundouriotis's assertion, though, does seem to backtrack from Goldsworthy's appreciation of the Count's European identity, and underscores his defeat with the customary polarities that will inevitably accentuate the subtle differences that disqualify this close relation of the West from absorption within its own 'imaginative whirlpool'.

Matthew Gibson's analysis of Stoker's novel in *Dracula and the Eastern Question* (2005) represents both a response to Coundouriotis's article and a revisiting of the author's Liberal politics. Whilst acknowledging Stoker's friendship with Gladstone and his professed interest in Irish Home Rule, Gibson argues that the author took a more pragmatic line with regard to the Balkans – a stance, indeed, which Gibson judges as 'decidedly Conservative'.[64] This apparent contradiction in Stoker's

seemingly orthodox Liberalism is explained by Gibson through reference to the author's biography. Stoker's younger brother George, who,
like the author, lived in London, had served as a surgeon in the Russo-
Turkish War of 1877–78, where he apparently 'became unashamedly
pro-Turkish in his sympathies'.[65]

Gibson's statement may be supported by reference to George Stoker's
own writings, quoted in Haining and Tremayne's semi-biographical study
of Bram Stoker, *The Un-Dead*. Haining and Tremayne see George Stoker's
decision to join the Turkish Army as quite in keeping with British foreign
policy in the time of Disraeli's premiership of 1874–80. They question:

■ Why did George decide to volunteer to serve the Turks? It is clear from
his writings that he was very supportive of the Turks and had a dislike
for Greeks, Bulgarians, Rumanians and the other small nationalities under
Turkish rule. Certainly, England's foreign policy at this time, as it had been
in the Crimean War, was to support the Turkish empire against what was
seen as the potential danger of the Russian empire. George seemed to
share his father's Unionist and High Tory background and this could have
made him into a blind supporter of Empire. He seems to have believed in
the 'civilising vocation' of the Ottoman empire.[66] □

Hence, where the archetypal Turk was, for George Stoker, 'educated as
a thoroughly honest and trustworthy man', the Greek, a Christian liberated from Ottoman rule, was less honourable: he states, 'my experience is that lying is more natural to the Greeks than truth, and, to my
sorrow, I know that they never failed to swindle me when such a chance
presented itself.'[67]

Gibson, though, further credits Bram Stoker with a knowledge of
the implications of the 1878 Treaty of Berlin, the agreement, brokered
on Britain's part by Disraeli and his Foreign Secretary Lord Salisbury
(1830–1903), under which the Ottoman Sultan Abdul Hamid II (1842–
1918) was deprived of the control of the majority of his Balkan possessions. Among the nations liberated from Turkish rule by the Treaty was
Romania, albeit with the loss of some territory to Russia. The 'traditions of Turkish rule' (9), however, arguably remained strong in nations
such as Romania after 1878. The Turkish heritage of the liberated,
Christian Balkans is thus the centre of Gibson's argument, as it was that
of Coundouriotis's before it. The corruption associated with a degenerate Ottoman East, though, is rendered somewhat differently in Gibson's
account, the Turks taking on a more favourable position in respect of
policing not merely Russian ambition but also the potentially anarchic
behaviour of the Balkan Christians. Thus, for Gibson:

■ *Dracula* does not represent a condemnation of Turkish influence upon
areas that have fallen under its sway so much as a complaint that the

natural degeneracy of Balkan Christians requires [i.e., justifies the presence of] their Ottoman rulers[68] □

For Coundouriotis, Count Dracula is condemned in the novel because he represents an aspiring European who cannot be accepted into that political identity because of his Turkish heritage. For Gibson, the Count is condemned because he represents those liberated Balkan peoples who have fallen into anarchy and degeneration as a consequence of their resistance to the law and order (brutal though it may have been) imposed upon them by Ottoman rule. Again, it is worth recalling here George Stoker's polemic: 'There is no doubt that the Oriental Christians, especially the Bulgarians, have been oppressed for centuries, but they have prospered and become rich.'[69]

Gibson's account thus reads *Dracula* as a text whose sentiments are decidedly at odds with Gladstonian Liberalism's sympathy for the Balkan Christian nations. As he suggests:

■ Turcophilia [love of Turks] in the novel seems to go beyond simple vilification of Balkan Christians to an implicit comparison between British Victorians and the Turks, as well as a bizarre exemption of the Turks from the West/East divide which otherwise is so important in the novel.[70] □

In support of this contention, Gibson draws attention to Van Helsing's historical survey of the Count's repeated incursions into Ottoman territory, where the Christian, European warrior had gone 'again and again [...] over the Great River into Turkey Land', and 'when beaten back, came again, and again, and again' (295). Here, the psychology of criminal deviance becomes momentarily intimate to racial stereotyping. When viewed through the psychology of Lombroso and Nordau, as it is in the exchange between Mina and Van Helsing, the Count's heroic actions become the repetitive and selfish gestures of a 'child-brain' (296) that can learn but slowly. One might further recall here how Harker comments upon the frequency of goitre – associated in Victorian England with degenerative cretinism – in the domestic population which supplied the Count's soldiery (15).

If the Count is, racially as well as individually, 'a criminal and of criminal type' (296), the text effectively reschedules the Turks – historically the enemies of Christian Europe – in more positive terms as

■ policemen and keepers of the peace, rather than occupiers and torturers, the view of them held by [the Romantic poets Lord Byron (1788–1824) and Percy Bysshe Shelley (1792–1822), by Gladstone, and by] most men who believed in the right to independence of either the Greeks, or other Balkan nations.[71] □

Stoker is taking liberties with history here – the Ottoman Turks, after all, were invaders of these Balkan nations – but it is apparent that a subtle equation is being drawn between the Van Helsing circle and Turkey, as much as it is between the Count and the Balkan nations:

> ■ in looking for patterns of behaviour in Dracula's past and comparing the present situation with his previous fights against the Turks, Van Helsing is surreptitiously identifying himself, Seward, Mina Harker and the others with the Turks, as being the containers of criminals, and London as having been 'invaded' in the same way that Turkey was repeatedly 'invaded' by the monster (conveniently ignoring the fact that Turkey was the aggressor at that time).[72] □

Gibson emphasises that *Dracula* does not represent an outright or explicit endorsement of Turkish policy in the Balkans. The novel does, though, appear to show 'a pro-Ottoman position on the question of Balkan independence, presenting the Christians they have fought as being irrational, and dangerous to Western society'.[73] Though Gibson's account is premised upon political knowledge and the biographical influence of George Stoker, one might also note how Stoker's political message is arguably underpinned by the scientific criminology (or, in this context, scientific racism) that medical critics of *Dracula* have discerned at work in the novel.

ANGLO-SAXON ALLIANCES

The scientific racism of *Dracula* – and, indeed, the scientific racism that may be discerned across the breadth of Stoker's writings – characteristically aligns Britain with the United States through possession of a common Anglo-Saxon heritage. As Stoker insists in *A Glimpse of America* (1885), the United States might well be regarded as 'England's first-born child', with the alliance between 'the English on both sides of the Atlantic' being a matter of 'the instinct of a common race, which makes brotherhood and the love of brothers a natural law'. Remarkably, the slippage between paternity and fraternity that concludes *A Glimpse of America* seems scarcely noticeable in the hyperbole of common history, common pride and the reflected glory of transatlantic advancement.[74] It is arguably this racial heritage, as much as his personal wealth and physical virility, that makes Quincey Morris a credible suitor for an English heiress – in much the same way as the wealthy American heroines of Stoker's *The Mystery of the Sea* (1902) and *Lady Athlyne* (1908) are scripted as appropriate marital partners to those novels' English heroes. With the heroic, sacrificial death of Quincey Morris in the service of both Mina Harker and England, the favourable association might seem to have gained its fictional apotheosis. Stoker, it would appear, admired America and favoured Americans, even when their behaviour was as gauche as it was heroic.[75]

The indulgent eulogy of *A Glimpse of America*, the sacrifice of Quincey Morris and the consistent tone of biography have all contributed to a pervasive critical consensus that regards Stoker as an enthusiast, if not an apologist, for America. Stoker's commitment to the United States has, however, twice been challenged in criticism. In a frequently anthologised chapter of *Signs Taken for Wonders* (1983), Franco Moretti appears to present at the outset a quite conventional interpretation of the Count as a European threat. Intriguingly, Moretti's Count is perceived not as a conventional feudal aristocrat, but rather as a reader of Adam Smith – the Count, Moretti notes, keeps no unproductive servants, indulges in no pomp, show or leisure, and, in the act of harvesting blood, never squanders his resources: 'His ultimate aim is not to destroy the lives of others according to whim, to waste them, but to *use* them.'[76]

With the Count reconfigured in Moretti's analysis as 'a saver, an ascetic, an upholder of the Protestant ethic', and with reference to the contention of Karl Marx (1818–1883) that 'Capital is dead labour which, vampire-like, lives only by sucking living labour', it is but a small development to argue that the Un-Dead in *Dracula* symbolises not an anachronistic feudal nobility, but an ascendant and wholly contemporary monopoly capitalism.[77] The Count, apparently, represents the resurgence, in 1897, of capital that has laid ' "buried" for twenty long years of recession', and which has now set out upon its ordained path of monopoly. Quoting Marx's *Capital*, Moretti states:

> ■ The *stronger* the vampire becomes, the *weaker* the living become: 'the capitalist gets rich, not, like the miser, in proportion to his personal labour and restricted consumption, but at the same rate as he squeezes out labour power from others, and compels the worker to renounce all the enjoyments of life'. Like capital, Dracula is compelled towards a continuous growth, an unlimited expansion of his domain: accumulation is inherent in his nature. [original italics][78] □

Jonathan Harker, it seems, has missed the point: the Count is, for all his primitive surroundings, 'nineteenth century up-to-date with a vengeance' (40) with regard to his plans for the 'teeming millions' (53) of London. 'Dracula', Moretti concludes, 'is the final product of the bourgeois century and its negation'.[79]

Moretti's subsequent assertion that monopoly capitalism was not highly developed in *fin-de-siècle* Britain, and, indeed, that it might well be regarded as 'foreign' or Other, facilitates his eventual association of the Transylvanian Count with the American adventurer. Moretti's assertion that 'The American, Morris, must die, because Morris is a vampire' comes initially as a surprise, though the critic rapidly assembles a number of parallels between the two apparently opposing figures who meet their end in Transylvania. This tabulation of Morris's mysterious origins, youthful appearance, and past history of adventures, however, is too rapidly compared to the Count's depiction, and lacks conviction. Moretti further credits Morris with possibly inflicting vampirism upon Lucy, given that her condition becomes active and aggressive following his final transfusion – though the critic is incorrect when he states that it is Morris who first mentions the word 'vampire' in *Dracula*: Harker translates the term from both Slovak and Serbian (13–14) in the first chapter of the novel.[80]

What is more convincing, though, is Moretti's suggestion that the American at first covertly supports the vampire, and then effectively strives to supersede him. Noting Morris's surprising inability either to track or shoot the Count in London. Moretti states:

■ [Morris] would be a totally superfluous character, if, unlike the others, he were not characterised by this mysterious connivance with the world of vampires. So long as things go well for Dracula, Morris acts like an accomplice. As soon as there is a reversal of fortunes, he turns into his staunchest enemy. Morris enters into competition with Dracula; he would like to replace him in the conquest of the Old World. He does not succeed in the novel but he will succeed, in 'real' history, a few years afterwards. □

As the final sentence suggests, the implications of Morris's shifting allegiance ought rightly to be read on a symbolic level: 'nobody suspects' – to borrow a phrase which Moretti insistently utilises in his demolition of Morris's altruism and racial fraternity – the American's motives.[81]

As Moretti eventually admits, Morris is not a vampire in the literal sense that the Count is, though he partakes of many of the metaphoric associations that Western culture has gathered around the evocative activity of the un-dead. If anything is made clear by Moretti's oscillation between reading Morris first as a literal, and then as a figurative, vampire, it is the strain under which Stoker's affinity for America is progressively placed as the United States gains in economic and strategic prominence. Stoker is, in Moretti's final account, pulled in two directions, his publicly stated racial allegiance being tested by the United States' association with the perceptibly 'foreign' threat of monopoly capitalism. Hence, Stoker must maintain the one whilst somehow dispelling the other. Moretti explains:

■ For Stoker, monopoly *must* be feudal, oriental, tyrannical. It cannot be the product of that very society he wants to defend. And Morris, naturally, is by contrast a product of Western civilisation, just as America is a rib of Britain and American capitalism a consequence of British capitalism. To make Morris a vampire would mean accusing capitalism directly; or rather accusing Britain, admitting that it is Britain herself that has given birth to the monster. This cannot be. For the good of Britain, then, Morris must be sacrificed.[82] □

Even the killing is occluded, as Morris dies at the hands of a gypsy (324) who is, none the less allowed to escape retributive British justice. The novel ends, Moretti concludes, not with the death of the Count but with that of Morris, 'the American financier', though Harker's coda might also serve to integrate the outsider safely within the altruistic and anti-monopolistic bourgeois British family. In the emblematically named son of Jonathan and Mina, the American becomes once again reassuringly British.[83]

Andrew Smith's 'Demonising the Americans: Bram Stoker's Postcolonial Gothic' (2003) has much to say about British and American relations as depicted within *Dracula*, even though the greater part of its argument is premised upon readings of 'The Squaw' (1893), *The Mystery of the Sea* and *The Lady of the Shroud*. Recalling Moretti's argument from the outset, Smith links Stoker's apparently contradictory attitude towards America in *Dracula* and elsewhere with the author's Anglo-Irish origins. Smith, like Gibson, interrogates Stoker's acknowledged Gladstonian Liberalism, and clarifies also his Home Rule politics, seeing the latter as far from separatist.[84] Smith's suggestion that Stoker envisaged an Ireland still redolent with a distinct, Celtic identity yet committed to a tolerant multinational British state based upon the British Isles is certainly credible, given the sentiments of the final phase of *The Snake's Pass* in particular.[85]

This idealised authorial vision of Ireland as 'a postcolonial country which is able to benefit from its alliance with the British Union' is, however, threatened by Britain's shifting position within the military and mercantile worlds.[86] The specific invasive threat posed by the Count suggests for Smith, as much as it does for Moretti, an occluded American Other:

■ The support for a unified Britain in which Ireland acquires some form of cultural autonomy and economic advancement at the expense of real political power is potentially threatened by the presence of those who could destabilise Britain's position within a global, and colonial, economy. In *Dracula*, it seems as though it is the Count who represents such a threat, although behind this ostensible danger there is the more palpable, and plausible, danger posed by America. Ultimately it is for this reason that Stoker revises his view of America as he comes to perceive it as a threat to

Britain's own colonial ambitions and consequently to Ireland's economic progress.[87] ☐

Smith is arguing here for a change in perception between *A Glimpse of America* and *Dracula*, albeit a change of perception that is subtle and coded rather than overt and polemical:

> ■ *A Glimpse of America* can be read as a taxonomic reading of America which stresses the similarities between the two nations. *Dracula*, however, is a novel that dwells on differences; in particular it focuses on such registers as history, culture and race in order to establish this difference, the same registers which in *A Glimpse of America* are used to establish similarity. These issues of Otherness in *Dracula* might appear to be ones that revolve around the image of the vampire; however, if Morris can be linked to this figure then America, by association, is also demonised.[88] ☐

Smith does not need to clarify the details of Morris's cultural difference, or indeed the factors which facilitate his association with the vampire: Moretti has already done this, though arguably in a far less thorough way than Smith might have done. Instead, Smith's article turns first to 'The Squaw' with its dialectal, sadistic American tourist, and then to *The Mystery of the Sea* (which juxtaposes an American heroine of English descent with a rapacious New Orleans negro and a Spanish Morisco nobleman) and, finally, to *The Lady of the Shroud*.

This latter novel, which imbricates the literary conventions of vampirism with a Balkan political fable, represents possibly the most thorough exposition of the ideas and fears that Smith identifies in *Dracula*. If America is present at all in *The Lady of the Shroud*, it is as an even more occluded presence, coded within Balka, a rising United States of the East, which, through European-derived technology, innovation and foresight, assembles an Empire of the Air to rival Britain's mastery of the seas. As Smith notes, the rise of a Celtic King, a former British subject, in the fictional Balkan nation that gathers Balka around itself, represents a 'triumph of the colonial oppressed'.[89] Britain's control over its former subjects is seemingly far from assured, whether these be individuals or nations. Indeed, as the closing words of *The Lady of the Shroud* underline, the modern nation encompassed about by hostile powers ought to aspire to an 'irresistible unity' that ensures an identification not merely with national leadership but also with the very concept of nationhood and national identity.[90] Perversely, that nation – styled in *The Lady of the Shroud* as The Land of the Blue Mountains – may be either Britain or America: an exemplar of how diverse nationalities may be formed into unity, a projection of how such a federal body might become a foe to fear. Certainly, the East-West oppositions of *Dracula* are not those of *The Lady of the Shroud*: in the latter the Van Helsing circle is replaced by a thinly disguised Edward VII, the individualist Count becoming the leader of a coalition determined to resist colonisation and eclipse. There is certainly sufficient evidence to develop the suggestion that Stoker's outlook changed as much between his two vampire novels as it did between *A Glimpse of America* and *Dracula*.

★   ★   ★

The concept of empire is complicated in British history by the contested status of Ireland, Stoker's birthplace. As ancient Celtic nation, provincial component of the British Isles and aspirant to Home Rule, Ireland is a muted though discernible presence throughout Stoker's fictional and non-fictional writings. Chapter 4 further explores the important issues of race and empire discussed in Chapter 3 in its consideration of how Irish Studies has developed a distinctive critique of *Dracula* in the context of British influence and Hibernian identity.

CHAPTER FOUR

Landlords and Disputed Territories: *Dracula* and Irish Studies

According to Joseph Valente, 'The decade of the Irish *Dracula* ended in 2000.'[1] Valente's terse valediction of a significant branch of the critical response to Stoker's novel appears, at first sight, to be both arbitrary and extraordinary. The statement, after all, prefaces a book-length study – tellingly entitled *Dracula's Crypt: Bram Stoker, Irishness, and the Question of Blood* – published some two years after the turn of the twenty-first century, making that work itself an anachronism, a mere superfluity by its author's own admission. Inevitably, Valente is teasing his readership here: his own distinctive – and, indeed, revisionist – response to 'the Irish *Dracula*' forms the substance of the work which follows that provocative opening statement. It rapidly becomes clear, though, that the term 'the Irish *Dracula*' has implications far beyond the novel's status as a fiction written by an Irishman. 'The Irish *Dracula*', for Valente, is arguably not the *Dracula* written by Stoker the Victorian Irishman, but rather an appropriated text circulating within the discipline of post-Victorian (and thus post-colonial) Irish Studies: *Dracula's Crypt* is as much a study of how *Dracula* has become an interpretative standard, a pattern of dense and recurrent signification in the discipline of Irish Studies, as it is a reconsideration of the Irish contexts of Stoker's fiction.

Valente's achievement is to identify how Irish Studies, having first liberated *Dracula* from its customary places in both Gothic criticism and Anglocentric English Studies, has come to inhibit its own ongoing commentary upon the potential meanings of Stoker's novel in general, and his vampire in particular. 'The Irish *Dracula*' is precisely what its prefatory 'the' suggests: a singular entity, a critical monolith that draws on certain shibboleths central to the highly politicised discourse that is Irish Studies. Consideration of Valente's work, because of its revisionist nature, necessarily occupies a significant proportion of the current chapter. To read the implications of *Dracula's Crypt* effectively, though, it is necessary to begin by identifying the critical consenius that forms its immediate context. This reading in turn invites a consideration not merely of how Irish Studies has appropriated and criticised Stoker's novel, but also of the criteria behind that discipline's characteristic conventions of selection and exclusion, its canons of relevance and aesthetic excellence, and its preoccupations, historical as well as critical and cultural.

DRACULA IN IRISH STUDIES

The ambiguous – if not awkward – place which *Dracula* occupies within the modern Irish Studies canon can be ascertained from the somewhat grudging tone of an assessment made at the very start of 'The decade of the Irish *Dracula*'. *The Field Day Anthology of Irish Writing* (1991), ostensibly both representative and authoritative yet frequently controversial in its assertion of a broad Irish canon, assigns *Dracula* to a relatively short survey embracing the breadth of the 'Irish Gothic and After (1820–1945)', under the editorship of W. J. McCormack, a critic firmly grounded in the study of Stoker's near contemporary, the Gothic author J. S. Le Fanu. Acknowledging the expertise of this editor, it is surprising to find that McCormack is insistent that 'the Irish tradition of Gothic fiction' might turn out on closer inspection to be 'a slender one', persisting in 'a fugitive and discontinuous manner throughout the nineteenth century' and at the point of 'expiring' when taken up by Stoker at the *fin de siècle*.[2] Its only redeeming factor, it would seem, is its potential for a distinctively Irish politicisation, something which apparently saves it from the ignominy of being merely a derivative, subaltern expression of a colonialist literary form. McCormack notes:

> ■ Whereas the origins of English Gothic are diverse and obscure [...] Irish Gothic fiction is remarkably explicit in the way it demonstrates its attachment to history and to politics.[3] □

This 'attachment' canonises Le Fanu, who was 'first thought of as an Irish historical novelist', and whose earlier works depicted incidents in County Dublin 'before he was obliged by his publisher to adopt contemporary English settings and the other trappings of sensational fiction', while it problematises the merely 'commercial novelist', Bram Stoker.[4] McCormack's rendering of Stoker throughout his chapter of the *Anthology* insistently underplays the novelist's Irish origins, locating the residual Irishness of *Dracula* not in its originality or its political commitment, but rather in its derivative status. According to McCormack, 'Stoker borrowed from a story of Le Fanu's ("Carmilla") when he came to write *Dracula*', and, even more damningly, 'Stoker's prose eschews the stylistic resourcefulness of its predecessor' in Le Fanu's vampire novella.[5] *Dracula*'s other correlative, as McCormack tellingly asserts, is 'the sensationalist immediacy' of 'Wilkie Collins's crime-novel *The Moonstone*', a thoroughly English work, crafted in an English literary tradition which was also to claim an impoverished Le Fanu as one of its exponents, an Irish martyr to the generic demands imposed 'by his London publisher'.[6]

Stoker's writing is thus flavoured not with a distinctive Irishness, but expresses, rather, a blandness of taste that disqualifies the author's entitlement to any Irish identity other than 'The smallness of Dublin's middle-class society, or at least that portion of it which adhered to the reformed churches.'[7] Thus for McCormack, and indeed for many other critics, the author of *Dracula* might be conveniently dismissed as 'an upright and unremarkable citizen', a man contextualised not by a revivalist national identity but rather by a trans-national or infra-national social identity. What else but complacency and conservatism could be expected of a man whose 'background was conventionally middle-class'?[8]

Both *Dracula* and Stoker thus seem to be compromised by a multiplicity of connections with Anglocentric culture, and to such an extent that neither can be easily assimilated to the Irish Studies canon. Though *Dracula* is impossible to ignore because of its commercial success, it makes no immediate or explicit statement about Ireland and has no obvious 'attachment to history and to politics'.[9] It is bound up with a genre which, though appropriated at times by Irish writers and adapted to Irish locales, remains intertwined with more broadly British (rather than discretely Irish) issues of society, politics and religion. Indeed, *all* Irish Gothic might be justifiably discarded from the Irish canon under this judgement, the genre being a literary form which 'engages quite promiscuously with other literary subgenres', leaving its authors 'far from exclusive in their loyalties' and compromised by 'the wide-ranging implications of their indiscriminate commerce'.[10] The purity of the canon would seem to resist the text's status as a fiction implicated not merely in the literary stylistics of a broader, English-speaking world, but equally in its shaping by issues – racial, social, cultural, political and medical – that project far beyond strictly Anglophone sources. *Dracula* the novel, like Dracula the vampire, is too promiscuous to be unequivocally acceptable to the academic guardians of a culture jealous of its integrity.

Likewise, there is no convincing sense in which Stoker himself can be easily appropriated by a nationalistic discourse in the way that the poet W. B. Yeats (1865–1939) or the playwright J. M. Synge (1871–1909) might be. The author's much-quoted description of himself as 'a philosophical Home-Ruler' is, as David Glover and others have demonstrated, generated by the tenets of Gladstonian Liberalism rather than separatist aspirations.[11] As *The Snake's Pass* – the author's first novel and his only full-length fiction set in Ireland – testifies, Stoker's vision of Home Rule was a form of semi-independence within the United Kingdom, with local governance stabilised through the imposition of English models and paternalistic leadership reconciling ancient differences. Such sentiments also underpin Stoker's commentary upon the 1907 International Exhibition in Dublin.[12] Stoker's relative conservatism, with its freighting of English liberalism and Anglo-Irish paternalism, thus effectively contributes to the exclusion of *Dracula* from the radical, political tradition that is – or ought to be, as McCormack's rhetoric implies – the hallmark of an approved Irish Gothic canon.[13] The heart of the problem is succinctly revealed in McCormack's reflection that 'Essentially, Stoker aligns himself with the London exiles [...] as against the home-based revivalists'.[14]

Though *Dracula* is a work that does not sit easily within the canon of Irish Studies, its place within the criticism of Irish Gothic remains assured because of the very nature of the critical processes that define Irish Studies as a practice. The place of *Dracula* within Irish Studies depends not upon the national origins of the author, nor indeed his conscious politics, but rather upon the availability of the text as an allegory capable of being interpreted in terms acceptable to the discipline. The place of the text within the discipline, in other words, is far from fixed, far from final. Notably, critics writing in the decade following McCormack's provocative keynote gesture have been characteristically less dismissive of both author and novel, seeing in the latter possibilities for the coded expression of the complex cultural ambiguities that apparently structure the existence of that most liminal of national identities, the Anglo-Irish.

THE ANGLO-IRISH INTERPRETATION

The conventional (though now frequently questioned) location of Stoker within an Anglo-Irish cultural identity opens up his life and work to an interpretation based upon an assumed liminal relationship to both power and national identity. The Anglo-Irish are not Irish, 'the "Anglo" part of the designation' referring not to mother tongue but rather to 'place of origin, immediate or ancestral'.[15] As Joseph Valente observes:

> ■ Stoker has generally been regarded as a member in good standing of the creole Anglo-Protestant garrison class in Ireland: a man of English ancestry on both sides of his family whose social intimacies, cultural sympathies, preferred creative genres, and institutional affiliations linked him closely with the Ascendancy. □

Valente correctly underplays Stoker's connection with the governing Protestant Ascendancy of his time: as he notes subsequently, the family's Anglican Protestantism made them eligible for

■ a wide range of sectarian advantages, but they were by no means members of the Ascendancy, or even of the true bourgeoisie, to whom their professional-managerial aspirations must have seemed decidedly arriviste.[16] □

Those 'sectarian advantages' were by no means assured in the Ireland of Stoker's upbringing, however. In professional life, the rise of an educated Roman Catholic middle class, eligible to apply for and demonstrably able to undertake the offices and responsibilities of governance and social leadership, threatened Anglo-Irish hegemony. Stoker had first-hand knowledge of this, being advised by his father not to apply for the post of Treasurer to the City of Dublin as 'none but an advanced Liberal or a Roman Catholic would be elected'.[17] Stoker's father's rhetoric schedules social change here as a new preferment rather than the exercise of a nascent meritocracy. By contrast, Stoker's biographer, Paul Murray, is quick to note how the author's progress within the Civil Service was a result of the reform of aristocratic patronage and that *Dracula*, consciously or not, embodies similar 'middle-class meritocratic values'.[18] Stoker is not, unequivocally, either a smug beneficiary or a resentful victim of the changes sweeping Irish politics, culture and society in the second half of the nineteenth century. He is, though, a writer arguably conscious not merely of the relativity of his position within that society, but also of that society's relationship to greater national and imperial contexts.

The relativity of Stoker's position as an Anglicised Protestant in a milieu rapidly reshaping itself by way of Roman Catholic and Celtic paradigms and standards is further complicated by his long-term residence in England, where much of *Dracula* was planned, drafted and revised. The subtle niceties that differentiate the Ascendancy from the Anglo-Irish bourgeoisie, and that bourgeoisie from the parvenus and the arrivistes, and all of these from the equally stratified urban and Roman Catholic populations within Ireland simply do not function in London, or indeed anywhere else in the United Kingdom. An Irishman in London was, arguably, simply an Irishman – all other forms of distinction being irrelevant to the context of a capital city largely dismissive of Irish distinctions and issues, whether sectarian or social. Such a vagueness of national identity characterises Stoker as seen by his contemporaries: he was 'a big, red-bearded untidy Irishman', a man possessed of a distinctive brogue whose inflections attracted not attention but mockery. Barbara Belford suggests that this brogue might itself have been an affectation: if so, Stoker appears not to have aspired to the social invisibility desired by his Count.[19]

Thus apparently, as Joseph Valente argues,

■ In the land of the Anglos, Stoker came to discover, Anglo-Irish usually translated as 'mere' Irish. Consequently, in *occupying* the metropolitan centre he paradoxically came to *embody* the Celtic fringe.[20] □

This is a tempting hypothesis, and one which might profitably explain many of the motifs of cultural and social uncertainty, of invasion and siege, which undoubtedly trouble those opposing the Count. Their central position, as it were, is under threat – and the comprehension of that threat induces an unease which destabilises confidence and consciousness, even when one enjoys the full privileges of a citizen rather than the less privileged lot of an immigrant. It is, however, not a hypothesis which has gained universal acceptance. Paul Murray is but the most recent of several commentators who have questioned the very application of the term 'Anglo-Irish' to Bram Stoker and his family. As he summarises, the 'aristocratic connotations' of the terms 'Anglo-Irish' and 'Protestant Ascendancy' are 'at odds with the relative humility of [Stoker's] background':

■ Roy Foster [...] admonished a previous biographer on this score: 'Bram Stoker was a middle-class Irish Protestant from the professional classes – not, as [Barbara] Belford repeatedly states, Anglo-Irish.' Much the same point is made by other modern critics: Chris Morash points out that 'Stoker's family were middle-class civil servants, not landowners' and David Glover [...] sees Stoker's middle-class Irish Protestant origins as having provided him with models of respectability and penury that remained with him all his life.[21] □

Paradoxically, Valente himself comes to refine Stoker's assumed Anglo-Irish ancestry with the more radical suggestion that only Stoker's father could claim a 'strictly Anglo-Saxon, or even British descent', the author therefore being 'an Anglo-Celtic rather than a traditionally Anglo-Irish subject'.[22] Valente's argument, as will be demonstrated below, has particular implications for the novel's engagement with issues of race and degeneration. Whatever the nature of the Irish identity associated with Stoker by the individual critic, the constant factor in the ascription is always that of reflection: as Haining and Tremayne suggest, the critical consensus is that 'Stoker's own Irish cultural consciousness is an integral part of his masterpiece'.[23]

Irish identity, however, is not coded or expressed exclusively in racial terms. Roy Foster concludes, quite correctly, in *Paddy and Mr Punch: Connections in Irish and English History* (1993) that 'Irish Protestantism, even in its non-Ulster, non-demotic mode, is as much a social and cultural identity as a religious one'.[24] This reasonable conclusion at least permits the critical retention of *Dracula* within what David Glover terms 'the Anglo-Irish Gothic tradition, a predominantly nineteenth-century mode of writing which struggled obsessively with the cultural meaning of Ireland and Irishness'.[25] One may be deemed Anglo-Irish not merely through documented racial origins or a verified connection to the familial network of the Ascendancy, but because one shares the preoccupations of writers legitimately included in this category because of an adherence to the strict interpretation of those qualifications. Stoker, if he was not unequivocally Anglo-Irish by birth, may at least lay claim to be Anglo-Irish in its status as a cultural identity bound up with a distinctive Protestant consciousness.

SECTARIANISM IN IRISH GOTHIC

It is impossible to ignore the often strident Protestant content of *Dracula*. As Victor Sage points out in *Horror Fiction in the Protestant Tradition* (1988), the opening of the novel is an exercise in the power of Protestant apologetics, the scene in which Harker accepts the crucifix from the Transylvanian peasant woman being particularly emphatic. Harker, of course, almost refuses the crucifix, for 'as an English Churchman, I have been taught to regard such things as in some measure idolatrous' (13).[26] As Sage notes, 'The *frisson* of [...] the passage is often lost on the modern reader', though 'in 1897, the source of insecurity was still raw in the audience'.[27] That conscious insecurity is vested in the seemingly fragile state of British Protestantism in the age of the Oxford Movement. The Oxford Movement was an organised and intellectual attempt to return the Church of England to its Roman Catholic roots, both with regard to ritual and authority. This aspiration was not universally accepted within the Anglican Communion, and a vociferous Protestant opposition was quick to depict the Oxford Movement as complicit in the surrender of English independence to a seductive Continental monster, the Church of Rome. Notably, as Patrick R. O'Malley has recently indicated, *Dracula* was published in the same year as Walter Walsh's polemical attack on Anglican ritualism, *The Secret History of the Oxford Movement*, which depicted the unreformed Church as vampiric, bloodthirsty and autocratic.[28]

As the novel opens, the polite and deferential Harker, an unassuming representative of everyday British Protestantism, risks being drawn into a compromise which does no credit to his Protestant origins. Harker's acceptance of the crucifix despite the misgivings of his Protestant conscience signals a change in his cultural and epistemological identity. As Sage argues:

■ Harker is a fall-guy, an unvigilant Protestant who is a born victim. His sense of duty forces him to continue on to the Count's castle, but from this moment he has been tainted by superstition.[29] □

'Superstition' here, of course, may ambiguously refer both to Roman Catholicism and to the occult Other. This latter is invisible to the Protestant Harker, but all too evident to the innkeeper's wife and the superstitious peasantry who surround his departing coach. Harker sees only a 'crowd of picturesque characters, all crossing themselves' (14) as he leaves the inn. What he does not appreciate is the intention behind the presentation of the crucifix. The innkeeper's wife wishes to protect Harker from certain damnation at the hands of the vampire, admittedly, but by implication she desires also to inform him of the sincerity and efficacy of her own sectarian beliefs. She may just as easily be attempting to save him from the doctrinal ignorance she associates with Protestantism, to prevent a damnation consequent upon his being an adherent to an apostate church beyond the 'true' faith.[30]

One might see in this early scene a foreshadowing of the novel's greater programme of epistemological and theological accommodation. Subsequently in *Dracula*, the empiricist Seward comes to accept Van Helsing's theories (179) as, later, do Holmwood and Morris. Holmwood, in particular, is disinclined to participate in any activity which may compromise his 'faith as a Christian' (182), though the word 'Protestant' might equally be substituted in this personal description. Only Van Helsing's gilding of academic titles, proclaiming his proficiency in the secular disciplines of medicine and law, authenticates his initial assertions. The Roman Catholic paraphernalia with which these titles are associated are authenticated only by the twofold act of witnessing: Van Helsing's verbal witness (or expression of faith) as to what the Host may do is upheld as the group visually witnesses its efficacy against the un-dead Lucy (186–7, 189). This is not persuasion by tract, but rather conviction by example – a form of empiricism. It is not so much that the Protestant forces under the Roman Catholic's leadership convert to the ascendancy of Rome, as that they accommodate the beliefs of this authoritative and persuasive Roman Catholic more subtly into their world-view after they are exemplified. It is the absolutism of Protestant belief, its singular purity vested in the conviction that the ceremonies and doctrines of Rome are, collectively, 'a fond thing vainly invented' that is undermined as *Dracula* progresses.[31] The cultural fear is that such accommodations represent 'the thin end of the wedge', the weakness through which further surrenders might be gained.[32]

Demotic, ignorant superstition – as opposed to the elegant apostasy of English high-churchmanship – was, of course, a stigma frequently associated with the Roman Catholic population of Ireland, both by the Protestant citizens of that island and by Anglicans and dissenters across the rest of Britain. Roy Foster's contention, though, that 'the superstitiousness of Irish Protestants was legendary' is worthy of comment.[33] Foster appears to argue that superstition is a context of Gothic in its Irish aspect, and in this sense he takes the Irish (or Anglo-Irish) tradition away from the British (or, at least, European) literariness that defines the genre for many critics, substituting in its place a more mythic, more localised complex of origins. The Irish Gothic, as it were, comes out of Ireland, and forms a parallel tradition to the other revivals that have come to structure Irish writing as being discrete from British paradigms.

Inevitably, under this interpretation, Protestant writing in the Gothic tradition becomes a chronicling of a declining hegemony, even where the writer has become physically distanced from the often violent immediacy of an issue being negotiated on the opposite side of the British archipelago. It is a preoccupation that connects what Foster perceives as a tradition not so much determined by genre and cliché as by the need to voice one's consciousness of a changing Ireland, and an Ireland whose political centre is rapidly moving away from the ancestral circle of the writer. Foster asserts that this 'line of Irish Protestant supernatural fiction'

■ leads from Maturin and Le Fanu to Bram Stoker and [the novelist and short-story writer] Elizabeth Bowen [1899–1973] and Yeats – marginalized Irish Protestants all, often living in England but regretting Ireland, stemming from families with strong clerical and professional colorations, whose occult preoccupations surely mirror a sense of displacement, a loss of social and psychological integration, and an escapism motivated by the threat of a takeover by the Catholic middle classes – a threat all the more inexorable because it is being accomplished by peaceful means and with the free legal aid of British governments.[34] □

Foster terms this preoccupation a phase of the 'Protestant magic', where Protestant Gothic mobilises on the one level a political commentary (or an expression of political fears), and on the other a yearning for an occultism that was in many respects culturally denied to them by the cliché of a prosaic, non-mystical sectarian identity. As Foster asserts, Yeats, in his guise as a political and cultural animal, identified Irish occultism 'for public purposes, as part of the Celtic mind-set': yet privately, it seems, he believed the Protestant mind more ready to accept such beliefs.[35]

Though it takes a somewhat more conventional view of 'Anglo-Irish writers from [the novelist] Regina Maria Roche [1764–1845], Maturin and Sheridan Le Fanu to Bram Stoker, Wilde, Yeats and Elizabeth Bowen' as being integral to 'a notoriously hard-headed social class which habitually chided the Catholic masses for their infantile superstition', Terry Eagleton's *Heathcliff and the Great Hunger: Studies in Irish Culture* (1995) makes much the same point regarding the 'surprising' interest in the supernatural evinced by Protestant writers.[36] Indeed, Eagleton's

'Protestant Gothic' shares many of the preoccupations of Foster's earlier 'Protestant magic', albeit in terms more forcibly reminiscent of Fredric Jameson's concept of a political unconscious.[37] The core belief that links Foster and Eagleton is the notion that, in Eagleton's words, 'Protestant Gothic might be dubbed the political unconscious of Anglo-Irish society', being in effect an 'entirely imaginary place' in which 'our everyday social practices and relations, with all their implicit violence, longing and anxiety' are involuntarily expressed: for Anglo-Irish society, it is 'the place where its fears and fantasies most definitively emerge'.[38] An Anglo-Irish Protestant author, in other words, is as much a writer about Ireland, and about Irish change, as one writing out of a Celtic or Roman Catholic milieu.

The problem is, though, that the unacknowledged sectarian bias of Irish Studies ensures that the Protestant author is never adequate for this rhetorical task. Foster's insistence that 'a strong theme in Protestant gothic is a mingled repulsion and *envy* where Catholic magic is concerned' (my italics), is both acknowledged and amplified by Eagleton into a statement whereby the Protestant author is seemingly nothing other than a wannabe Catholic, an aspiring and yearning convert to Rome whatever his public persona might otherwise say. Eagleton states:

■ And it seems plausible, as R. F. Foster argues, that much of the Anglo-Irish obsession with magic, the occult, secret societies and the rest was an attempt to surmount the solitude of the Protestant self – to find in ritual and mystical brotherhood a consoling substitute for that sense of system and solidarity which the Catholic Church was able to bestow on its adherents.[39] □

Eagleton's subsequent exploration of the 'paradox in the idea of the Anglo-Irish as victims of persecution' is equally telling. 'How come', Eagleton asks rhetorically, 'that those in power should feel so wretched – should share in some measure the spiritual impoverishment of those they oppress?'[40] The reason is that the Anglo-Irish feel an unconscious guilt or remorse in spite of their public justification, and they are compelled to number their sins, from the present inequity of society to the 'aboriginal crime' or 'initial trespass', 'the original crime of forcible settlement and expulsion'. Eagleton exemplifies this encounter between Marxism and the divided national identity of the Irish through Maturin's *Melmoth the Wanderer*, though it is clear from his subsequent argument that virtually any Anglo-Irish Gothic narrative may be regarded as being 'a nightmarish image of the relations between the Ascendancy and the people'.[41]

The problem attendant upon Eagleton's vision of Irish Gothic is its relative crudeness as an interpretative tool when applied to a complex situation. Effectively, its deployment unduly reduces that complexity to a polarity, obscuring the gradations of allegiance between the extreme limits of Protestantism and Roman Catholicism, of unequivocating Unionism and that nationalism which is culturally and linguistically as well as territorially separatist. Complexity is rationalised into a simple matter of Othering, and any chance of accommodation is seriously undermined by the polemical rhetoric that brands one side of the equation a 'lineage [...] tainted to its root'.[42] One might regard such an approach in its Irish Studies context as a critical equivalent of 'Vulgar Marxism', an interpretative convention, in other words, 'in which art is seen directly and unproblematically to mirror or reflect a society's class structure or economic base'.[43] Eagleton's rhetoric, for all its subtlety and undoubted erudition, still imposes a too-rigid, almost unforgiving, dichotomy premised upon the utter difference between Ascendancy and populace. This dichotomy can only be bridged by the critical convention that Anglo-Irish fiction both comments upon and effectively confirms their part in the social, cultural, religious and political wrongs of the past and the present.

THE DEMONS OF IRISH HISTORY

In its application to *Dracula* specifically, such an interpretative approach makes free – arguably too free – a use of that demon of nineteenth-century Irish history, the absentee landlord. Eagleton finds *Dracula* rich in symbolism supporting his contention that the vampire is a coded representation of the landlord class. He argues that

> ■ Dracula is an absentee landlord, deserting his Transylvanian castle to buy up property in London. Like many an Ascendancy aristocrat he is a devout Anglophile, given to poring over maps of the metropolis; and this gory-toothed vampire plans, a touch bathetically, to settle in Purfleet, as a number of the Anglo-Irish gentry were to migrate from the wilds of Connaught to the watering-holes of the English south coast.[44] □

Transylvania, here, is presumably a representation of Gladstonian Ireland, though it is not made clear how the Count continues to enforce his rule of fear over the peasantry there once he has departed for a landlord's exile within London society. The devil is in the detail, though: Eagleton's allegory is somewhat destabilised by the geographical location of Purfleet, which lies not on the English south coast but in Essex, to the east of London, and upon the north bank of the Thames. The construction of the allegory, though, carries within it a further reassuring function within nationalist discourse. Eagleton continues:

> ■ But Dracula, like the Ascendancy, is running out of land: by the end of the novel he is being hotly pursued around Europe, furnished only with

the crates of Transylvanian soil he needs to bed down in for the night. His material base is rapidly dwindling, and without this soil he will die. The Ascendancy, too, will evaporate once their earth is removed from them, though to wrench it from them will demand rather more than a sprig of garlic and rather less than a stake through the heart.[45] □

Eagleton's allegory here recalls the inevitability of social and political change associated with a classical Marxist vision of history. Whether or not Stoker and his associates perceived themselves as 'a dying social class' in 1897 is immaterial here: what is important is that this novel is seen to be linked, however unconsciously, to the nascent changes that have established the celebrated, liberated and democratic Ireland of the present.[46]

Much the same point is made by other critics who associate the vampire with the absentee landlord. Seamus Deane, for example, in *Strange Country: Modernity and Nationhood in Irish Writing since 1790* (1997) makes a far more detailed case regarding the symbolic nature of the soil which the Count brings with him to London, even though his ascription of meaning to symbol is at times somewhat obscure. If the Count represents the absentee landlord in London, then the soil represents 'the native material that is imported into the "foreign" legal system of English property relations'. Where Dracula moves the soil literally from his home country, the landlord merely takes with him legal title and the right to the profit and well-being of the land.[47] With Deane's suggestion that the soil is also a 'contaminated cargo', rendered unclean by the vampire's presence or proprietorship, comes an imperative to liberate and to cleanse, to return the soil to what it was when it was totally 'at home' and thus unconnected with the 'foreign' or with those who have taken themselves to foreign places. Deane, like Eagleton, though, concludes his argument with a reading of the novel as an allegory not of localised capitalism but of impending nationhood, and in terms more redolent of mass politics than of literary criticism. Of the Count, he states:

■ landlord that he is, with all his enslaved victims, his Celtic twilight is endangered by the approach of a nationalist dawn, a Home Rule sun rising behind the old Irish parliament. Dracula's dwindling soil and his vampiric appetites consort well enough with the image of the Irish landlord current in the nineteenth century. Running out of soil, this peculiar version of the absentee landlord in London will flee the light of day and be consigned to the only territory left to him, that of legend.[48] □

Though evocative as political rhetoric, this stridence makes for problematic criticism. It *is* true that the vampire was used as a signifier for unacceptable landlordism in Victorian Ireland. Declan Kiberd, for example, recalls Michael Davitt's description of landlords as 'cormorant vampires'. Again, the grotesque and ironic cartoon bat, labelled 'British Rule' and published in *The Irish Pilot* as a rejoinder to 'The Irish Vampire', printed in *Punch* in October 1885, is now arguably as well-known to critics as the original by Sir John Tenniel (1820–1914).[49] Irish Studies, though, has characteristically tended to tone down this Victorian context whilst appropriating *Dracula* to support a rhetorical reflection upon the inevitable downfall of the landlord class. Arguably, too much emphasis has been placed in Irish criticism upon historical events subsequent to *Dracula* – events which the novel did not shape and did not anticipate. The allegory, if it is there at all, is surely that of a crucial moment in the academic criticism of the last decade of the twentieth century.

Count Dracula, however, is a notorious shape-shifter, and likewise can accommodate many symbolisms in his comings and goings between nations, his links to the soil, and his sudden and spectacular downfall at the hands of a collective moral force. If not seen as a generalised figure such as the landlord, it seems inevitable that the Count should also be capable of interpretation as any one of a number of historical figures associated with Ireland. Irish Studies has concentrated upon but one of these possibilities, and that figure is Charles Stewart Parnell (1846–1891), the charismatic Anglo-Irish figurehead of nationalist ambitions in Ireland between the late 1870s and his fall from favour, following a divorce scandal, in 1890. Stoker, certainly, was aware of the at-times tense relationship between Parnell and the statesman William Ewart Gladstone, the latter a slight acquaintance of Stoker, upon whom the author bestowed a presentation copy of *Dracula*, among other novels.[50]

According to Michael Valdez Moses, 'Stoker's Dracula does not simply recapitulate the life of Charles Stewart Parnell in a straightforward allegorical fashion'. Indeed, Moses is laudably pluralist in his insistence that 'there is no single source for Dracula, who is a composite and free transformation of his many originals', among whom is Parnell.[51] Moses suggests that what Parnell shares with the vampire is 'a protean capability to assume whatever shape or image his audience found most deeply (and even illicitly) appealing'. Parnell is thus a contradictory figure, a charismatic and perplexingly attractive embodiment of 'the inchoate and conflicting dreams and desires of his followers (and, it might be added, the deepest fears and paranoid fantasies of his enemies)'.[52] There is an obvious rhetorical resemblance in Moses's assertion to the psychoanalytical criticism of *Dracula*, and the critical construction of the vampire as a simultaneous focus for taboo desires and the fear of taboo. That said, it *is* conceivable that, in Moses's words, 'Dracula [...] not only incarnates the attributes of Parnell as radical nationalist, dangerous leader of the Catholic masses (though himself a Protestant), and secret ally of violent revolutionary movements, he also incarnates a demonized version of the very sort of traditional and conservative Anglo-Irish Ascendancy landlord who despised Parnell as a traitor to his class.'[53]

Intriguingly, the symbolic relationship between the vampire and the politician, as tabulated by Moses, demonstrates the presence of signifiers and interpretations shared between the broad Victorian camps of unionist and nationalist, as well as other associations only pertinent to one or the other. Stoker, an English-domiciled Gladstonian liberal though not an outright supporter of the Irish-based Parnell, had a foot in both camps, as it were, and there are, according to Moses,

■ abundant and suggestive parallels between Parnell and Dracula that may be mobilized by the politically attentive reader of Stoker's novel. For example, both Parnell and Dracula are known for their haughty and reserved aristocratic bearing and for their uncanny power of commanding respect and attention [...] Moreover, like Dracula, Parnell was often viewed in England as a *foreign* threat, as a hostile alien presence who [...] pursued his designs against British rule in Ireland while safely ensconced at the very heart of the British Empire [...] Like Dracula, Parnell was said to possess an almost hypnotic gaze [...] Both Parnell and Dracula are also distinguished by a propensity for disguise [...] In particular, the foreign aristocrat always conceals or transforms his appearance in order to make possible his clandestine visits to his English women (original italics).[54] □

The resemblances listed by Moses are not absolute, though they are suggestive. Thus, as Moses concludes:

■ The cumulative effect of these many shadowy resemblances is a demonized portrait of Parnell as criminal, sensualist, adulterer, aristocrat and demon, who threatens the domestic harmony, legal structures, political institutions, and moral conventions that undergird Victorian society and the British Empire.[55] □

Moses's account somewhat qualifies the notoriously vague definition of Stoker's self-confessed status as a 'philosophical Home-Ruler'.[56] Stoker's is not an unequivocal nationalism, but is 'qualified by his disapproval of violent Fenianism and many of Parnell's tactics'.[57] It is bound up with an approval of the ideals of Empire, and rejects the vampire's self-appointed status as a would-be liberator of the people, which Moses emblematises particularly in the vampire's appearance to Mina as a suggestive 'pillar of cloud', the very device that led the Israelites out of their bondage to the adjoining imperial power of Egypt.[58] Moses further sees Renfield 'as a stand-in for the Irish adherents of Parnell and the nationalist cause', advancing further parallels in the behaviour of the Irish peasantry, who reputedly kneeled before the orator as Renfield abased himself before the Count, and who might well be regarded as 'crazed' or 'insane' under the politician's rhetorical direction.[59] As Moses concludes, nationalism embodies both an 'appeal' and a 'threat', and the encoding of Parnell through the Count appears to incorporate both.[60]

As Moses's work suggests, allegory can be a somewhat problematic tool when wielded in the name of literary criticism. *Dracula* is not *Animal Farm* (1945), and Stoker's alleged characterisations cannot be accepted with the certitude associated with pointed twentieth-century satire by George Orwell (1903–1950). But, if the move from the general to the specific, from the cultural or the historical to the biographical, is a dangerous one, then so too is the ready adoption of an apparently obvious issue or long-term event as a sort of key to the novel's allegorical script. Bruce Stewart, in 'Bram Stoker's *Dracula*: Possessed by the Spirit of the Nation?' (1998), written after the contributions of Eagleton, Foster and Moses, is mindful of the vampire's conventional signification as an alternately repressive or renegade member of the landlord class. Stewart's distinctive contribution to the debate, though, is to recall *The Snake's Pass*, Stoker's most substantial fictionalisation of Irish life and English intervention, and the striking evocation in that work of another demonised 'figure in the agrarian Irish landscape', the '"gombeen man" whom William Gladstone loved to hate'.[61] The gombeen man, largely overlooked in twentieth-century criticism of *Dracula*, is an unregulated usurer, an individual who lends money on the guarantee of property or land, and who is not bound by the conventions of banking and regular commerce. One of Stoker's Irish peasants in *The Snake's Pass* depicts the gombeen man in no uncertain terms:

> ■ 'He's a man that linds you a few shilling's or a few pounds whin ye want it bad, and thin niver laves ye till he has tuk all ye've got – yer land an' yer shanty an' yer holdin' and yer money an' yer craps; an' he would take the blood out of yer body if he could sell it or use it anyhow!'[62] □

Problematically, though, as Stewart points out, the gombeen man – 'the very model of a vampire, if we are truly seeking one' – is characteristically neither Anglo-Irish nor a landlord in the Ascendancy sense. Rather, 'So far from being a landlord in his own person (though perhaps a surrogate of sorts), he is one of the peasant class who has made such a success of usury that he could easily prey upon that economically-troubled grouping [i.e., landlords] also.'[63] One might therefore as easily discern in the vampire a critique of the indigenous community, which both spawns and sustains the debilitating activities of gombeenism, as an allegory of rapacious landlordism. Count

Dracula, after all, drains both his co-religionists and his own racial blood-pool first before venturing into the West. Gombeenism is, arguably, as likely a context for the vampire as landlordism – but it is a far less fashionable one, in critical terms. Stewart is right to counsel caution in any critical endorsement or adoption of 'a merely nationalistic interpretation of the novel, seen as an allegorical disclosure of the historical crimes of the Protestant ascendancy in Ireland'. As he suggests, 'The images of Bram Stoker and his most famous creation recently offered in this spirit are all too much like Count Dracula's reflection in Jonathan Harker's shaving mirror: the original is strangely absent.'[64]

If the vampire *is* an allegory of anything, it is, arguably, one of division, polarisation and bitter opposition. This much is suggested by Joseph Valente's magisterial assessment of ten years of criticism of *Dracula* conducted from an Irish Studies perspective. The characteristic Irish Studies appreciation of *Dracula*, for Valente, says as much about the culture of criticism as it does regarding the novel:

> ■ The Irish Studies take on Dracula [*sic*] [...] has greatly emphasized one of the conflicting aspects of the vampire's doppelgänger function, polarization. Following in the wake of mainstream postcolonial theory, the Irish school of criticism has typically found in the novel the Manichean oppositions dear to imperialist ideology – self and other, ruler and ruled, enlightened and backward, superior and subaltern – and has ascribed them to Stoker's anxiously normalizing impulses made articulate in the bourgeois pieties of Little England. This approach's momentum has been to credit the protagonists' official narrative of diametric opposition between the living and the undead, as epitomized in their repeated pledges to free the world of the vampiric enemy.[65] □

'Little England' is Valente's subtly ironic name for the cultural as much as physical opposition which both enacts and chronicles the war against a seeming outsider who is simultaneously physically literal and richly symbolic, excluded though intimate, and an anachronism whose presence bears witness against the hegemony of modernity. 'Little England', though, remains an ambiguous, if not downright troubling, term, hence its ironic inflection in *Dracula's Crypt*. 'Little England', after all, embodies a Roman Catholic Dutchman and a déclassé though wealthy American, and it is troubled and fractured by issues of social class – Harker is noticeably excluded from one foray against the vampire – as well as gender – Mina is doubly excluded, by class and sex, disqualified both from the conferences of the group and from receiving any revivifying transfusion such as those given to her friend, Lucy.[66] Thus, 'Little England' is convenient, critically expedient, even, though not necessarily a sufficiently compulsive concept upon which to premise either the perceived oppositions of *Dracula*, or the author's reflections upon the culture of the subaltern country in which he was born.

In going beyond the conventional reading of the Anglo-Irish as a liminal, hyphenated people throughout *Dracula's Crypt*, Valente desta-bilises further not merely the standard critical perception of the author's relationship to his culture, but also the very integrity of the oppositions conventionally associated with it. Valente argues that

■ Stoker was not a standard issue middle-class Anglo-Irish Protestant, as has been almost universally imagined, but an interethnic Anglo-Celt and hence a member of a conquering and a conquered race, a ruling and a subject people, an imperial and an occupied nation.[67] □

Stoker's mother's ancestry, which Valente assumes would have been known to the author, implicated him with the Norman Blake (or La Blaca) family but also with '*a native Irish family* whose original Connacht moniker was O Blathnhaic' (original italics).[68] This would make the author Anglo-Celtic rather than Irish by descent, though, Valente asserts, this racial lineage would probably be tempered by a cultural and narrative input associated with profession, education and religion: 'Using the very narrative means that would eventually earn Stoker accolades, his parents combined to transmit a sense of their subtle ethnic difference to their youngest son and thus to convert hybrid racial status into a dual cultural inheritance.'[69] As Valente suggests, if Stoker was aware of his hybrid ancestry, and was engaged in negotiating the two sides of his parentage through his writing, then this 'surely under-cuts the popular position that Stoker substantially shared the anxiety of Anglo-Irish intellectuals like the historian W. E. H. Lecky (1838–1903) or imperialist politicians like Lord Salisbury at the prospect of Celtic racial pollution, atavism or degeneration'.[70] This does *not* mean that Stoker did not maintain an interest in degeneration – the ambiguously clinical and anthropological eugenics of Lombroso and Nordau inform not merely *Dracula* but also *The Mystery of the Sea* (1902) and *The Lair of the White Worm* (1911) – but it does suggest that the Celt was never the focus of Stoker's interest in the *fin du globe*.[71]

The Irishness of Stoker, and hence of his writings also, is both com-plex and contradictory, and thus resists what Valente terms the 'unitary allegorical framework' that has hitherto oversimplified Stoker's hybrid or 'metrocolonial' consciousness:

■ Instead of a coherent design that shades into multiple indetermin-acies, as Moses suggests, the Irish *Dracula* represents something like a coherent indeterminacy, a semiotic space doubling and dividing against itself, obeying what Jacques Lacan calls the logic of the *vel*, 'more than one, and not quite two'.[72] □

If, among the many points of his compelling argument, Valente produces but one essential image that might stand for the complexity of Stoker's cultural consciousness, then it is the notion of the author's life – as a social being, as well as a writer – being a form of 'cultural performance'. This performance both exemplifies and undermines the parameters of an Anglo-Irish distinctiveness in a continual alternation of provocative display and ironic accommodation.[73] Stoker, it would appear, has been the victim of a 'one-size-fits-all' view of the Protestant Irish, a view that resists subtleties, inconvenient contradictions and indeed the breakdown of a highly politicised polarity which has for too long choked debate.

The climax of Valente's revisioning of the Irish Studies critique of *Dracula* comes in his concluding chapter, 'Beyond Blood', and its sparse though sustained analysis of the role that sanguine fluid may play in the rhetoric of nationalism and national identity. Though wide-ranging, the focus of this chapter is undoubtedly Quincey Harker, Mina's child. Quincey is born following Mina's ingestion of the Count's blood and he is thus, symbolically if not physiologically, associated with the Count far more intimately than with the mortals whose names he bears as a memorial (326). Much of what Valente has to say on the symbolics of blood in this concluding chapter has its parallel in the work of Punter, Sage and Hughes, critics of whom Valente appears to be ignorant.[74] What sets Valente's account aside from these – and, indeed, from the analyses by Daniel Pick and Stephen Arata, whom he selects as representative of 'a number of critics' who comment upon Quincey Harker's hybrid vampire-human bloodline – is its inflection of a distinctly Irish symbolism. Conventional Irish Studies logic – in line, it has to be said, with the rhetoric employed elsewhere when bloods (and races) mix – might well regard Quincey Harker as a contaminated or compromised individual, infected or debased by the blood he has taken on by his mother's promiscuous encounter with the Othered vampire. The body of the child, as it were, reproduces and reminds us of the miscegenation that has already troubled his mother. Strangely, though, there is no recollection, in the rhetoric of Harker's coda to *Dracula* (326–7), of the 'agony of abasement' (259) that earlier signalled Mina's revulsion at the knowledge of her intimacies with the Count.

Valente, uniquely, reads Mina Harker not as an unequivocal English heroine, but rather as a Celt by implication, her maiden name, Murray (55), being an Anglicised form of the native Celtic name O'Muireadhaigh.[75] With Mina distanced from conventional

Saxon rhetoric, and with the vampire (whether regarded as Landlord, immigrant or even Fenian rebel)[76] still implicated in prejudicial visions of the Irish, Valente is able to conclude, radically, that 'this final admixture of blood need not be construed as bearing any significance, as making any objective difference in a *racial* or *ethnic* sense' (original italics).[77] Thus, *Dracula* is 'not finally about blood distinction but blood consciousness'.[78] Twentieth-century critics have feverishly concentrated upon a conventional racial rhetoric of blood, insisting upon its fearful vulnerability, where the novel's protagonists by contrast, have serenely passed beyond such anxieties of signification:[79]

> ■ Indeed, Harker's ease of mind on this score is the political burden of the novel's happy ending. It is precisely in relinquishing the mania or obsession with blood that the men of Little England have freed themselves from the enthrallment with vampirism, which is but the Gothic literalization of that mania. To accept the influx of Dracula's blood, his racial otherness, is to escape the influence of Dracula's vampirism, his racist obsession with blood as the vehicle of identity. The vampire fighters have, in Harker's words, gone 'through the flames', the Christian symbol of purgation, and it is they who have been purified, not of Dracula's blood [...] but of their own liability to blood 'hate'.[80] □

Valente, indeed, might have drawn a further parallel with Stoker's 1909 *faux* vampire novel, *The Lady of the Shroud*, which concludes with the celebration of Balka, a unified consciousness for the Balkans, overwriting the historical differences of Christian and Muslim, brokered by an English adventurer and ratified by a thinly disguised Edward VII.[81] *Dracula* and *The Lady of the Shroud* (and, no doubt, *The Snake's Pass*, as well) might thus be said to be fictions of Gladstonian liberal unity, all of them being theoretical predications of 'a shift [...] from emulous rivalry among the various parties to the Irish Question to coexistence within a multinational state embracing Home Rule for its several constituencies'.[82] For all this, Stoker, a Gladstonian well into the twentieth century, remains dissonant to a political and cultural nationalism that has evolved almost beyond recognition through partition, independence, and the rise of a new federal Europe.

What must be said regarding Irish Studies criticism of *Dracula* is that the critical discourse has failed to evolve in quite the same way as the culture upon which it is focused. The 'decade of the Irish *Dracula*' arguably concretised in criticism the harsh bifurcations between Celtic and Saxon, Unionist and Republican, landlord and tenantry, English and Irish, at a time when, in politically liberal circles, such oppositions were undergoing radical renegotiation. The retention of such views in twenty-first century critical discourse might thus almost appear to be a form of nostalgia for more simple days – a time when enemies were evocative and, most of all, identifiable, when to be Irish (as an author or a text under study) could all to easily mean to be 'not English' or 'not Anglo-Irish'. This generalisation (or speculation), potentially, is as much a gross simplification as the critical approach it discusses, but it is as influenced by the political culture of the post-Good Friday Agreement world, just as earlier opinions were shaped by the turmoil of Bloody Sunday in 1972 or Drumcree in the mid-1990s. One thing is clear, though: Irish Studies in the twenty-first century is increasingly under pressure to evolve, to renegotiate and to treat with greater delicacy the texts of that island's often troubled past. Valente's conclusions will no doubt be superseded, but it is to be hoped that their successors will be as subtly iconoclastic as their author's original project in the first decade of the twenty-first century.

★   ★   ★

The final chapter of this Guide considers the significant contribution to the critical analysis of *Dracula* achieved in the field of Gender Studies. This aspect of the debate is not limited to readings of the novel's central female characters. In recent years critical attention has been brought to bear upon the alternately strident and troubled masculinities of the male protagonists, and the debate has been greatly enhanced by the rise of a Queer critique whose focus contemplates the sexualities of the vampire, the vampire hunters – and Stoker himself.

CHAPTER FIVE

Assertive Women and Gay Men: Gender Studies and *Dracula*

The plot of *Dracula*, if Clive Leatherdale (2001) is to be believed, hinges upon the fate of two women – Lucy Westenra and Mina Harker. Concurring with the work of other critics in the field, Leatherdale argues that *Dracula* is 'essentially [...] the same story told twice: first through Lucy, then Mina'.[1] The novel, in this respect, would appear to advance, first and foremost, a judgemental, comparative view of disparate female behaviours – two women are subjected to a similar ordeal, but react in dissimilar ways, their individual characters being held up to a standard based upon both moral behaviour and innate, approved femininity. The contrasts appear obvious. Lucy, who naively wishes to marry three men, demonstrates, in her seemingly light-hearted confession (60), an apparent predisposition to a sexual promiscuity which – criticism insists – parallels vampirism.[2] Mina, by contrast, resists the coded polygamy of the un-dead, setting herself aside from her husband upon her conscious equation of vampirism with 'unclean' and infectious sin (248). Lucy is complicit, and even culpable: because of her sensual predisposition, however unconscious it may be, she may be purified only in death. The businesslike Mina, in contrast, is victimised rather than seduced, and gains redemption through personal experience and reflection, reinforced by the sacrifices of the surrounding menfolk. If *Dracula* is 'the same story told twice', then the moral apotheosis of Mina might be read as a commentary upon the cautionary tale of Lucy, a corrective, didactic reminder of what is acceptable or 'true' femininity, a dispelling of the assertive, selfish sexuality critically associated with vampiric predation. As Leatherdale concludes, the novel's conclusion, where Mina produces a baby rather than 'a mass of type-writing' (326), signals approval of a return to the patriarchal status quo: 'The maternal', he contends, 'has seen off the carnal.'[3]

This juxtaposition of two women, representing, alternately, two forms of female consciousness and two extremes of femininity as perceived by a hypothetical male gaze, has undoubtedly shaped the gender critique of *Dracula*. Leatherdale, though he inevitably differs in the emphasis and textual detail of his study, remains broadly typical of a critical tendency that has shaped – and possibly limited – the gendered criticism of *Dracula* from the 1970s to the turn of the twenty-first century. Criticism has arguably dwelled too long and in too great a detail upon the evocative pair, and on the limited range of incidents in which the two heroines participate, in order to make a relatively consistent point about the repression of women. The novel, as it were, is understood to be an expression, variously, of Stoker's general misogyny, his prurience or his distaste for a certain movement within late-Victorian feminism. These fixations have characteristically been evidenced through the author's biography – his 'strong-willed' mother and 'frigid' wife – as well as by way of the two central heroines, juxtaposed against each other, or taken singly, before and after vampiric contact.[4] The focus of the gendered critique of *Dracula* is also substantially premised, as Foucault might argue, upon the twentieth century's desire to validate its own liberated status by demonstrating its ability to expose the repression and coded expression of sexuality, to transform effectively all signifiers into a discourse upon sex.[5] The ambivalence towards women which many critics detect in Stoker's portrayals, not merely of Lucy and Mina but also of the three female consorts of the Count, might well reflect not so much Victorian equivocation, but rather the twentieth century's own scarce-concealed fascination with the presence of transgression in the midst of conformity.

CONSCIOUS AND UNCONSCIOUS SEXUALITIES

A gendered double narrative, comparable to that proposed by Leatherdale, structures Alan Johnson's influential 1984 study '"Dual Life": The Status of Women in Stoker's *Dracula*'. Johnson liberally interprets Van Helsing's notion of 'dual life' (179) – the term with which the Dutch physician describes Lucy's post-mortem alternation between passive humanity and active vampirism – developing it into a tense interface of the conscious and unconscious forces at play within the two central heroines. For Van Helsing, Lucy's 'dual life' is exceptional, or, in the Dutchman's broken English, 'not as the common' (179). For Johnson, however, the condition projects beyond Lucy to Mina, and through Mina implicitly to the Victorian woman in general. Johnson argues that in the dual narrative or 'diptych' of the novel,

■ each woman develops [...] a life of conscious and willing conformity to her society and yet also a life of largely subconscious rebellion against it.

In the case of each woman, Dracula symbolises her inner rebelliousness, and its crisis coincides with her commerce with Dracula. The diptych also shows, however, that each woman's rebellion is justified and has been provoked by the undue constraints and condescension which have been inflicted upon her by society, chiefly by the men around her and chiefly because the thinking of the society is dominated by anachronistic notions of social class and chivalry.[6] □

Johnson, notably, associates the development of this progressive rebellion not with twentieth-century psychoanalytical models of the mind, but with the Victorian psychology of *Dracula* – a largely unexplored topic in 1982:

■ The rebellious selves of Lucy and Mina seem to be largely the product of their unconscious cerebration as they respond to their social surroundings. After their discontentment develops to the stage of strong rebellion, Dracula appears and attacks each character. He is thus in this context a symbolic double of each woman's rebellious egoism, and the literal vampirism which results from his bite represents the change in personality produced by the egoism.[7] □

This model of unconscious cerebration, based as it is on a somewhat shallow reading of Thomas Laycock (1812–1876) rather than of William Carpenter, lacks the historicist specificity of later accounts such as those by David Glover and William Hughes.[8] It does, though, raise an intriguing implication for Gender Studies, albeit one unacknowledged by Johnson. The association between unconscious cerebration, egotism and deviant psychology in *Dracula* – rendered by way of Renfield's progressive neurosis and Seward's obsessive introspection (69, 71, 237) – implicitly classes the growth of even the most rudimentary feminist consciousness as a neurosis. Read in the context of Carpenterian unconscious cerebration, such a development might be best impeded by keeping the mind distracted from the focus of the disorder. This is, signally, what Seward fails to do with respect to Renfield's *idée fixe* and, arguably, the attentions of the chivalrous males in the novel reinforce Lucy's psychological position in a similar way. One might draw a comparison here not merely with the plight of Renfield but also with the treatment of Laura Fairlie in Collins's *The Woman in White*. Johnson draws a comparison between Stoker's Mina and Collins's Marian Halcombe, though he might equally have considered associating Lucy with Laura Fairlie, a heroine re-educated by Carpenterian methods into a psychological simulacrum of another person.[9] Lucy's apparent rebellion, the argument runs, might easily be cured by distractions which do not recall for her subconscious the enclosed and dependent nature of her life.

Whilst largely concurring with the unconscious development of Lucy's rebellion, other critics are less committed to the contextual medical discourses of the novel. Writing in *Dracula: Between Tradition and Modernism*, for example, Carol Senf contends that:

> ■ In Lucy, Stoker paints a portrait of a young woman who is all convention on the surface, certainly of one who seems to accept the traditional roles of wife and mother that are laid out for her. During the day, Lucy never admits her rebellion about the constraints placed on women, but at night her rebellion surfaces as she wanders around Whitby in her sleep and eventually meets Dracula.[10] □

That meeting is itself a matter of contention: criticism has at different times embraced the notion that the Count has called Lucy to him, based upon their psychological sympathy or compatible deviance, as well as the suggestion that their meeting might have been nothing more than an accident.[11] If the latter, Lucy's victim status is assured: she is an opportune rather than an obvious conquest. If the former, then her predisposition to deviance, social, sexual or mental, implicates her in her own downfall.

To return to Senf's contention, though: even if Lucy enjoys an occluded sensual predisposition, she might well still become for the reader the innocent victim she appears to be in the eyes of her chivalric trio of suitors:

> ■ Because Lucy never realizes her own desire to escape from rigid nineteenth-century constraints on women, she cannot protect herself from temptation when it occurs. She is thus two times a victim, first of Dracula's seduction, and second, of her society's desire to purify her.[12] □

The violence which is scripted as being redemptive in the novel thus becomes a troubling reminder of the perils of female ignorance. Lucy joins a long list of innocents imperilled through ignorance of sin and sexuality – from Antonia in *The Monk* (1796) by Matthew Lewis (1775–1818), who reads a Bible expurgated of its sexual passages, to Stoker's own feminist heroine, Stephen Norman, in *The Man* (1905), whose gendered education fails to prepare her adequately for a conventional, let alone revisionist, womanhood.[13] Innocence and ignorance are thus simultaneously both reassuring and fearful: the innocent – or ignorant – heroine is idealised, and yet may carry beneath her demure surface an unconscious that links her all too easily to desire. Desire, it may be added, may be conventionally appropriated to the possession of the male proprietor-perceiver. The assertive or forward heroine is thus not merely a projection of male desire but also constitutes a threat to its gendered power base, its conventional sexual prerogative.

The novel itself seems remarkably coy regarding the latent sexual beast apparently hidden within every woman. As Phyllis Roth argues in 'Suddenly Sexual Women in Bram Stoker's *Dracula*' (1977):

> ■ only relations with vampires are sexualized in this novel; indeed, a deliberate attempt is made to make sexuality seem unthinkable in 'normal relations' between the sexes. Only when Lucy becomes a vampire is she allowed to be 'voluptuous', yet she must have been so long before, judging from her effect on men and from Mina's descriptions of her [...] Clearly, then, vampirism is associated not only with death, immortality and orality; it is equivalent to sexuality.[14] □

The vampire, indeed, seems a suitably distant vehicle through which to dissipate the ambivalent emotions that arise in the male conscious-ness when a treasured demure icon becomes, upon sexual initiation, a demanding sexual being. Roth, notably, follows the above assessment with the statement that 'in psychoanalytic terms, the vampirism [*sic*] is a disguise for greatly desired and equally strongly feared fantasies'. What cannot be spoken of through marriage or sexual initiation, lest it disturb the demure façade of the conventional heroine, may safely be vocalised through the figure of the vampire. The sexualised violence of Lucy's ritual disposal (192), which critics have conventionally regarded as a hardly oblique encoding of gang rape or defloration, in effect achieves two related ends.[15] Reading vampirism as sexuality, as Roth does, the promiscuity consequent upon initiation is permanently halted by the act, and the desired woman appropriated to one man alone *in perpetuam* – not as a demanding sexual partner but, englobed within the male gaze, as a holy and truthful image, an abiding memory (192–3).[16] As David Punter and Glennis Byron assert in *The Gothic* (2004), 'The staking of Lucy provides the most brutal enactment of the restoration of gendered boundaries'.[17]

This is, very much, the critical consensus with regard to Lucy: conventionally, she is a woman whose latent eroticism is unleashed from passivity, rather than an asexual being to whom a sexuality is added through vampirism. Hence, similar assessments can be found equally at the high-point of gendered *Dracula* criticism in the 1980s as much as in the more critically plural twenty-first century. Christopher Craft, in the influential '"Kiss me with those red lips": Gender and Inversion in Bram Stoker's *Dracula*' (1984) may begin by suggesting with regard to both Lucy and Mina that the Count 'kisses these women out of their passivity', though he is quick to note that this 'passivity' is a façade rather than an unequivocal asexual state of being.[18] The woman imbued with a latent sexuality is, here as elsewhere in *Dracula* criticism, a threat to the sexualised male, a disruption to conventional, polarised, gender compatibilities:

■ Dracula's authorizing kiss, like that of a demonic Prince Charming, triggers the release of this latent power and excites in these women a sexuality so mobile, so aggressive, that it thoroughly disrupts Van Helsing's compartmental conception of gender. Kissed into a sudden sexuality, Lucy grows 'voluptuous' (a word used to describe her only during the vampiric process), her lips redden, and she kisses with a new interest. This sexualization of Lucy [...] terrifies her suitors because it entails a reversal or inversion of sexual identity; Lucy, now toothed like the Count, usurps the function of penetration that Van Helsing's moralized taxonomy of gender reserves for males.[19] □

More recently, though in much the same vein, Catherine Lanone has argued in 'Bram Stoker's *Dracula*, or Femininity as a Forsaken Fairy Tale' (2005), that:

■ From the start, the fair-haired lovely Lucy is no Victorian angel. The letter she addresses to Mina [57–61] becomes the playful text articulating unspeakable female desire, as she wishes she could marry all of her suitors [...] The restless Lucy, whose sleepwalking may be seen as a metaphor of desire, is granted her wish for pre-marital sex through vampiric intercourse and blood transfusions [20] □

Lucy, whose liberation from monogamy into promiscuity might make her a heroine for less prudish times, cannot seem to evade condemnation in a novel whose every strategy appears calculated either to uphold or restore gender, class and racial boundaries.

THE AMBIVALENT SEXUAL MORALITY OF THE VAMPIRE HUNTERS

The repulsion which *ought*, conventionally, to be displayed at the prospect of 'unfeminine' or 'abnormal' desires such as those manifested in Lucy, theoretically insists that the reader identify 'himself' with the righteous and redemptive indignation associated with the Van Helsing circle rather than the transgressive indulgence of the Count and his minions. The too-easily assumed demarcation between the 'selfishness' (297) of the vampire and the 'high duty' (192) of the vampire hunters is, however, arguably but another manifestation of criticism's tendency to render the novel through polarities or absolutes. Tempting though such critical gestures might be, their imposed boundaries and oppositions do not sit well with the novel's portrayal of the at-times equivocal response of the group to the vampires' behaviour. As Phyllis Roth notes,

■ the split between the sexual vampire family and the asexual Van Helsing group is not at all clear-cut; Jonathan, Van Helsing, Seward and Holmwood are all overwhelmingly attracted to the vampires, to sexuality. Fearing this, they employ two defenses, projection and denial: it is not we who want the vampires, it is they who want us (to eat us, to seduce us, to kill us).[21] □

One might discern in Roth's evocation of a Freudian 'projection and denial' an explanation for the almost joyful male sexuality manifested in the ritual disposal of Lucy. The staking of Lucy is not merely a coded *jus primae noctis* – the feudal right to take a woman's virginity – apparently enacted on the day after the wedding which never was. It is equally a manifestation of the desire to be as penetrative as the vampire, to shed blood, to convert 'one of them' to 'one of us'. Hence, for Roth, the Count

■ acts out the repressed fantasies of the others, [and] since those others wish to do what he can do, we have no difficulty in recognizing an identifi- cation with the aggressor on the part of characters and reader alike.[22] □

Possibly, the triumphant disposal of the male vampire, through a war-like knife cut rather than a phallic penetration, is the eleventh-hour gesture that disperses the perverse identification between character/reader and vampire. Perverse, indeed, is that identification in an age which celebrated, through the code of the Victorian gentleman, the revival of chivalry and deference to women: as Roth concludes, after all, 'In accepting the notion of identification with the aggressor in *Dracula* […] what we accept is an understanding of the reader's identification with the aggressor's victimization of women.'[23]

The induction of Mina Harker into vampirism – though that vampirism never actually becomes active – presents the reader with a further set of difficulties. Mina is the focus of male chivalry and devotion in the final phase of the novel, though she does not attract the open sexual desire which three of her defenders have previously associated with Lucy. Carol Senf suggests that, had *Dracula* ended with the ritual, sexualised disposal of Lucy, then 'it would be tempting to conclude that Stoker was an antifeminist who simply hated women or that he was a traditionalist who hated the sexually assertive women who were gain- ing prominence in the 1890s'.[24] Mina's significance within the novel considerably exceeds any simplistic suggestion that she is nothing more than a conventional, virtuous and redeemable foil to Lucy's depravity. Credible arguments may indeed be advanced in favour of Mina's status as, in Phyllis Roth's words, 'the saint and the mother [...] all good, all pure, all true'.[25] Indeed, the Mina of Stoker's novel lacks the latent sexuality evoked by Winona Ryder's portrayal of the same character in Francis Ford Coppola's 1992 film, *Bram Stoker's Dracula*. But, if Stoker's Mina fails to display the sexual content that vampirism releases from the repressed Lucy of *Dracula*, her characterisation in the novel, however, is not without its suggestion of a passive femininity compromised from the outset. Mina embodies her own discrete version of a rebellion against gendered constraints, an emphasised difference that has underpinned a significant body of criticism.

If Lucy has not been openly embraced as a heroine of sexual liberation (or, at least a martyr to its cause), then Mina has only fleetingly been accepted as a protofeminist. This is surprising. Mina's rebellion, unlike that of her friend and former pupil, Lucy, is both conscious and independent of the vampire.[26] It is intellectual rather than sexual, and is based upon her conscious, supportive deployment of talents (memory, organisation) and skills (shorthand, typing) rather than any attempt to appropriate the prerogatives and powers of the male sex. Even when she is compromised by the vampire's bite, and her subsequent ingestion of his sexualised bodily fluids, Mina displays conscious shame rather than provocative voluptuousness. Indeed, it is she who imposes a form of quarantine between herself and Jonathan for his own protection, with the statement 'I must touch him or kiss him no more' (248). If she has a sexuality, it is safely contained, first within marriage and latterly by the act of child-bearing. If Mina's abilities and independence proclaim her oblique feminism, then her gender conservatism, her submission to male power and utility as a tool in male hands (whether these be the violent hands of the Count or the hypnotist's hands of Van Helsing), surely disqualify her from any iconic status in twentieth- or twenty-first-century feminist assessments.

THE NEW WOMAN

Mina's disqualification is further underwritten by her rather equivocal relationship to that most controversial of figures in the gender politics of the Victorian *fin de siècle*, the New Woman. Popularly associated – particularly in the verbal polemic of *Punch* and through the cartoons of George du Maurier – with progressive attitudes towards rational dress, educational achievement and sporting prowess, the New Woman existed as an unstable and shifting cultural shorthand for the assertive female.[27] The instability of the concept was in part a consequence of the New Woman's lack of central organisation or systematic policy: a woman calling herself a New Woman might embrace any combination of perceived preoccupations, from the right to bicycle unchaperoned, to the championing of more serious issues associated with sexuality, contraception and marriage. Equally, though, the uncertain identity of the New Woman was caused by her simultaneous depiction in the work of both advocates and opponents. Thus, as Lyn Pykett suggests in *The Improper Feminine* (1992), 'The New Woman was the embodiment of a complex of social tendencies. The title named a beacon of progress or beast of regression, depending on who was doing the naming.'[28] Both advocates and protagonists appear to agree upon the novelty of the figure and, with varying degrees of approval, upon her archetypal appetite *for* novelty and change.[29] Whether viewed with approval or disapprobation, one thing was certain, as Sally Ledger notes: 'she was dangerous, a threat to the status quo'.[30]

The New Woman is mentioned by name twice in *Dracula*, both references being contained within a single entry in the unmarried Mina's journal, dated 8 August. This is, in itself, arguably significant. Mina's references to the New Woman are essentially private remarks, the indexes of a comparison made for her own purposes and for her own eyes, rather than as a part of public discourse. These brief remarks, though, are contextualised in criticism through reference to Mina's own fictional biography. As Matthew Brennan notes in 'Repression, Knowledge, and Saving Souls: The Role of the "New Woman" in Stoker's *Dracula* and Murnau's *Nosferatu*' (1992):

> ■ In contrast to Lucy, who gives in to the dark power of her unconscious that Dracula symbolizes, Mina achieves considerable self-development through her commitment to knowledge. Despite her jokes about the New Woman [86–7], Mina herself resembles one in several ways: for one thing, she supports herself, before marriage, by working as an assistant school-mistress; for another, she knows stenography and can type, modern skills that help her complement her husband's law career, as does her memorizing train schedules.[31] □

Brennan's summation is in itself an index of how Mina's fictional biography modifies the relationship between her character and the polemical figure of the New Woman. Mina's resemblance to the New Woman waxes and wanes as she progresses from employee to wife, and from virginity to an active sexuality which may produce, variously, vampires or babies. Mina is not a New Woman, arguably, but exists in relationship to the New Woman throughout *Dracula*: she is, as it were, a commentary upon the evocative feminist as much as the New Woman's clichéd behaviour forms a background to her own drama.

The 'jokes' that Brennan identifies are a muted reflection of the strident anti-New Woman polemic of the last decade of the nineteenth century; Mina's referencing of the figure serves to exemplify the difference between approved and unorthodox female deportment. Mina first mentions the New Woman in her recollection of a meal enjoyed after a walk along the still-extant coastal path between Whitby and Robin Hood's Bay in North Yorkshire:

> ■ We had a capital 'severe tea' at Robin Hood's Bay in a sweet little old-fashioned inn, with a bow-window right over the seaweed-covered rocks of the strand. I believe we should have shocked the 'New Woman' with our appetites. Men are more tolerant, bless them! (86) □

Leaving aside the sarcasm integral to this recollection, which scripts the conventional male as being more 'tolerant' of women than the New Woman is herself, Mina's remark serves immediately to locate her within the culture of her time. As Carol Senf notes, in '*Dracula*: Stoker's Response to the New Woman' (1982), 'Because the New Woman was a subject of controversy in journalism, fiction, and – presumably, at least – drawing rooms, Mina's initial reference merely characterizes her as a well-informed young woman of the 1890s.'[32] Senf is quite correct in her conclusion that this allusion to the New Woman is rhetorically 'neutral' rather than hostile or condemnatory, for, as she asserts immediately after, the primary focus of the remark is the New Woman's 'insistence on greater freedom and physical activity'. Mina, in effect, is making selective use of the cliché: the sexual frankness associated with the New Woman is neither stressed nor referenced here, though, as Matthew Brennan notes, it almost invariably accompanies any critical appreciation of that figure.[33]

For all its absence of a sexual focus, Mina's remark is still curious. Though the 'appetites' exhibited by the two female travellers appear to be the consequence of recent strenuous activity – a 'severe tea' in this context meaning a 'large tea' – Mina is manoeuvring the two into a rhetorical position that situates them at an extreme *beyond* that of the New Woman. Because she does this, it is possible for criticism to project other (unspoken but known) attributes of the New Woman onto Lucy, the primary focus here (as elsewhere) of Mina's recollections. Sally Ledger, for example, argues in *The New Woman* (1997) that this:

> ■ reference to New Women ironically prefigures the fact that shortly after this scene Lucy goes on to develop 'appetites' of an altogether more wanton kind than those indulged in at tea-time; decadent sexual appetites associated in the periodical press of the 1890s with one particular construction of the New Woman.[34] □

The proleptic emphasis of Ledger's assertion adds, at first sight, authority to the conclusion towards which it draws. On closer inspection, however, it differs markedly from the seemingly innocent aside written by Mina. Ledger, it would appear, has prioritised the carnal appetites of some New Women over the conventional ones of others – and has overlooked, also, how Mina's remark aligns approval of the behaviour of Lucy and herself taking tea at Robin Hood's Bay with an observer who, though abstracted and hypothetical, is rendered as a conventional male rather than a progressive feminist.

Mina's second allusion to the New Woman, though, embodies a more telling reference to the sexuality associated with progressive feminism in the 1890s. With the exhausted Lucy 'asleep and breathing softly', Mina queries:

> ■ If Mr Holmwood fell in love with her seeing her only in the drawing room, I wonder what he would say if he saw her now. Some of the 'New Women' writers will some day start an idea that men and women should be allowed to see each other asleep before proposing or accepting. But I suppose the New Woman won't condescend in future to accept; she will do the proposing herself. And a nice job she will make of it too! (87) □

Carol Senf interprets this remark as a firm rejection, on Mina's part, of 'both the forwardness and the sexual openness of the New Woman writers'.[35] Though this would seem to ring true in the context of subsequent expressions of Mina's character – specifically, her revulsion at the sexualised posturing of the three vampires in Transylvania (317) – one wonders whether Mina experiences distaste rather than the 'discomfort' Senf perceives at this juncture.[36] The gesture itself, with its emphatic coda that anticipates the bathetic marriage proposal by the heroine of Stoker's *The Man*, certainly suggests a mocking rather than fearful tone, quite in keeping with a holiday that, though eventful, remains far from tragic. In essence, criticism has taken up this projected disturbance to the male prerogative of proposing marriage to underscore once more the convention, associated with anti-New Woman polemic, of a world inverted if not perverted.[37] Oddly, through this recurrent preoccupation, criticism has perversely come superficially to resemble the regressive tendencies which it, as a liberated and modern discourse, ought to dispel.

If Mina's words, in this second allusion to the New Woman, serve to distance her both from fictional characters and contemporary free-thinking feminists, then her scripted actions also redeploy the New Woman's independent attributes in the service of conventional sexual and social relations. Sally Ledger suggests that Lucy might be viewed within the compass of the New Woman because of her 'unnatural' treatment of the child she abducts immediately prior to her confinement within the tomb by Van Helsing (188).[38] Invoking the customary critical juxtaposition of the two heroines, Ledger further argues that 'The second half of *Dracula* shifts from a presentation of women as vampires to focus on a woman who, firmly rooted in the maternal paradigm, settles for the "ideal" of middle-class Victorian womanhood.'[39] Like Senf, Ledger contends that Mina's progress in *Dracula* represents not an aggression towards all women but rather an opportune rebuff to a specific and identifiable facet of late-Victorian female consciousness. Mina is thus an updated version of the ideal woman represented in the influential poem *The Angel in the House* (1854–63) by Coventry Patmore (1823–1896). According to Ledger:

■ Stoker, like so many writers and novelists at the *fin de siècle*, wanted to terminate the career of the sexualised New Woman and to reinstate in her place a modernised version of the 'angel in the house' – in this case Mina Harker.[40] □

Hence, as Matthew Brennan notes, Mina's career and independence are eclipsed by her marriage, her commercial skills becoming in context domestic skills, as she supports her husband in sickness, in employment and finally in his active pursuit of revenge and closure. Perversely, her redeployment of these skills in the pursuit of Count Dracula forces their retention, and disrupts Mina's relationship to Patmore's angelic ideal. Ironically, the tone of Brennan's assessment evokes Mina's difference at the same time as it asserts her aspiration to a conventional femininity:

■ So, though a New Woman would typically reject marriage, Mina does *choose* to marry, unlike Lucy whose marriage is basically arranged for her; moreover, Mina marries someone she can help intellectually and professionally, and furthermore someone who welcomes and values her help. More important, though, are her abilities to write and to edit – in other words, to create the knowledge by which Dracula is destroyed. (original italics)[41] □

Brennan's stress upon the word '*choose*' is crucial here. Though he does not develop the point, Mina is at her strongest and most useful to the forces of mortal, masculine orthodoxy when she is endowed with the power of choice. It is her choice to transfer the emotional phonograph records made by Seward into a neutral, passionless, carbon-paper copy which initiates the monumental task of producing a body of documents that may withstand the vampire's attacks (197, 249). It is the removal of her chosen participation within the coalition, however, that facilitates the Count's disruption of the group's plans and his predation upon Mina herself (213–14). Finally, it is Mina's choice to counsel Van Helsing to direct the vampire's hypnotic connection back against himself that eases their passage east (271). As Seward notes, these latter periods of 'absolute freedom' for Mina grant her 'complete control of herself' (286) – a control arguably as hard won from the vampire as it was earlier from her own associates. Mina may attain the final endorsement of sexual and social female orthodoxy in her production of an heir at the close of the novel, but it seems somewhat unfair to view her as one who abdicates her power either upon marriage or through absorption into a male-dominated coalition. In her construction and her recollections, Mina neither wholly opposes nor satisfactorily embraces the New Woman: she is, as it were, a referencing mid-point between the orthodox and the progressive, balancing, as Van Helsing intimates in the concluding sentence of *Dracula*, the 'brave and gallant' with 'sweetness and loving care' (327).

THE HOMOSOCIAL AND THE HOMOSEXUAL

Though Mina's initiative and mental acuity are not unequivocally associated with the New Woman in *Dracula*, these qualities remain somewhat problematic in their relationship to approved, separate-spheres models of gender demarcation. Where the novel does not explicitly tie Mina Harker to the deviance of the New Woman, it does in a sense both excuse her difference whilst acknowledging her perceived abnormality through Van Helsing's insistence that 'She has a man's brain – a brain that a man should have were he much gifted – and woman's heart' (207). Whilst Van Helsing's assessment of Mina has implications for her relationship to contextual perceptions of female psychology, it is also but one example of the blurring of gender boundaries within *Dracula*. Notably, as the gendered critique of *Dracula* has gradually shifted from analyses founded upon feminist-influenced readings of Stoker's heroines towards a consideration of the novel's male protagonists, attention has been brought to bear not merely upon the masculinity of the Count and his opponents, but also upon their homosexual and homoerotic implications.

The main focus of critical interest in this respect has not been the orthodox chivalric masculinity which the male protagonists consciously deploy in both their self-definition and defence of Mina.[42] Rather, criticism has come to focus upon the many subtle deviations from that social and sexual standard which the novel presents as consequences of the encounter with the vampire. The vampire's contact with men as much as with women confuses the accustomed certainties of who should penetrate or be penetrated. As Christopher Craft suggests, 'the vampiric kiss excites a sexuality so mobile, so insistent, that it threatens to overwhelm the distinctions of gender'.[43] Craft's contention needs further qualification, however: where Lucy and Mina are the literal recipients of that catalytic kiss, the Van Helsing circle are merely witnesses to its application (in the case of Mina) or consequences (for both heroines). Implicitly, therefore, it is simply knowledge of the vampire, rather than actual intimate contact that may query the integrity of masculinity in the bodies of those who outwardly and emphatically project their gendered orthodoxy.

For Craft, the Count's mouth is a synecdoche of the sexual confusion caused by vampirism within the novel. As he suggests:

■ As the primary site of erotic experience in *Dracula*, this mouth equivocates, giving the lie to the easy separation of the masculine and the feminine. Luring at first with an inviting orifice, a promise of red softness, but delivering instead a piercing bone, the vampire mouth fuses and confuses what Dracula's civilized nemesis, Van Helsing, and his Crew of Light, works so hard to separate – the gender-based categories of the penetrating and the receptive [...] With its soft flesh barred by hard bone, its red crossed by white, this mouth compels opposites and contrasts into a frightening unity, and it asks some disturbing questions. Are we male or are we female? Do we have penetrators or orifices? And if both, what does that mean?[44] □

Indeed, given that this 'inviting orifice' is first viewed by a male observer, Craft is quite correct in suggesting that:

■ the novel's opening anxiety, its first articulation of the vampiric threat, derives from Dracula's hovering interest in Jonathan Harker; the sexual threat that this novel first evokes, manipulates, sustains, but never finally represents is that Dracula will seduce, penetrate, drain another male.[45] □

That 'interest', though, cannot be openly expressed in a culture whose distaste for active homosexual relations might best be typified by the furore (and, indeed, confusion) surrounding the trials of Stoker's former Trinity College associate, Oscar Wilde, some two years before the publication of *Dracula*.[46] Hence, Craft perceives in the anti-vampiric campaign of *Dracula* a deflection of the vampire's sexual identity and energy onto other characters whose biological sex might render them less controversial intimates for the Van Helsing circle.

Through the novel's evasion of the homosexual script first established during Harker's sojourn in Castle Dracula, the vampire himself is transformed from an apparently homosexual male – he proclaims of Harker, 'This man belongs to me!' (43) – into a body of 'monstrous heterosexuality'. Effectively, the three female vampires function as both a heterosexual (though still sexually deviant) substitute for the male Count, and impose a hiatus upon the consummation of Harker's seduction at his hands. 'This moment is interrupted, this penetration denied', notes Craft: that which has *almost* happened is empowered to haunt the remainder of the text.[47]

For all this equivocation and displacement, the incorporation of both heterosexual and homosexual desire within the body of the Count generates important implications for the ritual disposal of Lucy Westenra. Craft views the blood transfusions which are administered to counteract the vampire's predation as an 'anxious reassertion of the conventionally male prerogative of penetration'. The transfusions effectively become a sort of prolepsis for the subsequent staking of Lucy, particularly where both interventions into her body are seen to change her from an undesired state to an idealised one. The second, though, is enacted with 'added emphasis', being 'an enthusiastic correction' which counters the homoeroticism as well as the heterosexuality of vampirism by literally 'reinscribing (upon Lucy's chest) the line dividing the male who penetrates and the woman who receives'.[48]

Craft's earlier suggestion that, for Harker, the three female vampires function as a heterosexual substitute for the homosexual Count should be recalled here. The penetration of Lucy well might here be a displaced substitute for the penetration of quite another vampire. The Count's disposal at the close of the novel is muted in comparison to Lucy's despatch. As Craft suggests, because 'Stoker could not represent so explicitly a violent phallic interchange between the Crew of Light and Dracula', a displacement is necessarily inserted so that 'Lucy receives the phallic correction that Dracula deserves'.[49]

Craft's study is concerned with the sexual politics and identities of the novel rather than with those of the author. It evades any strident suggestion of a homosexual identity on the part of Stoker, though its exploration of what Craft terms 'a pivotal anxiety of late-Victorian culture' perhaps suggests more than it actually says.[50] Stoker's critics have, for the most part, concurred with the bluff masculinity presented by the author's public persona – if only to avail themselves of the 'guilt' associated with his alleged syphilis and proclivity for prostitutes.[51] A small number of critics, however, have argued that this over-emphasised physicality concealed a fearful homosexual identity – an identity which, because of its 'unspeakable' nature during the British *fin de siècle*, informed the novel's construction of both male community and individual deviance.

Talia Schaffer, in '"A Wilde Desire Took Me": The Homoerotic History of *Dracula*' (1994), goes so far as to suggest that Stoker was a closeted homosexual, and his novel represented an anxious reflection upon a 'unique moment in gay history'.[52] That 'moment' was the final trial of Oscar Wilde in May 1895, or, rather, the trial and its repercussions both for Wilde as a felon legally and socially condemned and for other gay men who occupied an 'un-dead' borderland between two visibly conflicting sexual identities. Schaffer is not the first critic to identify the trace of the Wilde trials in Stoker's novel. Nina Auerbach, some twelve months earlier, contended 'that Dracula's primary progenitor is not Lord Ruthven, Varney, or Carmilla, but Oscar Wilde in the dock' – the Count is not derived from the demons of novelistic fiction, in other words, but from the horrors conjured up by the popular press.[53] As Schaffer notes, though, Stoker's relationship with Wilde was far more intimate than that of a public who encountered the disgraced author and playwright mediated through polemic. The two men were college associates in Dublin, they courted the same woman, Florence Balcombe, whom Stoker ultimately married, and they revolved in essentially the same social and theatrical circles in the London of the 1880s and 1890s. Wilde was sentenced on the day that both Irving and Stoker's brother, William Thornley, received their knighthoods – and Oscar's 'vanity and conceit' were explicitly recalled in a letter from his elder brother Willie Wilde (1852–1899) to Stoker, written two months' after the trial's conclusion. Yet, as Schaffer rightly points out, Wilde's name does not appear in Stoker's semi-autobiographical *Personal Reminiscences of Henry Irving*, nor in any of his twentieth-century essays upon fiction or the theatre. It is almost as if, in the words of Schaffer, Stoker had undertaken a 'careful erasure of Wilde's name from all his published (and unpublished) texts'.[54]

Stoker's omission of Wilde's name from his biography of Irving may well have indicated a delicacy of feeling in keeping with the author's reverence both for the theatre as a 'pure' or respectable art form and for Irving as its chief exponent – neither, as it were, should be sullied by association with the disgraced playwright, nor indeed the financial success of the book be imperilled by Wilde's inclusion.[55] Stoker's silence here may, admittedly, imply a heterosexist disdain for Wilde and all he had been made to stand for. But, if Stoker *was* gay, then the closing five years of the nineteenth century must have strained not merely his friendship with Wilde but also his own sense of security. Silence may here indicate fear rather than distaste. As Schaffer notes:

■ Oscar Wilde's trial set up a stark set of alternatives – safe concealment, or tempting revelation – yet forbade anyone to choose between the two. The trial's own interplay of disguise, half-admission, defense, and denial placed Wilde on the threshold of the closet. Thus the two extremes acquired value from their unattainability; the closet seemed like perfect sanctuary; coming out seemed like liberatory honesty. For a gay observer like Stoker, secrecy and self-assertion both became desirable goals even as Wilde's trial constructed 1890s homosexual identity as a delicate negotiation between them.[56] □

With the potentially ambivalent feelings surrounding this negotiation as its starting point, Schaffer's argument is a compulsive one. There is much evidence to support Schaffer's contentions not merely in the novel but also in Stoker's biography and the autobiographical statements of the *Personal Reminiscences of Henry Irving.* The density of evidence in '"A Wilde Desire Took Me"', though, is perhaps at times too intensively deployed, too laboriously linked to the unprovable hypothesis of Stoker's own homosexuality: it is in many respects a monumental edifice reared upon too slight a foundation.[57]

Be this as it may, Schaffer makes excellent use of the belief in Stoker's capacity for hero-worship common to both biography and criticism. Nina Auerbach, for example, considers 'Dracula [...] a proud servant's offering of friendship to a great man: the actor Henry Irving', proclaiming an identity between the Count and the thespian which she was again to affirm through the cover of the 1997 Norton Critical Edition of *Dracula,* which displays Irving's Mephistopheles as its cover artwork.[58] Noting Stoker's adulation of Walt Whitman and Hall Caine, as well as Irving, Schaffer argues that *Dracula* is effectively a discourse upon gay men – or, rather, upon men whom gay observers find attractive. Thus, for Schaffer, the relationship between Irving and Dracula is less interesting than that between the author and the actor because the same languages effectively structure, reveal and conceal both. Stoker's often effusive admiration for Irving – Schaffer quotes a letter in which Stoker proclaims 'my own love for the man' to a reporter – though it admits to a scarce concealed attraction, can be openly voiced by the author because the relationship was almost certainly never consummated: 'he could be open because he had nothing to hide'.[59] Indeed, Stoker's effusiveness had its own function in dispelling repression as well as proclaiming interest: 'Literary orgasm', as Schaffer puts it, 'avoids the dangers of homosexual sex'.[60]

Schaffer's innovation is not merely to amplify Auerbach's allusion to Wilde as a source for the novel, thus expelling Irving from the vampire's discursive ancestry. It is, more significantly, to question how earlier criticism has narrowly imposed a source upon a single character rather than on that character and his associates. For Schaffer, Wilde is both Dracula and Harker. In an intense section of '"A Wilde Desire Took Me"', Schaffer envisages the vampire not as Wilde himself, but as Wilde in the demonised persona imposed upon him during and after the trial. Thus, the Count on one level 'represents the ghoulishly inflated vision of Wilde produced by Wilde's prosecutors; the corrupting, evil, secretive, manipulative, magnetic devourer of innocent boys'. Behind this demonic biography, though, lies a further set of implications, in fact the very discourses that facilitate Wilde's structuring in this fearful light. The Count is simultaneously, therefore, a representation of 'the complex of fears, desires, secrecies, repressions and punishments that Wilde's name evoked in 1895'.[61] *Dracula*, in this respect, appears to be almost a collusion with the homophobia that condemned and convicted Wilde.

However, for Schaffer, Wilde is also Harker – a man who might well see Dracula's 'monstrous' face in his own shaving mirror.[62] There is an intimacy between the two in the novel, to be sure, though not quite the intimacy that Gary Oldman imposes upon Keanu Reeves in Coppola's *Bram Stoker's Dracula* when he shaves him, substituting his gaze for the solicitor's absent mirror. The two exchange clothes, sharing an identity in the perception of others (47); the Count undresses Harker (44), and Harker himself searches within the Count's own clothing (53).[63] Harker, though, is imprisoned, like Wilde, both within a literal building and beneath the demonisation that is embodied, in the novel, in the Count. Schaffer draws other comparisons – the censorship imposed upon the letters which both Harker and Wilde write from their respective prisons, the difficulties faced by both men when attempting to shave, and the greying hair which marks for both the horror of experience.[64] The related figures of the fictional vampire and his victim, the latter imprisoned rather than actually infected, embody the two poles of the debate around Wilde, which Schaffer terms, appropriately, 'Wilde-phobia' and 'Wilde-pity'. Whether or not the reader concurs with Schaffer's construction of Stoker as a gay man, the conclusion is inescapable: the same 'codes for the closet', as Schaffer terms them, appear to structure both Dracula and Harker.[65]

The critique of gender within *Dracula* has evolved in concert with the enclosing discipline of Gender Studies, graduating from a preoccupation with the depiction of women through to an engagement with both homosexual and heterosexual men. It must be noted, though, that critical works exclusively concerned with the representation of men and women in *Dracula* form but a proportion of the attention focused on that novel from a Gender Studies perspective. Gender is as mobile and pervasive a concept in modern criticism as it is in Stoker's 1897 novel. It informs other areas of the ongoing debate, from psychoanalytical studies to considerations of the medical context of *Dracula*, so that critics from Roth and Senf to Auerbach are referenced across the breath of the critical field. Some gaps, though, remain in the gendered critique of *Dracula*. There is no consideration of Renfield's masculinity, for example, nor of the indulgent sexism of the elderly sailors who hold the gaze of Lucy and Mina at Whitby. Much work remains to be done.

Conclusion

Scholarly editions of *Dracula* are a comparatively recent phenomenon, when viewed in the context of the novel's 110-year existence. Even in 1983, when Oxford University Press first added *Dracula* to its prestigious World's Classics series, the volume's editor, the novelist and essayist A. N. Wilson, felt somehow compelled to apologise for its inclusion therein. Stoker, throughout Wilson's introduction, is configured as a writer with 'little time – and, it must be firmly admitted, little aptitude – for letters'.[1] His novel is, equally, scripted as a derivative work, its perceived antecedents in 'The Vampyre' (1819) of John Polidori (1795–1821), *Varney the Vampire* (1845–47) by James Malcolm Rymer (1814–81), and, inevitably, J. S. Le Fanu's 'Carmilla', attracting almost as much emphasis in Wilson's introduction as *Dracula* itself. As Wilson insists, Stoker's

> ■ imagination was not a uniquely original one. Vampires from *Varney* and Le Fanu; a setting and a personage hastily 'got up' from a few hours in the British Museum. What is there left to say of Bram Stoker's originality or achievement? In what sense does *Dracula* deserve to be called a 'classic'?
>
> It is, patently, not a classic in the way that *Middlemarch* or *Madam Bovary* or *War and Peace* are classics. It is not a great work of literature. The writing is of a powerful, workaday sensationalist kind. No one in their right mind would think of Stoker as 'a great writer'.[2] □

Even more damningly, Wilson does not even bestow upon *Dracula* the dignity of an associated critical milieu. Though his select bibliography notes the biographies of Ludlam and Farson, literary criticism is represented only by the 1970 revision of Mario Praz's *The Romantic Agony* (1933), a work which does not consider *Dracula*, James Twitchell's *The Living Dead: A Study of the Vampire in Romantic Literature* (1981), which mentions it only in passing, and David Punter's relatively short interrogation in the (admittedly influential) *The Literature of Terror* (1980). In the Introduction itself, only Montague Summers's frenetic work of modern occultism, *The Vampire in Europe* (1929) is mentioned.[3] Stoker's novel, it seems, is hardly worthy of critical acknowledgement. *Dracula* is, indeed, for Wilson, 'a second-rate classic', one of many ephemeral 'great stories of the second-rate type'.[4]

It would be unthinkable today to preface *Dracula* with such faint praise and, indeed, with so little reference to the substantial body of criticism which has accumulated around the novel both before and following Wilson's 1983 Introduction. Yet one point made by Wilson, almost in passing, appears to retain some currency in contemporary literary discourse. Wilson concedes that Stoker's 'classic gift was that of a mythologist', and that 'His classic distinction is not artistic, but mythopoeic'.[5] At the centre of both the myth invented by Stoker, and of the burgeoning 'second-rate sub-culture' that Wilson associates with it, is the vampire himself: 'Count Dracula is as familiar a figure to us as Robin Hood or King Arthur were to an earlier generation.'[6] Curiously, Wilson is essentially in accord here with many more open-minded critics of *Dracula*. Writing just 12 months before Wilson, Carol Senf, for example, takes a slightly more positive view of the author's 'classic gift' when she suggests that 'Stoker's genius is that Dracula is the supreme bogeyman – a creature who means different things to different people.'[7] This persistent and directed focus upon the Count is surely what has kept the novel in the critical gaze for so long.

Senf's 'different people' comprise both fictional characters and commentating critics. Both, as it were, endow the vampire with meaning, so that, perversely, he returns a reflection that is as much a commentary upon the interpreter as the focus of interpretation. In a critical field that is now characteristically as reflective upon its own practice as it is interrogative with regard to its central text, it should be evident that the Count may no longer be considered in isolation. When Senf suggests that Dracula 'represents the power of the isolated individual', she proclaims the paradox of the Vampire's disdainful singularity.[8] The very presence of power militates against isolation. In *Dracula*, the Count has implications not merely for those who actively oppose him, but for all those who may know of him or come into his presence, however unknowingly. His power is not held in reserve, but is always on the point of breaking out as a catalyst, its potential being to change not merely the physicality of self but also the manner in which the self may be viewed. Moreover, the Count exists in a reciprocal relationship with mortal humanity, emulating its achievements and aspirations, responding to its resistance, becoming progressively subject to its accumulating laws and perceptive gaze. His change is, equally, a commentary upon his time.

If the Count absorbs meaning from criticism, as much as he reflects, apparently, the coded meanings of the *fin de siècle*, then he is active, too, in the transfer of meaning: through the bite, through an osmotic ingestion of his essence, through his very existence or the impending threat of his presence. He is an icon of change, and a yardstick by which the mutability and resistance of others might yet be measured. The Count, as it were, circulates his substance, his meanings, not merely amongst those he has bitten, but equally amongst those he has not touched. It stands to reason, therefore, that those fictional 'others' are equally worthy of study, equally capable of signification, equally susceptible to critical analysis – though, strangely, the Count still at times appears to attract an undue proportion of attention, even in relatively recent critical discourse.

It is perilous, though, to speculate regarding the likely development of *Dracula* criticism, even where current work might offer tempting suggestions of its possible direction. The contemporary state of *Dracula* studies suggests a period of consolidation and reflection, with a plethora of respectable scholarly editions, many of which embody new or reprinted criticism, being paralleled by the relatively recent phenomenon of accessible 'literary lives' which interface biography with criticism. The latter, best represented by Andrew Maunder's *Bram Stoker* (2006) and Lisa Hopkins's *Bram Stoker: A Literary Life* (2007), are likely to form the context of twenty-first century writing upon *Dracula*, in much the same way as Phyllis Roth's seminal *Bram Stoker* (1982) supported criticism in the 1980s and 1990s.[9] The two studies, both excellent in their own right, arguably demonstrate how the critical field has changed in 25 years: there is less emphasis in the work of Maunder and Hopkins upon psychoanalysis and sexual symbolism, and a more protracted reading of social contexts such as Stoker's theatrical career, the commercial nature of his writing, and his participation in the discourses (rather than neuroses) of his day.

The specific themes explored over almost a half-century of *Dracula* criticism, as represented in this Guide, are likely to maintain their currency, at least in the foreseeable future. All continue to present opportunities for reflection, revisitation and development, As criticism of the novel has also benefited from the rise of newer theoretical disciplines such as Queer Studies, one might anticipate also the application of nascent theoretical fields to the novel in the future. Curiously, this has not always proved to be the case: ecocriticism, a critical approach which has proved highly influential in both published research and pedagogy from the 1980s, is yet to produce an assessment – or even a substantial acknowledgment – of *Dracula*. The possible reasons why this should be the case might well, in its own right, form the subject of an investigation into the complex relationships between *Dracula* and theory.

Whatever direction the future study of Stoker's novel takes, the criticism of *Dracula* is likely to retain both the enduring topicality, and the resistance to methodological closure and orthodoxy, that has distinguished its discourse from the 1960s to the present. 'Time', as the Count himself says, 'is on my side' (267) – and the criticism of *Dracula* is likely to remain as resistant to the debilitations and enfeeblement of age as the vampire is himself.

Notes

Introduction

1. *The Spectator*, 31 July 1897, p. 151; 'The Trail of the Vampire', *St James's Gazette*, 3 June 1897, p. 5; *The Bookman*, August 1897, p. 129.
2. *Athenaeum*, 6 June 1897, p. 835; *The Observer*, 1 August 1897, p. 7.
3. Hall Caine, 'Bram Stoker: The Story of a Great Friendship', *Daily Telegraph*, 24 April 1912, p. 16; *The Glasgow Herald*, 10 June 1897, p. 10; *Athenaeum*, 6 June 1897, p. 835.
4. 'Obituary: Mr Bram Stoker', *The Times*, 22 April 1912, p. 15.
5. The Sensation Novel, which juxtaposed domestic convention with melodramatic excess, flourished from the 1860s, its popular authors including Wilkie Collins, Mrs Henry Wood (1814–1887) and Mary Elizabeth Braddon (1837–1915). See Andrew Radford's forthcoming *Victorian Sensation Fiction: A Reader's Guide to Essential Criticism* (Basingstoke: Palgrave Macmillan, 2008). The French term *fin de siècle* (literally 'the end of the century') is often used to refer to European writings of the 1890s, particularly where these make reference to social change and cultural decadence.
6. The *Journal of Dracula Studies*, edited by Elizabeth Miller. Information on critical works concerned exclusively with *Dracula*, or in which *Dracula* occupies a significant proportion of the argument, can be found in Richard Dalby and William Hughes, *Bram Stoker: A Bibliography* (Westcliff-on-Sea: Desert Island Books, 2004), pp. 142–79.
7. Several bilingual critical collections have been published in support of the *CAPES* and *Agrégation* curriculum in France. These include Max Duperray and Dominique Sipière (eds), *Dracula: Bram Stoker et Francis Ford Coppola* (Paris: Armand Colin, 2005) and Gilles Menegaldo and Dominique Sipière (eds), *Dracula: Stoker/Coppola* (Paris: Ellipses, 2005).
8. *Dracula* was translated into Icelandic, with a preface by the author, as early as 1901, into German in 1908, into Russian around 1912, into French in 1920 and into Irish in 1933. Subsequent overseas editions have included reprints of these earlier translations, as well as new editions in Afrikaans, Japanese and Catalan. See Dalby and Hughes, (2004), pp, 102–11. Scholarly editions of the novel are invariably annotated, though few to the extent of Clive Leatherdale's encyclopaedic *Dracula Unearthed* (Westcliff-on-Sea: Desert Island Books, 1998).
9. For example, F. R. Leavis effectively dismissed 'the minor novelists' revived in 'the present vogue of the Victorian age' by focusing critical attention upon 'The great English novelists [...] Jane Austen, George Eliot, Henry James, and Joseph Conrad'. See F. R. Leavis, *The Great Tradition* (1948; London: Penguin, 1962), pp. 2, 1.
10. Michel Foucault, *The History of Sexuality: An Introduction*, trans. Robert Hurley (1976; London: Penguin, 1984), pp. 5–7, 10–12, and *passim*.
11. *The Publishers' Circular*, 7 August 1897, p. 131.
12. Maurice Richardson, 'The Psychoanalysis of Ghost Stories', *The Twentieth Century*, 166 (December 1959), pp. 419–31; extract reprinted as 'The Psychoanalysis of Count Dracula', in Christopher Frayling (ed.), *Vampires: Lord Byron to Count Dracula* (London: Faber & Faber, 1991), pp. 418–22.
13. Joseph S. Bierman, '*Dracula*: Prolonged Childhood Illness and the Oral Triad', *American Imago*, 29 (1972), pp. 186–98; Daniel Lapin, *The Vampire, Dracula and Incest* (San Francisco: Gargoyle, 1995), p. 31
14. Elisabeth Bronfen, *Over Her Dead Body: Death, Femininity and the Aesthetic* (Manchester: Manchester University Press, 1992).

15. C. F. Bentley, 'The Monster in the Bedroom: Sexual Symbolism in Bram Stoker's *Dracula*', *Literature and Psychology*, 22 (1972), pp. 27–34; Carol L. Fry, 'Fictional Conventions and Sexuality in *Dracula*', *Victorian Newsletter*, 42 (1972), pp. 20–2.

16. Christopher Craft, '"Kiss me with those red lips": Gender and Inversion in Stoker's *Dracula*', *Representations*, 8 (1984), pp. 107–33; H. L. Malchow, *Gothic Images of Race in Nineteenth-Century Britain* (Stanford: Stanford University Press, 1996), pp. 130–6; Talia Schaffer, 'A Wilde Desire Took Me: The Homoerotic History of *Dracula*', *ELH*, 61 (1994), pp. 381–425. Queer theory was identified as a discrete movement during the 1990s, though several studies of *Dracula*, and, indeed, of the broader Gothic, had discerned 'queer' relationships within that novel before that institutionalisation: see Donald E. Hall, *Queer Theories* (Basingstoke: Palgrave, 2003), pp. 1, 12–16.

17. Robert Mighall, 'Sex, History and the Vampire', in William Hughes and Andrew Smith (eds), *Bram Stoker: History, Psychoanalysis and the Gothic* (Basingstoke: Macmillan, 1998), pp. 62–77 at pp. 62–4.

18. Robert Mighall, *A Geography of Victorian Gothic Fiction: Mapping History's Nightmares* (Oxford: Oxford University Press, 1999), p. 227.

19. Sally Ledger, *The New Woman: Fiction and Feminism at the Fin de Siècle* (Manchester: Manchester University Press, 1997), pp. 100–6; Marie Mulvey-Roberts, '*Dracula* and the Doctors: Bad Blood, Menstrual Taboo and the New Woman', in Hughes and Smith (1998), pp. 78–95.

20. Jasmine Y. Hall, 'Solicitors Soliciting: The Dangerous Circulations of Professionalism in *Dracula*', in Barbara Leah Harman and Susan Meyer (eds), *The New Nineteenth Century: Feminist Readings of Underread Victorian Fiction* (New York: Garland, 1996), pp. 99–116; Anne McGillivray, '"What sort of grim adventure was it on which I had embarked?": Lawyers, Vampires and the Melancholy of Law', *Gothic Studies*, 4/2 (2002), pp. 116–32.

21. Ernest Fontana, 'Lombroso's Criminal Man and Stoker's Dracula', *Victorian Newsletter*, 66 (1984), pp. 25–7.

22. See, for example, Victor Sage, *Horror Fiction in the Protestant Tradition* (Basingstoke: Macmillan, 1988), pp. 180–3; William Hughes, *Beyond Dracula: Bram Stoker's Fiction and its Cultural Context* (Basingstoke: Macmillan, 2000), pp. 73–5.

23. See, for example, Daniel Pick, '"Terrors of the Night": *Dracula* and "Degeneration" in the Late Nineteenth Century', *Critical Quarterly*, 30 (1988), pp. 71–87; Stephen D. Arata, 'The Occidental Tourist: *Dracula* and the Anxiety of Reverse Colonisation', *Victorian Studies*, 33 (1990), pp. 621–45; Rhys Garnett, '*Dracula* and *The Beetle*: Imperial and Sexual Guilt and Fear in Late Victorian Fantasy', in Rhys Garnett and R. J. Ellis (eds), *Science Fiction Roots and Branches: Contemporary Critical Approaches* (New York: St Martin's Press, 1990), pp. 30–54; Jules Zanger, 'A Sympathetic Vibration: *Dracula* and the Jews', *ELT*, 34 (1991), pp. 33–43.

24. Mulvey-Roberts (1998), pp. 84–5.

25. Franco Moretti, *Signs Taken for Wonders: Essays in the Sociology of Literary Form* (London: Verso, 1983), pp. 83–98; Terry Eagleton, *Heathcliff and the Great Hunger* (London: Verso, 1995), pp. 215–16.

26. Joseph Valente, *Dracula's Crypt: Bram Stoker, Irishness and the Question of Blood* (Urbana: University of Illinois Press, 2002), p. 38.

27. Raymond T. McNally and Radu Florescu, *In Search of Dracula: A True History of Dracula and Vampire Legends* (New York: New York Graphic Society, 1972; reprinted London: Book Club Associates, 1979), pp. 20–2, 176–81.

28. See Elizabeth Miller, 'Filing for Divorce: Count Dracula vs Vlad Tepes', in Elizabeth Miller (ed.), *Dracula: The Shade and the Shadow* (Westcliff-on-Sea: Desert Island Books, 1998), pp. 166–79; Elizabeth Miller, *Dracula: Sense and Nonsense* (Westcliff-on-Sea: Desert Island Books, 2000), pp. 180–223.

29. Clive Leatherdale, *Dracula: The Novel and the Legend* (Wellingborough: Aquarian Press, 1985), p. 75; cf. Clive Leatherdale, *Dracula: The Novel and the Legend*, 3rd edn

(Westcliff-on-Sea: Desert Island Books, 2001), p. 77, where the author modifies this statement to make Stoker 'a *largely* hack writer' (my italics).

30. David Glover, *Vampires, Mummies, and Liberals: Bram Stoker and the Politics of Popular Fiction* (Durham, NC: Duke University Press, 1996), p. 5.

31. Fontana (1984), pp. 180–5; Pick (1988), pp. 71–87.

32. Carol A. Senf, *Science and Social Science in Bram Stoker's Fiction* (Westport, CT: Greenwood Press, 2002), pp. 3–5, 43; *Dracula: Between Tradition and Modernism* (New York: Twayne, 1998), pp. 74–98. Bram Stoker, 'The Censorship of Fiction' (1908), reprinted in Richard Dalby (ed.), *A Glimpse of America and Other Lectures, Interviews and Essays* (Westcliff-on-Sea: Desert Island Books, 2002), pp. 154–61 at pp. 157, 160.

33. Resources of this type include searchable critical articles archived as part of the JSTOR initiative (http://www.jstor.org), and the online publication of journals such as *Gothic Studies* (http://journals.mup.man.ac.uk/cgi-bin/MUP?COMval=journal&key=GOTH) and the *Journal of Dracula Studies* (http://www.blooferland.com/drc/index.php?title=Journal_of_Dracula_Studies). Biographical and critical articles published in *The Bram Stoker Society Journal* between 1989 and 2001 have also been archived on CD-ROM (http://www.brianjshowers.com/stokersociety.html).

34. Bram Stoker, *Personal Reminiscences of Henry Irving* (London: Heinemann, 1906), 2 vols, Vol. 1, p. 31.

35. See Peter Haining and Peter Tremayne, *The Un-Dead: The Legend of Bram Stoker and Dracula* (London: Constable, 1997), pp. 41, 43–4.

36. Stoker, *Personal Reminiscences*, Vol. 1, p. 32. The details of Stoker's academic achievements are contained in the Muniment Records and Catalogue of Graduates of the University of Dublin, archived at Trinity College. Stoker's alleged specialism has been accepted without question by Haining and Tremayne: see Haining and Tremayne (1997), p. 53.

37. Barbara Belford, *Bram Stoker: A Biography of the Author of Dracula* (London: Weidenfeld & Nicolson, 1996), p. 34.

38. Stoker (1906), Vol. 1, p. 32. These cups are briefly detailed in Daniel Farson, *The Man Who Wrote Dracula: A Biography of Bram Stoker* (London: Michael Joseph, 1975), p. 18.

39. Stoker (1906), Vol. 1, p. 32; Paul Murray, *From the Shadow of Dracula: A Life of Bram Stoker* (London: Jonathan Cape, 2004), pp. 34–5. The Historical Society funded a limited production of Stoker's presidential address, *The Necessity for Political Honesty*, in 1872, making this the author's first publication.

40. Harry Ludlam, *A Biography of Dracula: The Life Story of Bram Stoker* (London: Foulsham, 1962), p. 41.

41. Stoker (1906), Vol. 1, p. 6.

42. Stoker (1906), Vol. 1, pp. 28–33, at p. 33.

43. Leslie Shepard, 'The Stoker Family on the Move: The Changes of Address and Travels of the Stokers', *The Bram Stoker Society Journal*, 10 (1998), pp. 30–5, at pp. 34, 35.

44. Haining and Tremayne (1997), p. 181.

45. Haining and Tremayne (1997), p. 177.

46. 'The Funeral of Mr Bram Stoker', *The Times*, 25 April, 1912.

47. Ludlam's book was 'Published for The Fireside Press by W. Foulsham & Co.', according to its title page.

48. See, for example, Belford (1996), pp. 226, 246–7, 319.

49. W. N. Osborough, 'The Dublin Castle Career (1866–78) of Bram Stoker', *Gothic Studies*, 1/2 (1999), pp. 222–40; L. Shepard, 'The Library of Bram Stoker', *The Bram Stoker Society Journal*, 4 (1992), pp. 28–34; James Drummond, 'Bram Stoker's Cruden Bay', *The Scots' Magazine*, (April 1976), pp. 23–8.

50. Stoker (1906), Vol. 1, p. 31.

51. Ludlam (1962), p. 11; Farson (1975), p. 13.

52. Belford (1996), pp. 13–14.

53. Seymour Shuster, 'Dracula and Surgically Induced Trauma in Children', *British Journal of Medical Psychology*, 46 (1973), pp. 259–70, at pp. 261, 259.

54. Joseph Bierman (1972), pp. 195, 196–7.

55. Joseph S. Bierman, 'A Crucial Stage in the Writing of *Dracula*', in Hughes and Smith (1998), pp. 151–72, at pp. 151, 166. Bierman, remarkably, is the author of one of the most baldly factual accounts of the origins of *Dracula*, namely 'The Genesis and Dating of *Dracula* from Bram Stoker's Working Notes', *Notes and Queries*, 222 (1977), pp. 39–41.

56. Belford (1996), p. 152; Murray (2004), p. 113; 'Obituary: Mr Bram Stoker', *The Times*, 22 April 1912, p. 15, Achates was the friend and lieutenant of Aeneas in Virgil's *Aeneid*, being customarily known as 'fidus [faithful] Achates'.

57. Laurence Irving, *Henry Irving: The Actor and His World* (London: Columbus, 1989), p. 453; Farson (1975), pp. 215–16.

58. Belford (1996), p. 106; Maurice Hindle, 'Introduction' to Bram Stoker, *Dracula* (London: Penguin, 1993), pp. vii–xxx, at pp. xxix–xxx.

59. Belford (1996), p. 106.

60. Royce MacGillivray, '*Dracula*: Bram Stoker's Spoiled Masterpiece', *Queen's Quarterly*, 79 (1972), pp. 518–27; Richardson (1959), pp. 428, 429; Bierman (1972), p. 197.

61. See, for example, Joseph Valente's reading of Stoker's isolation as an Irishman in London, in *Dracula's Crypt: Bram Stoker, Irishness and the Question of Blood* (Urbana: University of Illinois Press, 2002), p. 38.

62. John D'Addario, 'We're all Suckers for Dracula: Bram Stoker and the Homoeroticism of Vampires', *The Advocate*, 24 October 1989, pp. 40–2 at pp. 41, 42.

63. Stoker (1906), Vol. 2, pp. 96–7.

64. Horace Traubel, *With Walt Whitman in Camden: January 21 to April 7, 1889* (Philadelphia: University of Pennsylvania Press, 1953), pp. 183, 185. The letter of 18 February 1872 was forwarded to the poet with a letter dated 14 February 1876. The author, presumably, had had second thoughts about sending it at the time of writing. The date of the second letter being St Valentine's day may be nothing more than a coincidence.

65. The first letter was drafted seven months before Stoker published his first short story in 1872. By the time of the second letter he had published three further stories.

66. Murray (2004), p. 78.

67. Belford (1996), p. 86.

68. Farson (1975), pp. 214, 234–5.

69. Penelope Shuttle and Peter Redgrove, *The Wise Wound: Menstruation and Everywoman* (London: HarperCollins, 1994), p. 252; Mulvey-Roberts (1998), pp. 78–95 at p. 79.

70. Stoker's Death Certificate is reproduced in Elizabeth Miller (ed.), *Bram Stoker's Dracula: A Documentary Volume* (Detroit: Thomson-Gale, 2005), p. 27.

71. Hall Caine, 'Bram Stoker: The Story of a Great Friendship', *The Daily Telegraph*, 24 April 1912, p. 16, reprinted in Miller (2005), pp. 24–6 at p. 24; Ludlam (1962), p. 150.

72. Farson (1975), pp. 214, 234.

73. Belford (1996), pp. 320–1; Leslie Shepard, 'A Note on the Death Certificate of Bram Stoker', in Leslie Shepard and Albert Power, eds *Dracula: Celebrating 100 Years* (Dublin: Mentor Press, 1997), pp. 178–80; Haining and Tremayne (1997), pp. 181–2; Murray (2004), pp. 267–9.

1 Psychoanalysis and Psychobiography: The Troubled Unconsciousness of *Dracula*

1. Robert Mighall, '"A pestilence which walketh in darkness": Diagnosing the Victorian Vampire', in Glennis Byron and David Punter (eds), *Spectral Readings: Towards a Gothic Geography* (Basingstoke: Macmillan, 1999), pp. 108–24, at p. 108.

2. For pre-Hammer cinematic adaptations and their sexual implications, see David Skal, *Hollywood Gothic: The Tangled Web of Dracula from Novel to Stage to Screen* (New York: Norton, 1990), pp. 54, 143–4, 190.

3. Ernest Jones, *On the Nightmare* (London: Hogarth Press and the Institute of Psycho-analysis, 1931). The sections of Jones's study most relevant to the literary vampire were reprinted as 'On the Vampire' in Christopher Frayling (ed.), *Vampyres: Lord Byron to Count Dracula* (London: Faber & Faber, 1991), pp. 398–417. Subsequent references to *On the Nightmare* are taken from this reprinted extract.

4. Jones (1931), pp. 399–400.

5. Jones (1931), p. 401.

6. Jones (1931), p. 412.

7. Jones (1931), p. 411.

8. Maurice Richardson, 'The Psychoanalysis of Ghost Stories', *The Twentieth Century*, 166 (1959), pp. 419–31. The portion of Richardson's article which considers *Dracula* has been reprinted as 'The Psychoanalysis of Count Dracula' in Frayling (1991), pp. 418–22. Subsequent references to 'The Psychoanalysis of Ghost Stories' are taken from this reprinted extract.

9. Richardson (1959), p. 420. The rather exaggerated tone of the article may be a teasingly ironic response to a number of complaints 'that there is too much about sex in *The Twentieth Century*': see 'To Our Readers', *The Twentieth Century*, 166 (1959), p. 418.

10. Richardson (1959), pp. 419, 418.

11. Jones (1931), p. 400.

12. Clive Leatherdale, though, interprets Lucy's actions as a knowing and immodest demonstration of her desirability. See Clive Leatherdale, *Dracula: The Novel and the Legend*, 3rd edn (Westcliff-on-Sea: Desert Island Books, 2001), p. 144.

13. Richardson (1959), p. 418.

14. Richardson (1959), p. 419.

15. Richardson (1959), p. 420.

16. Sigmund Freud, *Totem and Taboo* in *The Origins of Religion* (London: Penguin, n.d.), pp. 43–224 at pp. 202–6.

17. David Punter, *The Literature of Terror: A History of Gothic Fictions from 1765 to the Present Day*, 2nd edn (London: Longman, 1996), 2 vols, Vol. 2, pp. 15–22.

18. Richard Astle, 'Dracula as Totemic Monster: Lacan, Freud, Oedipus and History', *Sub-Stance*, 25 (1980), pp. 98–105.

19. Phyllis Roth, *Bram Stoker* (Boston: Twayne, 1982), p. 111.

20. Roth (1982), pp. 114, 115.

21. Roth (1982), p. 115.

22. Roth (1982), pp. 115, 116.

23. Roth (1982), p. 116.

24. Roth (1982), p. 117.

25. Roth (1982), pp. 118–19.

26. Roth (1982), p. 120.

27. C. F. Bentley, 'The Monster in the Bedroom: Sexual Symbolism in Bram Stoker's *Dracula*', *Literature and Psychology*, 22 (1972), pp. 27–33, at pp. 28, 29.

28. Bentley (1972), pp. 30–1.

29. Bentley (1972), p. 31

30. Daniel Farson, *The Man Who Wrote Dracula: A Biography of Bram Stoker* (London: Michael Joseph, 1975), pp. 234–5.

31. Penelope Shuttle and Peter Redgrove, *The Wise Wound: Menstruation and Everywoman* (London: HarperCollins, 1994), p. 252.

32. Marie Mulvey-Roberts, '*Dracula* and the Doctors: Bad Blood, Menstrual Taboo and the New Woman', in William Hughes and Andrew Smith (eds), *Bram Stoker: History, Psychoanalysis and the Gothic* (Basingstoke: Macmillan, 1998), pp. 78–95, at p. 79.

33. Mulvey-Roberts (1998), pp. 79, 84.

34. Mulvey-Roberts (1998), pp. 90–1.

35. Mulvey-Roberts (1998), p. 91.

36. Mulvey-Roberts (1998), p. 92.

37. Mulvey-Roberts (1998), pp. 84–5; Shuttle and Redgrove (1994), p. 252.

38. Bram Stoker, *Personal Reminiscences of Henry Irving* (London: William Heinemann, 1906), 2 vols, Vol. 1, p. 31.

39. Stoker (1906), Vol. 1, p. 32. Stoker drafted *Personal Reminiscences of Henry Irving*, in part at least, whilst convalescing from a paralytic stroke, this biographical detail arguably adding a further contextual layer of poignancy to the author's recollection of sporting glories past.

40. Barbara Belford, *Bram Stoker: A Biography of the Author of Dracula* (London: Weidenfeld & Nicolson, 1996), p. 14. Belford's account features quotations from the manuscript of the 1906 biography which did not appear in the published version.

41. Farson (1975), p. 13; Paul Murray, *From the Shadow of Dracula: A Life of Bram Stoker* (London: Jonathan Cape, 2004), pp. 24–5.

42. Joseph Bierman, '*Dracula*: Prolonged Childhood Illness, and the Oral Triad', *American Imago*, 29 (1972), pp. 186–98, at p. 192; Seymour Shuster, '*Dracula* and Surgically Induced Trauma in Children', *British Journal of Medical Psychology*, 46 (1973), pp. 259–70, at p. 259.

43. Stoker himself admitted that, during this period, 'I was naturally thoughtful and the leisure of long illness gave opportunity for many thoughts which were fruitful according to their kind in later years.' See Stoker (1906), Vol. 1, p. 31.

44. Bierman (1972), p. 192.

45. Farson (1975), pp. 155–6.

46. Bierman (1972), p. 197.

47. Bierman (1972), p. 193.

48. Bram Stoker, *The Jewel of Seven Stars* (Westcliff-on-Sea: Desert Island Books, 1996), pp. 64–5 and p. 65, n. 14.

49. Bierman (1972), p. 192.

50. Bierman (1972), p. 195; Shuster (1973), p. 259.

51. Shuster (1973), p. 259.

52. Shuster (1973), p. 259.

53. Bierman (1972), p. 197.

54. Shuster (1973), p. 268.

55. Joseph Bierman, 'The Genesis and Dating of *Dracula* from Bram Stoker's Working Notes', *Notes and Queries*, 222 (1977), pp. 39–41.

56. Joseph S. Bierman, 'A Crucial Stage in the Writing of *Dracula*', in Hughes and Smith (1998), pp. 151–72, at p. 153.

57. Bierman (1998), p. 151.

58. Bierman (1972), pp. 193, 195, 192–3.

59. Bierman (1998), p. 166.

60. Bierman (1998), p. 151.

61. See also Mulvey-Roberts (1998), p. 79; Bentley (1972), p. 32.

62. Bierman (1998), p. 168.

63. Daniel Lapin, *The Vampire, Dracula and Incest* (San Francisco: Gargoyle, 1995), p. xii.

64. Lapin (1995), pp. 35, 38–9.

65. Lapin (1995), pp. 13, 38–9.

66. Lapin (1995), pp. 6–7.

67. Lapin (1995), p. 6.

68. Lapin (1995), pp. 7–8.

69. Lapin (1995), p. 27.

70. Lapin (1995), p. 46.

71. Lapin (1995), pp. 15, 28.

72. Lapin (1995), pp. 15–16.

73. Lapin (1995), p. 17.

74. Lapin (1995), p. 24.

75. Lapin (1995), p. 39.

76. Lapin (1995), p. 31.

77. Lapin (1995), p. 43.

78. Elisabeth Bronfen, *Over Her Dead Body: Death, Femininity and the Aesthetic* (Manchester: Manchester University Press, 1992), pp. 313–22, at pp. 316, 319, 294.

79. Bronfen (1992), p. 313.

80. Damien Hirst, 'The Physical Impossibility of Death in the Mind of Someone Living' (Saatchi Gallery, 1992). See Damien Hirst, *Pictures from the Saatchi Gallery* (London: Booth-Clibborn Editions, 2001), pp. 10–12.

81. Bronfen (1992), p. 292.

82. Bronfen (1992), p. 295.

83. Bronfen (1992), p. 317.

84. Bronfen (1992), p. 314.

85. Bronfen (1992), p. 294.

86. Bronfen (1992), p. 320.

87. Bronfen (1992), pp. 295, 315, 319.

88. Bronfen (1992), p. 294.

89. Bronfen (1992), p. 318.

90. Bronfen (1992), p. 319. For Bronfen's gendered definitions of hysterical and obsessional discourse see pp. 314–15.

91. Bronfen (1992), p. 319.

92. Bronfen (1992), p. 319.

93. Julia Kristeva, *Powers of Horror: An Essay on Abjection* (New York: Columbia University Press, 1982), p. 4.

94. Kristeva (1982), p. 15.

95. Anne Williams, *Art of Darkness: A Poetics of Gothic* (Chicago: University of Chicago Press, 1995), pp. 126–9, at p. 128.

96. Williams (1995), p. 4. Jerrold E. Hogle, 'Introduction: The Gothic in Western Culture', in Jerrold E. Hogle (ed.), *The Cambridge Companion to Gothic Fiction* (Cambridge: Cambridge University Press, 2002), pp. 1–20, at p. 7.

97. Hogle (2002), p. 7.

98. Hogle (2002), p. 9.

2 Medicine, Mind and Body: The Physiological Study of *Dracula*

1. The *Studies on Hysteria* comprise a preliminary communication, case studies and theoretical commentaries, published in German in 1893 and 1895, which Freud wrote in collaboration with Joseph Breuer (1842–1925). Both were translated into English in 1909.

2. For information on these three influential medical figures, see Roy Porter, *The Greatest Benefit to Mankind: A Medical History of Humanity from Antiquity to the Present* (London: HarperCollins, 1997), pp. 510–15 .

3. Paul Murray, *From the Shadow of Dracula: A Life of Bram Stoker* (London: Jonathan Cape, 2004), p. 175.

4. Peter Haining and Peter Tremayne, *The Un-Dead: The Legend of Bram Stoker and Dracula* (London: Constable, 1997), pp. 62, 91.

5. William Benjamin Carpenter, *Principles of Mental Physiology* (London: Henry S. King, 1874), p. 516.

6. Leonard Wolf, *The Essential Dracula*, 1975, reprinted (New York: Plume, 1993), p. 93, n. 36.

7. A similar point is also made by John Greenway in ' "Unconscious Cerebration" and the Happy Ending of *Dracula*', *Journal of Dracula Studies*, 4 (2002), pp. 1–9, at p. 3.

8. Carpenter (1874), pp. 217–19, 671; William Hughes, ' "So unlike the normal lunatic": Abnormal Psychology in Bram Stoker's *Dracula*', *University of Mississippi Studies in English*, 11/12 (1993–95), pp. 1–10, at pp. 2–4.

9. William Hughes, *Beyond Dracula: Bram Stoker's Fiction and its Cultural Context* (Basingstoke: Palgrave Macmillan, 2000), pp. 144–8.

10. David Glover, *Vampires, Mummies and Liberals: Bram Stoker and the Politics of Popular Fiction* (Durham, NC: Duke University Press, 1996), p. 77.

11. Glover (1996), p. 78.

12. Glover (1996), p. 79.

13. See, for example, Clare A. Simmons, 'Fables of Continuity: Bram Stoker and Medievalism', in William Hughes and Andrew Smith (eds), *Bram Stoker: History, Psychoanalysis and the Gothic* (Basingstoke: Macmillan, 1998), pp. 29–46, at pp. 29–30.

14. Glover (1996), pp. 79–80.

15. Greenway (2002), p. 2.

16. Compare here, Holmwood's hysteria following the staking of Lucy, expressed to, and arguably dispelled by, the reassuring maternal presence of Mina Harker (*Dracula*, p. 203). See also Hughes (2000), pp. 160–2.

17. Glover (1996), p. 80.

18. Victor Sage, *Horror Fiction in the Protestant Tradition* (Basingstoke: Macmillan, 1988), p. 51.

19. David Punter, *The Literature of Terror*, 2nd edn (London: Longman, 1996), 2 vols, Vol. 2, pp. 16–17.

20. Sage (1988), p. 51.

21. Michel Foucault, *The History of Sexuality: An Introduction* (1976; London: Penguin, 1984), p. 147.

22. Sage (1988), p. 52.

23. Foucault (1976), p. 147.

24. Punter (1996), Vol. 2, p. 21.

25. Foucault (1976), p. 147.

26. Carpenter (1874), pp. 385, 636–52.

27. David Hume Flood, 'Blood and Transfusion in Bram Stoker's *Dracula*', *University of Mississippi Studies in English*, New Series, 7 (1989), pp. 180–92, at p. 186.

28. Flood (1989), p. 186. See also C. F. Bentley, 'The Monster in the Bedroom: Sexual Symbolism in Bram Stoker's *Dracula*', *Literature and Psychology*, 22/1 (1972), pp. 27–33, at p. 29.

29. Marie Mulvey-Roberts, among other critics, considers the 'dubious medical opinion' expressed in *Dracula* that the blood of the male is superior to that of the female. See Marie Mulvey-Roberts, '*Dracula* and the Doctors: Bad Blood, Menstrual Taboo and the New Woman', in Hughes and Smith (1998), pp. 78–95, at p. 81.

30. See Hughes (2000), pp. 174–5.

31. Sage (1988), p. 56.

32. Compare here the cinematic portrayal of Lucy in Francis Ford Coppola's *Bram Stoker's Dracula* (1992), where she deliberately and self-consciously teases Quincey Morris by fondling his phallic bowie knife.

33. Mulvey-Roberts (1988), pp. 82, 86.

34. Mulvey-Roberts (1988), p. 86.

35. Mulvey-Roberts (1988), p. 80.

36. Hughes (2000), p. 150.

37. Phyllis Roth, *Bram Stoker* (Boston, MA: Twayne, 1982), p. 113; Elaine Showalter, *Sexual Anarchy: Gender and Culture at the Fin de Siècle* (London: Bloomsbury, 1991), pp. 180–1.

38. See Ben Barker-Benfield, 'The Spermatic Economy: A Nineteenth-Century View of Sexuality', *Feminist Studies*, 1 (1972), pp. 45–74.

39. Diane Mason, '"A very devil with the men": The Pathology and Iconography of the Erotic Consumptive and the Attractive Masturbator', *Gothic Studies*, 2/2 (2000), pp. 205–17, at pp. 209, 207, 210, 213.

40. Leila S. May, '"Foul things of the night": Dread in the Victorian Body', *Modern Language Review*, 93/1 (1998), pp. 16–22, at p. 16.

41. From Mayhew's *London Labour and the London Poor* (1861), Volume 1, quoted in May (1998), p. 18.

42. Quoted in May (1998), p. 17.

43. Oscar Wilde, *The Picture of Dorian Gray* (Harmondsworth: Penguin, 1985), pp. 164–5.

44. Mason (2000), p. 209; Hughes (2000), pp. 154–5.

45. Alan P. Johnson, ' "Dual Life": The Status of Women in Stoker's Dracula', *Tennessee Studies in Literature*, 27 (1984), pp. 20–39, at p. 27.

46. Elizabeth Lynn Linton, 'The Wild Women: No. 1. As Politicians', *The Nineteenth Century*, 30 (1891), pp. 79–88, at p. 79.

47. Glover (1996), p. 77.

48. It is true that Van Helsing expresses respect for the Count's achievements, undertaken alone (279) and over an immense period of time, but he declines to celebrate the vampire as a corporeally or intellectually superior being, for all his longevity and extraordinary powers: see William Hughes, ' "The Fighting Quality": Physiognomy, Masculinity and Degeneration in Bram Stoker's Later Fiction', in Andrew Smith, Diane Mason and William Hughes (eds), *Fictions of Unease: The Gothic from Otranto to The X-Files* (Bath: Sulis Press, 2002), pp. 119–31.

49. The Count fails in this latter aspiration, being seen immediately before his return to Transylvania in 'a hat of straw which suit not him or the time' (276).

50. The racial context, which is particularly shaped by Stoker's somewhat insistent anti-Semitism, is discussed in Chapter 3 of this Guide.

51. Reprinted, with modifications, as Leonard Wolf, *The Essential Dracula* (New York: Plume, 1993), p. 403.

52. Wolf (1993), p. 403.

53. Victor Sage is one of the few critics to exploit the possibilities of Nordau's *Degeneration* (1895), by connecting it with Harker's collapse into an 'abnegation of the will' when confronted by the three female vampires: see Sage (1988), pp. 184–5.

54. Cesare Lombroso-Ferrero, *Criminal Man* (1875), quoted in Sage (1988), p. 181.

55. Ernest Fontana, 'Lombroso's Criminal Man and Stoker's Dracula', *Victorian Newsletter*, 66 (Fall 1984), pp. 25–7, at pp. 25–6.

56. See Hughes (2002), pp. 119–20, 129.

57. *Manchester Guardian*, 15 June 1897, p. 9.

58. Fontana (1984), p. 25.

59. Daniel Pick adds to this domestic risk the threat of foreign – specifically Jewish – invasion and intermarriage. See ' "Terrors of the Night": *Dracula* and "Degeneration" in the Late Nineteenth Century', *Critical Quarterly*, 30/4 (1988), pp. 71–87, at p. 80.

60. Fontana (1984), p. 26.

61. See, for example, Johnson (1984), p. 26

62. Fontana (1984), p. 26.

63. The symptoms of epilepsy include, according to one contemporary popular medical work, a momentary pallor, possibly followed by 'a sudden cry or groan' after which 'the patient then falls down perfectly unconscious [...] convulsions come on at once [...] and consist of firm contraction or rigidity of the muscles. The face is terribly distorted and the tongue thrust out, the limbs twisted into strange positions, the breathing arrested, and the face becomes blue and swollen.' See 'A Medical Man' [pseud.], *Cassell's Family Doctor* (London: Cassell and Company, 1897), p. 530.

64. Fontana (1984), p. 26.

65. Fontana (1984), pp. 25, 27.

66. Fontana (1984), p. 27.

67. For an assessment of the cultural as well as medical implications of brain fever, see Elaine Hartnell, ' "Thoughts too long and too intensively fixed on one object": Fictional Representations of "Brain Fever" ', in Nickianne Moody and Julia Hallam (eds), *Medical Fictions* (Liverpool: MCCA, 1998), pp. 201–12, *passim*.

68. Fontana (1984), p. 27. Fontana draws explicitly here upon Mark M. Hennelly Jnr, 'Dracula: The Gnostic Quest and Victorian Wasteland', *English Literature in Transition*, 20 (1977), pp. 13–26, at p. 23.

69. The Count's nostrils, indeed, broaden in a manner reminiscent of Van Helsing's, when the vampire is interrupted within the Harkers' bedchamber (247).

70. Lombroso, quoted in Sage (1988), p. 182. Teratology is the study of animal or vegetable monstrosity.

71. Sage (1988), pp. 182–3.

72. Though Van Helsing and the Count 'do not make records and keep diaries' (Sage [1988], p. 183), the two do contribute to the original narrative, though their words have an ephemeral quality due to the loss of the original media following the Count's entry to the asylum. The Count contributes a letter to Harker, Van Helsing a letter, a telegram, a note and a memorandum, all directed to Seward, as well as an entry on the doctor's phonograph (12, 106–7, 130, 181, 313–18, 273–4), all of which become embedded within the narratives of others.

73. Sage (1988), p. 177; cf. Pick (1988), p. 76.

74. Robert Mighall, *A Geography of Victorian Gothic Fiction: Mapping History's Nightmares* (Oxford: Oxford University Press, 1999), pp. 208–9.

75. Mighall (1999), p. 211.

76. Mighall (1999), p. 226.

77. Mighall (1999), p. 226.

78. Mighall (1999), pp. 226–7.

79. Compare here the opinion of Daniel Pick (1988), p. 78.

80. Mighall (1999), p. 246.

81. Mighall (1999), p. 247.

82. Full publication details for these are given in Clive Leatherdale, *The Origins of Dracula* (London: William Kimber, 1987), pp. 237–9. The volume includes extracts from several works named in Stoker's working notes for *Dracula*.

3 Invasion and Empire: The Racial and Colonial Politics of *Dracula*

1. Jules Zanger, 'Dracula and the Jews: A Sympathetic Vibration', *English Literature in Transition*, 34/1 (1991), p. 40.

2. For a discussion of Stoker's interest in gentlemanly culture, see William Hughes, *Beyond Dracula: Bram Stoker's Fiction and its Cultural Context* (Basingstoke: Palgrave Macmillan, 2000), pp. 54–7.

3. The Count, indeed, contributes to the narrative directly only once, and that in the written form of a letter welcoming Harker to the Carpathians (12).

4. Branka Arsić, 'On the Dark Side of the Twilight', *Social Identities*, 7/4 (2001), pp. 551–71, at p. 551. Arsić's title is a misquotation of Jonathan Harker's recollection of his arrival at Bistritz (11).

5. See Terry Phillips, 'The Rules of War: Gothic Transgressions in First World War Fictions', *Gothic Studies*, 2/2 (2000), pp. 222–44, at pp. 240–1.

6. The potential symbolism of Lucy's apparently curious surname has preoccupied critics from time to time. Clive Leatherdale, for example, arguing that 'Possibly it is an amalgam of "the West" (being under attack from the East) and "Ra" (the pagan sun-god). Lucy, in other words, is meant to be the Light of the West'. Cannon Schmitt regards Lucy as one 'whose very name signals her place as bearer of occidental identity'. A more prosaic, though quite convincing explanation of Lucy's surname is that Stoker merely adapted to his own purposes a distinctively Irish patronymic which he may have encountered during his travels in rural Ireland. See Clive Leatherdale, *Dracula: The Novel and the Legend* (Wellingborough: Aquarian, 1985), p. 136; Cannon Schmitt, *Alien Nation: Nineteenth-Century Gothic Fictions*

and English Identity (Philadelphia: University of Pennsylvania Press, 1997), p. 143; Mark Pinkerton, 'Why Westenra?', in Leslie Shepard and Albert Power (eds), *Dracula: Celebrating 100 Years* (Dublin: Mentor, 1997), pp. 43–6.

7. Henry Mayhew, *London Labour and the London Poor* (London: Newbolt, n.d.), 4 vols, Vol. 1, pp. 1–2; Patricia McKee, 'Racialization, Capitalism, and Aesthetics in Stoker's *Dracula*', *Novel*, 36/1 (2002), pp. 42–60.

8. See Gustave Doré and Blanchard Jerrold, *London: A Pilgrimage* (1872; New York: Dover, 1970), pp. 122, 124; James Greenwood, 'A Night in a Workhouse' (1866) in Peter Keating (ed.), *Into Unknown England 1866–1913: Selections from the Social Explorers* (London: Fontana, 1981), pp. 31–54, at pp. 40, 46.

9. One might note, also, here the readiness with which the professional classes in *Dracula* – solicitors and estate agents (79, 239), most notably – respond to the Count's proffered wealth. Those members of the bourgeoisie who do not enjoy independent means, it would appear, share the vulnerability of the proletariat.

10. Carol Senf, '*Dracula*: The Unseen Face in the Mirror', *Journal of Narrative Technique*, 9 (1979), pp. 160–70, at p. 164. The crucial scene in Stoker's novel is, of course, Harker's comprehension of the vampire's reasons for travelling to London (53–4).

11. Judith Wilt, *Ghosts of the Gothic: Austen, Eliot, and Lawrence* (Princeton: Princeton University Press, 1980), p. 92.

12. Patrick Brantlinger, *Rule of Darkness: British Literature and Imperialism, 1830–1914* (Ithaca, NY: Cornell University Press, 1988), pp. 227–53. Brantlinger briefly discusses *Dracula* as a 'demonic invasion' on pp. 233–4.

13. Stephen D. Arata, 'The Occidental Tourist: *Dracula* and the Anxiety of Reverse Colonization', *Victorian Studies*, 33 (1990), pp. 621–45, at p. 622.

14. Arata (1990), p. 623.

15. Arata (1990), p. 624; George Chesney, *The Battle of Dorking: Reminiscences of a Volunteer*, reprinted with Saki, *When William Came* (Oxford: Oxford University Press, 1997), p. 3. For further narratives of this type, see I. F. Clarke (ed.), *The Tale of the Next Great War, 1870–1914* (Liverpool: Liverpool University Press, 1995).

16. Arata (1990), p. 623.

17. Arata (1990), p. 623.

18. Arata (1990), p. 634..

19. David Glover, *Vampires, Mummies, and Liberals: Bram Stoker and the Politics of Popular Fiction* (Durham, NC: Duke University Press, 1996), pp. 12–13.

20. Glover (1996), pp. 50–1.

21. Rudyard Kipling, 'The Mark of the Beast', in Rudyard Kipling, *Strange Tales* (Ware: Wordsworth, 2006), pp. 3–25, at pp. 4–5, 9. Notably, Fleete's settler colleagues, who perform the exorcism that releases him from the curse put upon him by the Indian leper, consider themselves to have 'disgraced ourselves as Englishmen forever' (14). The very act of combating an invasive foreign or deviant threat brings with it the risk of compromise and contamination.

22. Rhys Garnett, '*Dracula* and *The Beetle*: Imperial and Sexual Guilt and Fear in Late-Victorian Fantasy', in Rhys Garnett and R. J. Ellis (eds), *Science Fiction Roots and Branches: Contemporary Critical Approaches* (New York: St Martin's Press, 1990), pp. 30–54.

23. Arata (1990), p. 624.

24. Arata (1990), p. 628.

25. Ludmilla Kostova, 'Straining the Limits of Interpretation: Bram Stoker's *Dracula* and its Eastern European Contexts', in John Bak (ed.), *Post/Modern Dracula: From Victorian Themes to Postmodern Praxis* (Newcastle: Cambridge Scholars Publishing, 2007), pp. 13–30, at pp. 15–16.

26. Arata (1990), p. 629.

27. Arata (1990), p. 630.

28. Arata (1990), p. 631. Arata is inaccurate here with regard to Stoker's precise source. Stoker's manuscript notes to *Dracula*, now preserved at the Rosenbach Museum and Library

in Philadelphia, refer to Gerard's 'Transylvanian Superstitions', *The Nineteenth Century*, (July 1885), pp. 130–50, rather than the two-volume work cited by Arata.

29. Jules Zanger, 'Dracula and the Jews: A Sympathetic Vibration', *English Literature in Transition*, 34/1 (1991), pp. 32–43, at p. 34.

30. Zanger (1991), pp. 34, 36.

31. Bram Stoker, *The Man* (London: Heinemann, 1905), p. 226. This phrase has been excised from the abridged reprint of *The Man* (*c*.2001), published by Wildside Press.

32. Nina Auerbach, *Woman and the Demon: The Life of a Victorian Myth* (Cambridge, MA: Harvard University Press, 1982), p. 16.

33. Zanger (1991), pp. 37–8.

34. Carol Margaret Davison, *Anti-Semitism and British Gothic Literature* (Basingstoke: Palgrave, 2004), p. 126. The further implications of 'Host' as a religious and military term are explored on p. 136.

35. Davison (2004), pp. 120–1; Harry Ludlam, *A Biography of Dracula: The Life Story of Bram Stoker* (London: Foulsham, 1962), p. 97.

36. Davison (2004), p. 128.

37. Zanger (1991), p. 35.

38. Davison (2004), p. 135.

39. Davison (2004), p. 136.

40. Davison (2004), p. 134.

41. Davison (2004), pp. 121–5; Zanger (1991), pp. 34–6.

42. Schmitt (1997), p. 141.

43. Davison (2004), pp. 123–4.

44. Davison (2004), p. 143.

45. Davison (2004), p. 144.

46. Sigmund Freud, 'The Uncanny' (1919), trans. James Strachey, reprinted in Victor Sage (ed.) *The Gothick Novel: A Selection of Critical Essays* (Basingstoke: Macmillan, 1990), pp. 76–87, at p. 78.

47. Emily Gerard, 'Transylvanian Superstitions' (1885), reprinted in Elizabeth Miller (ed.), *Bram Stoker's Dracula: A Documentary Volume* (Detroit: Thomson Gale, 2005), pp. 182–6, at p. 182.

48. Vesna Goldsworthy, *Inventing Ruritania: The Imperialism of the Imagination* (New Haven, CT: Yale University Press, 1998), p. 78.

49. Goldsworthy (1998), p. 77.

50. Goldsworthy (1998), p. 79.

51. Goldsworthy (1998), p. 79.

52. Goldsworthy (1998), p. 80.

53. Goldsworthy (1998), p. 79.

54. Goldsworthy (1998), p. 79.

55. Goldsworthy (1998), p. 80.

56. Goldsworthy (1998), p. 81.

57. Attempts to link Stoker's Count to Vlad Ţepeş recur sporadically in the criticism of *Dracula*, the earliest identifications between the two by Bacil Kirtley (1958), Harry Ludlam (1962) and Raymond McNally and Radu Florescu (1972) being rebuffed in particular by Elizabeth Miller. See Elizabeth Miller, 'Filing for Divorce: Count Dracula vs Vlad Tepes [*sic*]', in Elizabeth Miller (ed.), *Dracula: The Shade and the Shadow* (Westcliff-on-Sea: Desert Island Books, 1998), pp. 165–77.

58. Goldsworthy (1998), p. 82.

59. Goldsworthy (1998), p. 83.

60. Goldsworthy (1998), p. 84.

61. Goldsworthy (1998), p. 84.

62. Eleni Coundouriotis, '*Dracula* and the Idea of Europe', *Connotations*, 9/2 (1999–2000), pp. 143–59, at p. 144.

63. Coundouriotis (1999–2000), p. 154.

64. Matthew Gibson, *Dracula and the Eastern Question: British and French Vampire Narratives of the Nineteenth-Century Near East* (Basingstoke: Palgrave, 2006), p. 74.

65. Gibson (2006), p. 74.

66. Peter Haining and Peter Tremayne, *The Un-Dead: The Legend of Bram Stoker and Dracula* (London: Constable, 1997), p. 116.

67. Quoted in Haining and Tremayne (1997), p. 117. Haining and Tremayne's work is gratifyingly detailed but rather deficient in referencing, and these quotations, which probably have their origins in George Stoker's autobiographical work *With 'The Unspeakables'* (1878), are unattributed. Gibson is considerably more precise in his deployment of similar quotations from George Stoker's work: see Gibson (2006), p. 79.

68. Gibson (2006), pp. 74–5.

69. Quoted in Haining and Tremayne (1997), p. 117.

70. Gibson (2006), p. 81.

71. Gibson (2006), p. 82.

72. Gibson (2006), p. 82.

73. Gibson (2006), p. 83.

74. Bram Stoker, *A Glimpse of America*, in Richard Dalby (ed.), *A Glimpse of America and Other Lectures, Interviews and Essays* (Westcliff-on Sea: Desert Island Books, 2002), pp. 11–30, at p. 30.

75. See Hughes (2000), pp. 94–6.

76. Franco Moretti, *Signs Taken for Wonders: Essays in the Sociology of Literary Forms* (London: Verso, 1983), pp. 83–98. Anthologised as 'Dracula and Capitalism' in Glennis Byron (ed.), *Dracula: Contemporary Critical Essays* (Basingstoke: Macmillan, 1999), pp. 43–54, at p. 45. All subsequent references to *Signs Taken for Wonders* are taken from Byron's critical anthology.

77. Moretti (1983), p. 45.

78. Moretti (1983), p. 46.

79. Moretti (1983), p. 47.

80. Moretti (1983), p. 49.

81. Moretti (1983), p. 49.

82. Moretti (1983), p. 50.

83. Moretti (1983), pp. 50, 48, 54, n. 12.

84. Andrew Smith, 'Demonising the Americans: Bram Stoker's Postcolonial Gothic', *Gothic Studies*, 5/2 (2003), pp. 20–31, at pp. 21, 22.

85. See, for example, Nicholas Daly, *Modernism, Romance and the Fin de Siècle* (Cambridge: Cambridge University Press, 1999), p. 78; Hughes (2000), *Beyond Dracula*, pp. 64–6.

86. Smith (2003), p. 22.

87. Smith (2003), p. 23.

88. Smith (2003), p. 24.

89. Smith (2003), p. 29.

90. Bram Stoker, *The Lady of the Shroud* (Westcliff-on-Sea: Desert Island Books, 2001), p. 352.

4 Landlords and Disputed Territories:
Dracula and Irish Studies

1. Joseph Valente, *Dracula's Crypt* (Urbana: University of Illinois Press, 2002), p. 1.

2. W. J. McCormack, 'Irish Gothic and After (1820–1945)', in *The Field Day Anthology of Irish Writing*, Vol. 2, ed. Seamus Deane (Londonderry: Field Day Publications, 1991), pp. 831–54, at pp. 833, 831.

3. McCormack (1991), p. 833.

4. McCormack (1991), pp. 832, 840, 831.

5. McCormack (1991), pp. 842, 843.

6. McCormack (1991), pp. 843, 840. According to McCormack, 'Le Fanu depended for his income on London publishers': see W. J. McCormack, *Sheridan Le Fanu* (Stroud: Sutton, 1997), p. 200.

7. McCormack (1991), p. 842.

8. McCormack (1991), p. 842.

9. McCormack (1991), p. 833.

10. McCormack (1991), p. 833.

11. See Bram Stoker, *Personal Reminiscences of Henry Irving* (London: William Heinemann, 1906), 2 vols, Vol. 1, p. 343; Paul Murray, *From the Shadow of Dracula* (London: Jonathan Cape, 2004), p. 139; David Glover, *Vampires, Mummies, and Liberals* (Durham, NC: Duke University Press, 1996), pp. 12, 28–9.

12. See William Hughes, '"For Ireland's Good": The Reconstruction of Rural Ireland in Bram Stoker's *The Snake's Pass*', *Irish Studies Review*, No. 12 (Autumn 1995), pp. 17–21; and '"Introducing Patrick to his New Self": Bram Stoker and the 1907 Dublin Exhibition', *Irish Studies Review*, No. 19 (Summer 1997), pp. 9–14.

13. McCormack (1991), pp. 833, 842.

14. McCormack (1991), p. 845.

15. Julian Moynahan, *Anglo-Irish* (Princeton: Princeton University Press, 1995), p. 3.

16. Valente (2002), p. 15.

17. Quoted in Harry Ludlam, *A Biography of Dracula* (London: Foulsham 1962), p. 41.

18. Murray (2004), p. 45.

19. Horace Wyndham, quoted in Glover (1996), p. 26; Barbara Belford, *Bram Stoker* (London: Weidenfeld & Nicolson, 1996), p. 99.

20. Valente (2002), p. 38.

21. Murray (2004), pp. 20–1.

22. Valente (2002), p. 16.

23. Peter Haining and Peter Tremayne, *The Un-Dead* (London: Constable, 1997), p. 12.

24. Roy Foster, *Paddy and Mr Punch* (London: Penguin, 1995), p. 213.

25. Glover (1996), p. 25.

26. Stoker was himself an *Irish* churchman – a member of the Anglican Church in Ireland, and as such familiar with the generally Protestant tenor of its *Prayer Book* liturgy.

27. Victor Sage, *Horror Fiction in the Protestant Tradition* (Basingstoke: Macmillan, 1988), p. 51

28. Patrick R. O'Malley, *Catholicism, Sexual Deviance, and Victorian Gothic Culture* (Cambridge: Cambridge University Press, 2006), pp. 130–1.

29. Sage (1988), p. 51.

30. The Catholic doctrine whereby non-adherents to the Roman faith were *ipso facto* damned is a frequent topic in the Protestant polemic of the nineteenth century: see, for example, R. P. Blakeney, *A Manual of Romish Controversy* (Edinburgh: The Hope Trust, n.d. [1851]), p. 240.

31. 'Of Purgatory', Article 22 of the Church of England, *The Book of Common Prayer* (London: SPCK, n.d.), p. 581.

32. 'The thin end of the wedge' is the title of an evocative cartoon attack on the re-introduction of Roman Catholic archbishoprics to England in 1850. See *Punch*, 19 (July–December 1850), p. 207; reprinted in Sage (1988), Plate 7, between pp. 138–9.

33. Foster (1995), p. 221.

34. Foster (1995), p. 220.

35. Foster (1995), pp. 221, 220.

36. Terry Eagleton, *Heathcliff and the Great Hunger* (London: Verso, 1995), p. 187.

37. Eagleton admits he has adapted Jameson's *The Political Unconscious* (1981) 'somewhat freely' in *Heathcliff and the Great Hunger*, though he does take time to explain his adaptation at the outset of his analysis. See Eagleton (1995), pp. 187–8.

38. Eagleton (1995), p. 187.

39. Foster (1995), p. 220; Eagleton (1995), p. 189.

40. Eagleton (1995), pp. 189–90.
41. Eagleton (1995), p. 190.
42. Eagleton (1995), p. 216.
43. Jeremy Hawthorn, *A Glossary of Contemporary Literary Theory* (London: Arnold, 2003), p. 199.
44. Eagleton (1995), p. 215.
45. Eagleton (1995), p. 215.
46. Eagleton (1995), p. 194.
47. Seamus Deane, *Strange Country* (Oxford: Clarendon Press, 1998), p. 90.
48. Deane (1998), p. 90.
49. Declan Kiberd, *Irish Classics* (London: Granta, 2001), p. 394; Anon., 'The English Vampire', *The Irish Pilot*, 7 November 1885, and John Tenniel, 'The Irish Vampire', *Punch*, 7 November 1885, reprinted in Murray (2004), between pp. 180–1.
50. Stoker (1906), Vol. 2 pp. 26–33; Murray (2004), pp. 138–9.
51. Michael Valdez Moses, 'The Irish Vampire: *Dracula*, Parnell, and the Troubled Dreams of Nationhood', *Journal X*, 2/1 (1997), pp. 66–111, at p. 68. Among these 'originals', Moses lists 'Sir Henry Irving, Sir Richard Burton, Henry Morton Stanley, Franz Liszt [1811–1886], Jacques Damala [...] Oscar Wilde, Sir William Wilde, Walt Whitman [...] and Vlad the Impaler'.
52. Moses (1997), p. 68.
53. Moses (1997), p. 69.
54. Moses (1997), pp. 74–5.
55. Moses (1997), p. 76.
56. Stoker (1906), Vol. 2, p. 31.
57. Moses (1997), p. 83.
58. Moses (1997), p. 84.
59. Moses (1997), pp. 83–4.
60. Moses (1997), p. 103.
61. Bruce Stewart, 'Bram Stoker's *Dracula*: Possessed by the Spirit of the Nation?', in Bruce Stewart (ed.), *That Other World: The Supernatural and the Fantastic in Irish Literature and its Contexts* (Gerrards Cross: Colin Smythe, 1998), 2 vols, Vol. 2, pp. 65–83, at p. 77.
62. Bram Stoker, *The Snake's Pass* (Dingle: Brandon, 1990), p. 26. Stewart (1998) reprints this passage, with a misprint, on p. 77.
63. Stewart (1998), p. 77.
64. Stewart (1998), pp. 79, 80.
65. Valente (2002), p. 85.
66. See William Hughes, ' "For the Blood is the Life": The Construction of Purity in Bram Stoker's *Dracula*', in Tracey Hill (ed.), *Decadence and Danger: Writing, History and the Fin de Siècle* (Bath: Sulis Press, 1997), pp. 128–37, at p. 135.
67. Valente (2002), p. 4.
68. Valente (2002), p. 16; Haining and Tremayne (1997), p. 44.
69. Valente (2002), p. 16.
70. Valente (2002), p. 16. This 'popular position' is that adopted by David Glover, Chris Morash, Canon Schmitt and Daniel Pick: see Valente (2002), p. 151, n. 3.
71. See William Hughes, ' "The Fighting Quality": Physiognomy, Masculinity and Degeneration in Bram Stoker's Later Fiction', in Andrew Smith, Diane Mason and William Hughes (eds), *Fictions of Unease: The Gothic from Otranto to The X-Files* (Bath: Sulis Press, 2002), pp. 119–31.
72. Valente (2002), p. 4.
73. Valente (2002), p. 39.
74. David Punter, *The Literature of Terror* (London: Longman, 1996), 2 vols, Vol. 2., pp. 16–17; Sage (1988), p. 52; William Hughes, *Beyond Dracula: Bram Stoker's Fiction and its Cultural Context* (Basingstoke: Palgrave Macmillan, 2000), pp. 139–40.

75. Valente (2002), p. 66.
76. Valente (2002), pp. 55–6, 59–61, 58–9.
77. Valente (2002), p. 141.
78. Valente (2002), p. 141.
79. Michel Foucault, *The History of Sexuality: An Introduction* (London: Penguin, 1984), pp. 147–8.
80. Valente (2002), pp. 141–2.
81. Bram Stoker, *The Lady of the Shroud* (Westcliff-on-Sea: Desert Island Books, 2001), pp. 328–9, 336–7.
82. Valente (2002), p. 142.

5 Assertive Women and Gay Men: Gender Studies and *Dracula*

1. Clive Leatherdale, *Dracula: The Novel and the Legend*, 3rd edn (Westcliff-on-Sea: Desert Island Books, 2001), p. 151. Leatherdale cites only Phyllis Roth, *Bram Stoker* (Boston: Twayne, 1982), p. 102, in support of his contention: complementary readings may be found in Robert Frost, 'Virgins and Vampires', *The English Review*, 13 (2002), pp. 27–9, at p. 29; and Mark Hennelly, 'Twice-Told Tales of Two Counts: *The Woman in White* and *Dracula*', *Wilkie Collins Society Journal*, 2 (1982), pp. 15–31, at p. 22.
2. Robert Mighall, notably, takes issue with the unequivocal acceptance of Lucy's 'voluptuous' tendencies, and suggests that her description in *Dracula* stems largely from Seward's own medical interests: see Robert Mighall, *Victorian Gothic: Mapping History's Nightmares* (Oxford: Oxford University Press, 1999), pp. 232–3.
3. Leatherdale (2001), p. 152.
4. See, for example, Carol Senf, '*Dracula*: Stoker's Response to the New Woman', *Victorian Studies*, 26/1 (1982), pp. 33–49, at pp. 37–8.
5. Michel Foucault, *The History of Sexuality: An Introduction* (1976; London: Penguin, 1984), pp. 3–4, 6–7, 21, 33.
6. Alan P. Johnson, '"Dual Life": The Status of Women in Stoker's *Dracula*', *Tennessee Studies in Literature*, 27 (1984), pp. 20–39, at p. 21.
7. Johnson (1984), p. 26.
8. Indeed, Johnson's access to Laycock's *Treatise on the Nervous Diseases of Women* (1840) comes not directly, but via a footnote to Leonard Wolf's 1975 *Annotated Dracula*. See David Glover, *Vampires, Mummies, and Liberals: Bram Stoker and the Politics of Popular Fiction* (Durham, NC: Duke University Press, 1996), pp. 76–8; William Hughes, *Beyond Dracula: Bram Stoker's Fiction and its Cultural Contexts* (Basingstoke: Palgrave Macmillan, 2000), pp. 142–3.
9. Johnson (1984), pp. 24, 37, n. 9; William Hughes, 'Habituation and Incarceration: Mental Physiology and Asylum Abuse in *The Woman in White* and *Dracula*', in Andrew Mangham (ed.), *Wilkie Collins: Interdisciplinary Essays* (Newcastle: Cambridge Scholars Publishing, 2007), pp. 136–48.
10. Carol A. Senf, *Dracula: Between Tradition and Modernism* (New York: Twayne, 1998), p. 52.
11. Burton Hatlen, 'The Return of the Repressed/Oppressed in Bram Stoker's *Dracula*', in Margaret L. Carter (ed.), *Dracula: The Vampire and the Critics* (Ann Arbor, MI: UMI Research Press, 1988), pp. 117–35 at p. 123; Hughes (2000), p. 146.
12. Senf (1998), pp. 52–3.
13. M. G. Lewis, *The Monk* (Peterborough: Broadview, 2004), p. 230; Bram Stoker, *The Man* (London: Heinemann, 1905), pp. 83–4.
14. Phyllis A. Roth, 'Suddenly Sexual Women in Bram Stoker's *Dracula*', *Literature and Psychology*, 27 (1977), pp. 113–21, at p. 115.
15. See, for example, C. F. Bentley, 'The Monster in the Bedroom: Sexual Symbolism in Bram Stoker's *Dracula*', *Literature and Psychology*, 22 (1972), pp. 27–33, at p. 31; Victor Sage, '*Dracula* and the Codes of Victorian Pornography', in Gilles Menegaldo and Dominique Sipière (eds), *Dracula: Stoker/Coppola* (Paris: Ellipses, 2005), pp. 55–69, at p. 66.

16. Nina Auerbach, however, argues persuasively that Lucy's active vampirism may well be associated with a monogamous interest in her still-living fiancé: see *Our Vampires, Ourselves* (Chicago: University of Chicago Press, 1995), pp. 79–80.

17. David Punter and Glennis Byron, *The Gothic* (Oxford: Blackwell, 2004), p. 233.

18. Compare here Clive Leatherdale's assessment of Lucy as 'a woman/angel violated by the devil': Leatherdale (2001), p. 150.

19. Christopher Craft, '"Kiss me with those red lips": Gender and Inversion in Bram Stoker's *Dracula*', *Representations*, 8 (1984), pp. 107–33, at p. 120.

20. Catherine Lanone, 'Bram Stoker's *Dracula*, or Femininity as a Forsaken Fairy Tale', in Menegaldo and Sipière (2005), pp. 199–206, at p. 203.

21. Roth (1977), p. 116.

22. Roth (1977), p. 117. Stoker arguably enacts a similar equivocation between identification with a more conventional sexual predator and his chivalric counterpart in *The Mystery of the Sea* (1902). See Hughes (2000), pp. 108–12.

23. Roth (1977), p. 117.

24. Senf (1998), p. 53.

25. Roth (1977), p. 118; cf. Leatherdale (2001), pp. 146, 151.

26. Senf (1998), p. 55.

27. See, for example, Sally Ledger, *The New Woman: Fiction and Feminism at the Fin de Siècle* (Manchester: Manchester University Press, 1997), pp. 9–31, *passim*.

28. Lyn Pykett, *The Improper Feminine: The Women's Sensation Novel and the New Woman Writing* (London: Routledge, 1992), p. 139.

29. Pykett (1992), p. 138.

30. Ledger (1997), p. 11.

31. Matthew C. Brennan, 'Repression, Knowledge, and Saving Souls: The Role of the "New Woman" in Stoker's *Dracula* and Murnau's *Nosferatu*', *Studies in the Humanities*, 19 (1992), pp. 1–10, at p. 4.

32. Carol A. Senf, '*Dracula*: Stoker's Response to the New Woman', *Victorian Studies*, 26/1 (1982), pp. 33–49, at p. 35.

33. Brennan (1992), p. 1.

34. Ledger (1997), p. 102.

35. Senf (1982), p. 36.

36. Senf (1982), p. 37.

37. Pykett (1992), pp. 139, 140.

38. Ledger (1997), p. 104.

39. Ledger (1997), p. 105.

40. Ledger (1997), p. 106; cf. Senf (1982), p. 34.

41. Brennan (1992), p. 4.

42. For a reading of the conventional masculinities of *Dracula*, see Leatherdale (2001), p. 131. Sos Eltis, by contrast, augments the conventional masculine signification with ambiguous, though apparently manly, expressions of emotion: see 'Corruption of the Blood and Degeneration of the Race: *Dracula* and Policing the Borders of Gender', in John Paul Riquelme (ed.), Dracula *by Bram Stoker* (Boston: Bedford/St Martin's, 2002), pp. 450–65, at pp. 458–9.

43. Craft (1984), p. 117.

44. Craft (1984), p. 109. Craft's depiction of the inviting mouth of the Count appears to overlook Harker's own observations regarding its cruelty and the 'rank' (23–4) breath it exhales.

45. Craft (1984), pp. 109–10.

46. See Alan Sinfield, *The Wilde Century: Effeminacy, Oscar Wilde and the Queer Movement* (London: Cassell, 1994), pp. 1–3.

47. Craft (1984), p. 110.

48. Craft (1984), pp. 121, 122.

49. Craft (1984), p. 124.

50. Craft (1984), p. 108.

51. Daniel Farson, *The Man Who Wrote Dracula: A Biography of Bram Stoker* (London: Michael Joseph, 1975), pp. 233–4; –, 'The Sexual Torment of the Man Who Created Dracula', *The Mail on Sunday*, 3 January 1993, pp. 35–6.

52. Talia Schaffer, '"A Wilde Desire Took Me": The Homoerotic History of *Dracula*', *ELH*, 61 (1994), pp. 381–425, at p. 381.

53. Auerbach (1995), p. 84.

54. Schaffer (1994), p. 381.

55. See, for example, Bram Stoker, 'The Censorship of Stage Plays', *The Nineteenth Century*, 66 (1909), 974–89, at pp. 984–5.

56. Schaffer (1994), pp. 381–2.

57. See, for example, the rather awkward attempt to link an incident in Wilde's homosexual life with the death of the sailors on the Demeter (Schaffer [1994], p. 406), as well as the insistent punning upon the word 'wild' (Schaffer [1994], pp. 401, 420).

58. Auerbach (1995), p. 67. For a more hostile view of the relationship, see Laurence Irving, *Henry Irving: The Actor and His World* (London: Columbus Books, 1989), p. 453.

59. Schaffer (1994), p. 386.

60. Schaffer (1994), p. 387.

61. Schaffer (1994), p. 398.

62. Schaffer (1994), p. 388.

63. Schaffer (1994), pp. 401–2

64. Schaffer (1994), p. 405.

65. Schaffer (1994), pp. 402, 397.

Conclusion

1. A. N. Wilson, 'Introduction' to *Dracula*, by Bram Stoker (Oxford: Oxford University Press, 1983), pp. vi–xix, at p. x.

2. Wilson (1983), p. xiv.

3. Wilson (1983), pp. xiv, vii.

4. Wilson (1983), p. xiv. It is perhaps pertinent to observe at this juncture that Wilson's Introduction no longer prefaces the current Oxford World's Classics *Dracula*, having disappeared with the edition's final reprint in 1991. The current edition is edited, with an Introduction and notes, by the Cambridge academic Maud Ellmann.

5. Wilson (1983), pp. xix, xvi.

6. Wilson (1983), pp. xvi, xvii.

7. Carol A. Senf, '*Dracula*: Stoker's Response to the New Woman', *Victorian Studies*, 26/1 (1982), pp. 33–49 at p. 47.

8. Senf (1982), p. 47.

9. Andrew Maunder, *Bram Stoker* (Tavistock: Northcote House, 2007); Lisa Hopkins, *Bram Stoker: A Literary Life* (Basingstoke: Palgrave, 2007); Phyllis Roth, *Bram Stoker* (Boston: Twayne, 1982).

Bibliography

CRITICAL EDITIONS OF STOKER'S WORKS

Auerbach, Nina and David J. Skal (eds), *Dracula* (New York: Norton, 1997).

Byron, Glennis (ed.), *Dracula* (Peterborough: Broadview, 1998).

Dalby, Richard (ed.), *A Glimpse of America and Other Lectures, Interviews and Essays* (Westcliff-on-Sea: Desert Island Books, 2002).

Ellmann, Maud (ed.), *Dracula* (Oxford: Oxford University Press, 1998).

Hindle, Maurice (ed.), *Dracula* (London: Penguin, 1993).

Hughes, William (ed.), *The Lady of the Shroud* (Westcliff-on-Sea: Desert Island Books, 2001).

Hughes, William and Diane Mason (eds), *Dracula* (Bath: Artswork Books, 2007).

Leatherdale, Clive (ed.), *Dracula Unearthed* (Westcliff-on-Sea: Desert Island Books, 1998).

Leatherdale, Clive (ed.), *The Jewel of Seven Stars* (Westcliff-on-Sea: Desert Island Books, 1996).

Riquelme, John Paul (ed.), *Dracula* (Boston: Bedford/St Martin's, 2002).

Stoker, Bram, *Personal Reminiscences of Henry Irving* (London: William Heinemann, 1906), 2 vols.

Stoker, Bram, 'The Censorship of Stage Plays', *The Nineteenth Century*, 66 (1909), pp. 974–89.

Stoker, Bram, *The Man* (London: Heinemann, 1905).

Stoker, Bram, *The Snake's Pass* (Dingle: Brandon, 1990).

Wilson, A. N. (ed.), *Dracula* (Oxford: Oxford University Press, 1983).

Wolf, Leonard (ed.) *The Essential Dracula* (New York: Plume, 1993).

BIOGRAPHIES

Anon, 'Obituary: Mr Bram Stoker', *The Times*, 22 April 1912, p. 15.

Belford, Barbara, *Bram Stoker: A Biography of the Author of Dracula* (London: Weidenfeld & Nicolson, 1996).

Caine, Hall, 'Bram Stoker: The Story of a Great Friendship', *Daily Telegraph*, 24 April 1912, p. 16.

Drummond, James, 'Bram Stoker's Cruden Bay', *The Scots' Magazine* (April 1976), pp. 23–8.

Farson, Daniel, *The Man Who Wrote Dracula: A Biography of Bram Stoker* (London: Michael Joseph, 1975).

Farson, Daniel, 'The Sexual Torment of the Man Who Created Dracula', *The Mail on Sunday*, 3 January 1993, pp. 35–6.

Haining, Peter and Peter Tremayne, *The Un-Dead: The Legend of Bram Stoker and Dracula* (London: Constable, 1997).

Irving, Laurence, *Henry Irving: The Actor and His World* (London: Columbus, Books, 1989).

Ludlam, Harry, *A Biography of Dracula: The Life Story of Bram Stoker* (London: Foulsham, 1962).

Murray, Paul, *From the Shadow of Dracula: A Life of Bram Stoker* (London: Jonathan Cape, 2004).

Osborough, W. N., 'The Dublin Castle Career (1866–78) of Bram Stoker', *Gothic Studies*, 1/2 (1999), pp. 222–40.

Shepard, Leslie, 'The Library of Bram Stoker', *The Bram Stoker Society Journal*, 4 (1992), pp. 28–34.

Shepard, Leslie, 'A Note on the Death Certificate of Bram Stoker', in Leslie Shepard and Albert Power (eds), *Dracula: Celebrating 100 Years* (Dublin: Mentor Press, 1997) pp. 178–80.

Shepard, Leslie, 'The Stoker Family on the Move: The Changes of Address and Travels of the Stokers', *The Bram Stoker Society Journal*, 10 (1998), pp. 30–5.

Traubel, Horace, *With Walt Whitman in Camden: January 21 to April 7, 1889* (Philadelphia: University of Pennsylvania Press, 1953).

GENERAL STUDIES

Bak, John (ed.), *Post/Modern Dracula: From Victorian Themes to Postmodern Praxis* (Newcastle: Cambridge Scholars Publishing, 2007).

Bierman, Joseph S., 'The Genesis and Dating of *Dracula* from Bram Stoker's Working Notes', *Notes and Queries*, 222 (1977), pp. 39–41.

Byron, Glennis (ed.), *Dracula: Contemporary Critical Essays* (Basingstoke: Macmillan, 1999).

Carter, Margaret L. (ed.), *Dracula: The Vampire and the Critics* (Ann Arbor: UMI Research Press, 1988).

Dalby, Richard and William Hughes, *Bram Stoker: A Bibliography* (Westcliff-on-Sea: Desert Island Books, 2004).

Daly, Nicholas, *Modernism, Romance and the Fin de Siècle* (Cambridge: Cambridge University Press, 1999).

Duperray, Max and Dominique Sipière (eds), *Dracula: Bram Stoker et Francis Ford Coppola* (Paris: Armand Colin, 2005).

Frayling, Christopher (ed.), *Vampires: Lord Byron to Count Dracula* (London: Faber & Faber, 1991).

Glover, David, *Vampires, Mummies, and Liberals: Bram Stoker and the Politics of Popular Fiction* (Durham, NC: Duke University Press, 1996).

Hall, Jasmine Y., 'Solicitors Soliciting: The Dangerous Circulations of Professionalism in *Dracula*', in Barbara Leah Harman and Susan Meyer (eds), *The New Nineteenth Century: Feminist Readings of Underread Victorian Fiction* (New York: Garland, 1996), pp. 99–116.

Hennelly, Mark M., Jnr, '*Dracula*: The Gnostic Quest and Victorian Wasteland', *English Literature in Transition*, 20 (1977), pp. 13–26.

Hennelly, Mark M., Jnr, 'Twice-Told Tales of Two Counts: *The Woman in White* and *Dracula*', *Wilkie Collins Society Journal*, 2 (1982), pp. 15–31.

Hogle, Jerrold E. (ed.), *The Cambridge Companion to Gothic Fiction* (Cambridge: Cambridge University Press, 2002).

Hopkins, Lisa, *Bram Stoker: A Literary Life* (Basingstoke: Palgrave, 2007).

Hughes, William, *Beyond Dracula: Bram Stoker's Fiction and its Cultural Contexts* (Basingstoke: Palgrave Macmillan, 2000).

Hughes, William, ' "For the Blood is the Life": The Construction of Purity in Bram Stoker's *Dracula*', in Tracey Hill (ed.), *Decadence and Danger: Writing, History and the Fin de Siècle* (Bath: Sulis Press, 1997), pp. 128–37.

Leatherdale, Clive, *Dracula: The Novel and the Legend* (Wellingborough: Aquarian Press, 1985).

Leatherdale, Clive, *Dracula: The Novel and the Legend*, 3rd edn (Westcliff-on-Sea: Desert Island Books, 2001).

Leatherdale, Clive, *The Origins of Dracula* (London: William Kimber, 1987).

MacGillivray, Royce, '*Dracula*: Bram Stoker's Spoiled Masterpiece', *Queen's Quarterly*, 79 (1972), pp. 518–27.

Maunder, Andrew, *Bram Stoker* (Tavistock: Northcote House, 2007).

May, Leila S., ' "Foul things of the night": Dread in the Victorian Body', *Modern Language Review*, 93/1 (1998), pp. 16–22.

McNally, Raymond T. and Radu Florescu, *In Search of Dracula: A True History of Dracula and Vampire Legends* (London: Book Club Associates, 1979).

Menegaldo, Gilles, and Dominique Sipière (eds), *Dracula: Stoker/Coppola* (Paris: Ellipses, 2005).

Mighall, Robert, *A Geography of Victorian Gothic Fiction: Mapping History's Nightmares* (Oxford: Oxford University Press, 1999).

Miller, Elizabeth (ed.), *Dracula: The Shade and the Shadow* (Westcliff-on-Sea: Desert Island Books, 1998).

Miller, Elizabeth, 'Filing for Divorce: Count Dracula vs Vlad Tepes' in *Dracula: The Shade and the Shadow*, ed. Elizabeth Miller (Westcliff-on-Sea: Desert Island Books, 1998), pp. 166–79.

Miller, Elizabeth, *Dracula: Sense and Nonsense* (Westcliff-on-Sea: Desert Island Books, 2000).

Miller, Elizabeth (ed.), *Bram Stoker's Dracula: A Documentary Volume* (Detroit: Thomson Gale, 2005).

Moretti, Franco, *Signs Taken for Wonders: Essays in the Sociology of Literary Form* (London: Verso, 1983).

Punter, David and Glennis Byron, *The Gothic* (Oxford: Blackwell, 2004).

Roth, Phyllis, *Bram Stoker* (Boston, MA: Twayne, 1982).

Sage, Victor, *Horror Fiction in the Protestant Tradition* (Basingstoke: Macmillan, 1988).

Senf, Carol, '*Dracula*: The Unseen Face in the Mirror', *Journal of Narrative Technique*, 9 (1979), pp. 160–70.

Senf, Carol, *Dracula: Between Tradition and Modernism* (New York: Twayne, 1998).

Senf, Carol, *Science and Social Science in Bram Stoker's Fiction* (Westport, CT: Greenwood Press, 2002).

Shepard, Leslie, and Albert Power (eds), *Dracula: Celebrating 100 Years* (Dublin: Mentor Press, 1997).

Skal, David, *Hollywood Gothic: The Tangled Web of Dracula from Novel to Stage to Screen* (New York: Norton, 1990).

Williams, Anne, *Art of Darkness: A Poetics of Gothic* (Chicago: University of Chicago Press, 1995).

PSYCHOANALYTICAL STUDIES

Astle, Richard, 'Dracula as Totemic Monster: Lacan, Freud, Oedipus and History', *Sub-Stance*, 25 (1980), pp. 98–105.

Bentley, C. F., 'The Monster in the Bedroom: Sexual Symbolism in Bram Stoker's *Dracula*', *Literature and Psychology*, 22 (1972), pp. 27–34.

Bierman, Joseph, '*Dracula*: Prolonged Childhood Illness and the Oral Triad', *American Imago*, 29 (1972), pp. 186–98.

Bierman, Joseph, 'A Crucial Stage in the Writing of *Dracula*', in William Hughes and Andrew Smith (eds), *Bram Stoker: History, Psychoanalysis and the Gothic* (Basingstoke: Macmillan, 1998), pp. 151–72.

Bronfen, Elisabeth, *Over Her Dead Body: Death, Femininity and the Aesthetic* (Manchester: Manchester University Press, 1992).

Jones, Ernest, *On the Nightmare* (London: Hogarth Press and the Institute of Psycho-analysis, 1931).

Lapin, Daniel, *The Vampire, Dracula and Incest* (San Francisco: Gargoyle, 1995).

Punter, David, *The Literature of Terror: A History of Gothic Fictions from 1765 to the Present Day*, Second Edition (London: Longman, 1996), 2 vols, Vol. 2.

Richardson, Maurice, 'The Psychoanalysis of Ghost Stories', *The Twentieth Century*, 166 (December 1959), pp. 419–31.

Shuster, Seymour, '*Dracula* and Surgically Induced Trauma in Children', *British Journal of Medical Psychology*, 46 (1973), pp. 259–70.

MEDICAL STUDIES

Flood, David Hume, 'Blood and Transfusion in Bram Stoker's *Dracula*', *University of Mississippi Studies in English*, New Series, 7 (1989), pp. 180–92.

Fontana, Ernest, 'Lombroso's Criminal Man and Stoker's Dracula', *Victorian Newsletter*, 66 (1984), pp. 25–7.

Greenway, John, '"Unconscious Cerebration" and the Happy Ending of *Dracula*', *Journal of Dracula Studies*, 4 (2002), pp. 1–9 .

Hartnell, Elaine, '"Thoughts too long and too intensively fixed on one object": Fictional Representations of "Brain Fever"', in Nickianne Moody and Julia Hallam (eds), *Medical Fictions* (Liverpool: MCCA, 1998), pp. 201–12.

Hughes, William, '"So unlike the normal lunatic": Abnormal Psychology in Bram Stoker's *Dracula*', *University of Mississippi Studies in English*, 11/12 (1993–95), pp. 1–10.

Hughes, William, 'Habituation and Incarceration: Mental Physiology and Asylum Abuse in *The Woman in White* and *Dracula*', in Andrew Mangham (ed.), *Wilkie Collins: Interdisciplinary Essays* (Newcastle: Cambridge Scholars Publishing, 2007), pp. 136–48.

Mason, Diane, '"A very devil with the men": The Pathology and Iconography of the Erotic Consumptive and the Attractive Masturbator', *Gothic Studies*, 2/2 (2000), pp. 205–17.

Mighall, Robert, '"A pestilence which walketh in darkness": Diagnosing the Victorian Vampire', in Glennis Byron and David Punter (eds), *Spectral Readings: Towards a Gothic Geography* (Basingstoke: Macmillan, 1999), pp. 108–24.

Pick, Daniel, '"Terrors of the Night": *Dracula* and "Degeneration" in the Late Nineteenth Century', *Critical Quarterly*, 30 (1988), pp. 71–87.

RACE AND EMPIRE

Arata, Stephen D., 'The Occidental Tourist: *Dracula* and the Anxiety of Reverse Colonisation', *Victorian Studies*, 33 (1990), pp. 621–45.

Arsić, Branka, 'On the Dark Side of the Twilight', *Social Identities*, 7/4 (2001), pp. 551–71.

Brantlinger, Patrick, *Rule of Darkness: British Literature and Imperialism, 1830–1914* (Ithaca, NY: Cornell University Press, 1988).

Coundouriotis, Eleni, '*Dracula* and the Idea of Europe', *Connotations*, 9/2 (1999–2000), pp. 143–59.

Davison, Carol Margaret, *Anti-Semitism and British Gothic Literature* (Basingstoke: Palgrave, 2004).

Garnett, Rhys, '*Dracula* and *The Beetle*: Imperial and Sexual Guilt and Fear in Late Victorian Fantasy', in Rhys Garnett and R. J. Ellis (eds), *Science Fiction Roots and Branches: Contemporary Critical Approaches* (New York: St Martin's Press, 1990), pp. 30–54.

Gibson, Matthew, *Dracula and the Eastern Question: British and French Vampire Narratives of the Nineteenth-Century Near East* (Basingstoke: Palgrave, 2006).

Goldsworthy, Vesna, *Inventing Ruritania: The Imperialism of the Imagination* (New Haven: Yale University Press, 1998).

Hughes, William, 'A Singular Invasion: Revisiting the Postcoloniality of Bram Stoker's *Dracula*' in Andrew Smith and William Hughes (eds), *Empire and the Gothic: Studies in the Ideology of Genre* (Basingstoke: Palgrave, 2003), pp. 88–102.

Kostova, Ludmilla, 'Straining the Limits of Interpretation: Bram Stoker's *Dracula* and its Eastern European Contexts' in John Bak (ed.), *Post/Modern Dracula: From Victorian Themes to Postmodern Praxis* (Newcastle: Cambridge Scholars Publishing, 2007), pp. 13–30.

Malchow, H. L., *Gothic Images of Race in Nineteenth-Century Britain* (Stanford, CA: Stanford University Press, 1996).

Schmitt, Cannon, *Alien Nation: Nineteenth-Century Gothic Fictions and English Identity* (Philadelphia: University of Pennsylvania Press, 1997).

Smith, Andrew, 'Demonising the Americans: Bram Stoker's Postcolonial Gothic', *Gothic Studies*, 5/2 (2003), pp. 20–31.

Zanger, Jules, 'A Sympathetic Vibration: *Dracula* and the Jews', *ELT*, 34 (1991), pp. 33–43.

IRISH STUDIES

Deane, Seamus, *Strange Country* (Oxford: Clarendon Press, 1998).

Eagleton, Terry, *Heathcliff and the Great Hunger* (London: Verso, 1995).

Foster, Roy, *Paddy and Mr Punch* (London: Penguin, 1995).

Kiberd, Declan, *Irish Classics* (London: Granta, 2001).

McCormack, W. J., 'Irish Gothic and After (1820–1945)', in Seamus Deane (ed.), *The Field Day Anthology of Irish Writing* (Londonderry: Field Day Publications, 1991), Vol. 2, pp. 831–54.

McKee, Patricia, 'Racialization, Capitalism, and Aesthetics in Stoker's *Dracula*', *Novel*, 36/1 (2002), pp. 42–60.

Moses, Michael Valdez, 'The Irish Vampire: *Dracula*, Parnell, and the Troubled Dreams of Nationhood', *Journal X*, 2/1 (1997), pp. 66–111.

O'Malley, Patrick R., *Catholicism, Sexual Deviance, and Victorian Gothic Culture* (Cambridge: Cambridge University Press, 2006).

Pinkerton, Mark, 'Why Westenra?', in Leslie Shepard and Albert Power (eds), *Dracula: Celebrating 100 Years* (Dublin: Mentor, 1997).

Stewart, Bruce, 'Bram Stoker's *Dracula*: Possessed by the Spirit of the Nation?', in Bruce Stewart (ed.), *That Other World: The Supernatural and the Fantastic in Irish Literature and its Contexts* (Gerrards Cross: Colin Smythe, 1998), 2 vols, Vol. 2, pp. 65–83.

Valente, Joseph, *Dracula's Crypt: Bram Stoker, Irishness and the Question of Blood* (Urbana: University of Illinois Press, 2002).

GENDER AND QUEER STUDIES

Auerbach, Nina, *Our Vampires, Ourselves* (Chicago: University of Chicago Press, 1995).

Brennan, Matthew C., 'Repression, Knowledge, and Saving Souls: The Role of the "New Woman" in Stoker's *Dracula* and Murnau's *Nosferatu*', *Studies in the Humanities*, 19 (1992), pp. 1–10.

Craft, Christopher, '"Kiss me with those red lips": Gender and Inversion in Stoker's *Dracula*', *Representations*, 8 (1984), pp. 107–33.

D'Addario, John, 'We're all Suckers for Dracula: Bram Stoker and the Homoeroticism of Vampires', *The Advocate*, 24 October 1989, pp. 40–2.

Eltis, Sos, 'Corruption of the Blood and Degeneration of the Race: *Dracula* and Policing the Borders of Gender', in John Paul Riquelme (ed.), *Dracula* by Bram Stoker (Boston, MA: Bedford/St Martin's, 2002), pp. 450–65.

Foucault, Michel, *The History of Sexuality: An Introduction* (1976; London: Penguin, 1984).

Frost, Robert, 'Virgins and Vampires', *The English Review*, 13 (2002), pp. 27–9.

Fry, Carol L., 'Fictional Conventions and Sexuality in *Dracula*', *Victorian Newsletter*, 42 (1972), pp. 20–2.

Hughes, William, '"The Fighting Quality": Physiognomy, Masculinity and Degeneration in Bram Stoker's Later Fiction', in Andrew Smith, Diane Mason and William Hughes (eds), *Fictions of Unease: The Gothic from Otranto to The X-Files* (Bath: Sulis Press, 2002), pp. 119–31.

Johnson, Alan P., '"Dual Life": The Status of Women in Stoker's *Dracula*', *Tennessee Studies in Literature*, 27 (1984), pp. 20–39.

Lanone, Catherine, 'Bram Stoker's *Dracula*, or Femininity as a Forsaken Fairy Tale', in Gilles Menegaldo and Dominique Sipière (eds), *Dracula: Stoker/Coppola* (Paris: Ellipses, 2005), pp. 199–206.

Ledger, Sally, *The New Woman: Fiction and Feminism at the Fin de Siècle* (Manchester: Manchester University Press, 1997).

McGillivray, Anne, '"What sort of grim adventure was it on which I had embarked?": Lawyers, Vampires and the Melancholy of Law', *Gothic Studies*, 4/2 (2002), pp. 116–32.

Mighall, Robert, 'Sex, History and the Vampire', in William Hughes and Andrew Smith (eds), *Bram Stoker: History, Psychoanalysis and the Gothic* (Basingstoke: Macmillan, 1998), pp. 62–77.

Mulvey-Roberts, Marie, '*Dracula* and the Doctors: Bad Blood, Menstrual Taboo and the New Woman', in William Hughes and Andrew Smith (eds), *Bram Stoker: History, Psychoanalysis and the Gothic* (Basingstoke: Macmillan, 1998), pp. 78–95.

Pykett, Lyn, *The Improper Feminine: The Women's Sensation Novel and the New Woman Writing* (London: Routledge, 1992).

Roth, Phyllis A., 'Suddenly Sexual Women in Bram Stoker's *Dracula*', *Literature and Psychology*, 27 (1977), pp. 113–21.

Sage, Victor, '*Dracula* and the Codes of Victorian Pornography', in Gilles Menegaldo and Dominique Sipière (eds), *Dracula: Stoker/Coppola* (Paris: Ellipses, 2005), pp. 55–69.

Schaffer, Talia, 'A Wilde Desire Took Me: The Homoerotic History of *Dracula*', *ELH*, 61 (1994), pp. 381–425.

Senf, Carol A., '*Dracula*: Stoker's Response to the New Woman', *Victorian Studies*, 26/1 (1982), pp. 33–49.

Shuttle, Penelope and Peter Redgrove, *The Wise Wound: Menstruation and Everywoman* (London: HarperCollins, 1994).

Simmons, Clare A., 'Fables of Continuity: Bram Stoker and Medievalism' in William Hughes and Andrew Smith (eds), *Bram Stoker: History, Psychoanalysis and the Gothic* (Basingstoke: Macmillan, 1998), pp. 29–46.

Index